Panorama
of
Paris

LOUIS SEBASTIEN MERCIER,
Né à Paris.
Dessiné par Pujos
Gravé par B. L. Henriquez

Selections from *Le Tableau de Paris*

Louis-Sébastien Mercier

Panorama

of

Paris

Based on the translation by
Helen Simpson

Edited and with a new
preface and translations of additional articles by
Jeremy D. Popkin

The Pennsylvania State University Press
University Park, Pennsylvania

Library of Congress Cataloging-in-Publication Data

Mercier, Louis-Sébastien, 1740–1814.
  [Tableau de Paris. English. Selections]
  Panorama of Paris : selections from Tableau de Paris / Louis-
Sébastien Mercier ; based on the translation by Helen Simpson ;
edited and with a new preface and translations of additional
articles by Jeremy D. Popkin.

    p.   cm.
  Includes bibliographical references and index.
  ISBN 0-271-01930-1 (cloth : alk. paper)
  ISBN 0-271-01929-8 (pbk.: alk. paper)
  1. Paris (France)—Description and travel. 2. Paris (France)
—Social life and customs—18th century. 3. Feuilletons, French
—France—Paris. I. Popkin, Jeremy D., 1948– . II. Title.
DC729.M56513   1999
944'.361034—dc21   98-51840
                                                       CIP

It is the policy of The Pennsylvania State University Press to use acid-free
paper for the first printing of all clothbound books. Publications on un-
coated stock satisfy the minimum requirements of American National
Standard for Information Sciences—Permanence of Paper for Printed
Library Materials, ANSI Z39.48-1992.

Frontispiece: Louis-Sébastien Mercier (1740–1814): Frontispiece to the
1799 edition of *L'An 2440.* This is the only known portrait of Mercier, who
disdained the visual arts. (This item is reproduced by permission of The
Huntington Library, San Marino, California)

I would like to dedicate this new edition of an old classic about one of the world's most fascinating cities to my parents, Richard and Juliet Popkin, in whose company I first discovered Paris in 1952, at the age of three, and to the many friends with whom I have shared its pleasures in the years since.

Contents

Acknowledgments

I owe thanks to my research assistant, Alycia Bergmann, and to my son, Alex Popkin, for their invaluable aid in preparing the manuscript, to Jeffrey Peters for help with the translation, and to an old friend, Jack Censer, for help in obtaining many of the illustrations. My mother, Juliet Popkin, of the Popkin Literary Agency, provided vital encouragement for the project, and Peter Potter of Penn State Press has guided it to timely publication.

Editor's Preface

A City in Words: Louis-Sébastien Mercier's
Tableau de Paris

L ouis-Sébastien Mercier's *Le Tableau de Paris*, published from
1781 to 1788, is one of the forgotten treasures of French literature. For more than a century, historians have exploited its twelve
volumes of vivid pen-portraits of Parisian life,[1] and no anthology of
readings about the city can avoid borrowing from it. But Mercier's
masterpiece is more than a repository of historical local color. The
Tableau de Paris is an important and original work that helped
shape many kinds of French writing. Mercier was a pioneering
urban ethnograper, a participant-observer who described the society around him with the same sense of curiosity that drove the
period's explorers to portray the natives of remote Pacific islands.
He was also a philanthropically minded reformer, using his pages
to denounce ills ranging from inadequate garbage removal and
adulterated food to traffic jams, and thus the spiritual ancestor of
nineteenth-century campaigners for urban improvement such as
Louis-René Villermé and Alexandre Parent-Duchatelet. In his ability to distill the daily life of a city into short, incisive essays, Mercier
was the inventor of a new kind of urban journalism, known in
French as the *feuilleton,* and still practiced throughout the Western
world.

Above all, however, Mercier's *Tableau de Paris* is a fascinating
work of literature, which deserves a place in the great tradition of
imaginative writing about Paris that includes Balzac's *Human Comedy,* Victor Hugo's *Les Misérables,* Emile Zola's novels, and Georges
Perec's *Life: An Owner's Manual.* The *Tableau de Paris* "inaugurated

---

1. For examples of how contemporary social historians have used Mercier's
work, see Arlette Farge, *Fragile Lives: Violence, Power, and Solidarity in the Eighteenth-
Century Paris* (Cambridge, Mass.: Harvard University Press, 1993), and Daniel
Roche, *The People of Paris,* trans. Marie Evans (Berkeley and Los Angeles: University
of California Press, 1987).

a new genre and served at once as a model, standard, and norm for innumerable later works" about the city, the literary critic Priscilla Ferguson has written.[2] Like later authors in this tradition, Mercier aspired to include all of Parisian life in his pages: the rich, the poor, the young, the old, men and women, police and criminals, priests and philosophers, even the animals, from carriage-horses to canaries, that shared the banks of the Seine with the six hundred thousand or so human inhabitants of his day. And, like them, Mercier sought a method of writing that could convey the unique character of urban life: its intensity, its diversity, its quality of constant change, and its peculiar repetitive patterns.

Claiming for the *Tableau de Paris* a place on a level with the acknowledged masterpieces of writing about Paris requires a redefinition of the canon of French literature. The *Tableau de Paris* fits into none of the established categories of literature: it is not a novel, not a history, not a work of philosophy. The work fits poorly in a literary tradition famed for its devotion to form: it lacks any apparent pattern or organization. Furthermore, history played a cruel trick on the book. The French Revolution of 1789, which broke out just a year after Mercier published the final volumes of his portrait, overturned much of the world he had so carefully described. Mercier's innovative work was immediately transformed into a description of a vanished Old Regime, making it out of date almost from the moment it appeared. Still convinced of the importance of his subject and his method, Mercier tried again: in 1798, he published *Le Nouveau Paris,* the most thoroughgoing effort of the period to capture the spirit of the capital during the Revolution. Once again, history overtook the author: Napoleon Bonaparte seized power in 1799, and a regime and a public devoted to restoring social order had no interest in a book that reminded them of its successful subversion. Neither the *Tableau de Paris* nor the *Nouveau Paris* was completely reprinted again for two centuries. In 1994, a team of French scholars headed by Jean-Claude Bonnet made the full texts of both works available in new, carefully anno-

2. Priscilla Parkhurst Ferguson, *Paris as Revolution: Writing the Nineteenth-Century City* (Berkeley and Los Angeles: University of California Press, 1994), 54.

tated editions. Thanks to their efforts, the time is ripe for a new appreciation of Mercier's work.[3]

The time is also ripe for a new reading of the *Tableau de Paris* because today's readers are prepared to appreciate the literary virtues of unruly texts like Mercier's. Even the *Tableau*'s apparent lack of form can now be seen as Mercier's way of meeting the special challenges posed by his subject. The book has all the characteristics of a modern metropolis. Like a great city, it sprawls, it is crowded with people of all sorts, and it forms a seemingly unorganized chaos. It took Mercier more than a thousand chapters spread over 2,800 printed pages to write his portrait of France's capital and its daily life on the eve of the Revolution of 1789. To have put this mass of material together according to a system would have falsified the picture Mercier wanted to compose. Nothing seemed to him more characteristic of urban existence than its diversity and the way in which opposites like the rich and the poor, the law-abiding and the criminal, the clean and the dirty, were thrown together. When he put an article on used-clothes dealers next to one on aristocratic life, Mercier was conveying the sense of dissonance that made the great city unique. If Mercier had to invent a new form for the *Tableau de Paris*, it was because he aimed to do something truly novel. He was the first writer to set himself the goal of portraying a great city not as a collection of buildings or a system of political institutions but as a living being, of recording the thousands of daily interactions between its cells and organs through which it breathed, nourished itself, and grew. Mercier's pages recorded innumerable small human dramas, but his real

3. Louis-Sébastien Mercier, *Tableau de Paris*, ed. Jean-Claude Bonnet, 2 vols. (Paris: Mercure de France, 1994), and *Le Nouveau Paris*, ed. Jean-Claude Bonnet (Paris: Mercure de France, 1994). Bonnet and his colleagues have also published an important volume of essays on Mercier: *Louis-Sébastien Mercier (1740–1814): Un hérétique en littérature* (Paris: Mercure de France, 1995), which is now the starting point for any study of Mercier. I have drawn especially on the contributions of Bonnet himself and his collaborators Pierre Frantz, Shelly Charles, Jean-Rémy Mantion, and Anthony Vidler. Both these critical editions of Mercier's works and the collaborative volume include extensive bibliographies. See also *Le Paris de Louis-Sébastien Mercier: Cartes et Index Toponymique* (Paris: Mercure de France, 1994), a set of maps showing all the locations in Paris mentioned in Mercier's works.

subject was Paris as a whole—its streets, its markets, its churches, its jails—and the constant flow of activity that connected all its parts. Louis-Sébastien Mercier was uniquely suited to carry out this project. He was a native of Paris, born on June 6, 1740, the son of a respectable artisan, an armorer or weapons-maker. Mercier's mother also came from an artisan family. Her death in 1743 was the occasion for an inventory of the couple's property, which shows that the household stood halfway between the poverty of ordinary workers and the prosperity of those who had risen into the ranks of the true bourgeoisie. As Mercier's biographer, Léon Béclard, wrote, this middling position was "a good place to learn to observe Paris."[4] Mercier's social origins were thus very similar to those of his contemporary, the glass-fitter Jacques-Louis Ménétra, born in 1738, whose autobiography gives us a fascinating record of Parisian life from the point of view of a man who remained in this milieu all his life.[5] Mercier's destiny was different. He was sent to school and received a good education, although he later complained extensively about his years at the Collège de Quatre-Nations, and he also learned from the rich urban culture around him, becoming a precocious devotee of the theater and the capital's literary life. He read voraciously and, like so many of his generation, was especially influenced by the works of Jean-Jacques Rousseau.

After two years as a teacher in the provincial city of Bordeaux, where he completed his first major literary effort, an essay entitled "The Happiness of Men of Letters," published in 1763, Mercier, determined to become a man of letters himself, returned to Paris. He published several works in the 1760s, but the book that made his fame was his utopian fantasy, *The Year 2440*, which first appeared in 1771. Mercier imagined a Paris of the distant future, purged of all its defects. Its inhabitants would enjoy a city of broad boulevards and smoothly running traffic. The medieval fortress of the Bastille would have disappeared, the unsanitary and over-

4. Léon Béclard, *Sébastien Mercier: Sa vie, son oeuvre, son temps* (Paris: H. Champion, 1903; reprint Hildesheim: Georg Olms, 1982), 3. The volume covers Mercier's life up to the start of the French Revolution in 1789; Béclard died before he could finish the work.
5. Jacques-Louis Ménétra, *Journal of My Life*, ed. Daniel Roche, trans. Arthur Goldhammer (New York: Columbia University Press, 1986).

crowded central hospital would have been replaced by clean and modern clinics in the suburbs, and a purified religion of reason would have replaced the superstitions of Catholicism. Mercier's imagined France was still a monarchy, but its king was to have been brought up as a simple citizen, and the elaborate social hierarchy of Mercier's day would have disappeared.[6]

From the perspective of our day, Mercier's utopia seems surprisingly cautious. He failed to foresee the sweeping technological changes of the industrial era, and he never hinted that the Bastille might come down in his own lifetime. Nevertheless, the book's implied critique of Old Regime France's institutions was too radical for the censors. *The Year 2440* was promptly banned—a measure that did nothing to hinder its sales—and its author, although he remained undisturbed in Paris, now had the reputation of a dangerous radical. *The Year 2440* also marked Mercier's first venture into urban literature: the perfected Paris of the twenty-fifth century was an implicit critique of the real Paris of Mercier's own day. Before he turned to this latter subject, however, Mercier tried his hand at another literary genre that also served him well as preparation for the *Tableau*. His great ambition in the early 1770s was to succeed as a playwright, and specifically to replace the classical tragedies and comedies that dominated the French stage with a new form of theater, the *drame*, featuring characters and situations drawn from real life. Denis Diderot had made the case for the *drame* in the 1750s, but Mercier renewed the attack in a polemical work, *Du théâtre*, published in 1773, and in a series of original scripts. Mercier's theatrical works enjoyed success on stages in the French provinces and even abroad, but his stinging criticism of the capital's privileged theater company, the *Comédie française*, embroiled him in a bitter controversy with its actors and led them to refuse to perform his plays.

Despite this frustration, Mercier's experience as a playwright was valuable preparation for the *Tableau*. He came to conceive of Paris as a "grand and constantly changing stage" ("Preface"), its inhabitants as actors, and their interactions as so many dramas waiting to

6. For a discussion of *The Year 2440* and translations of excerpts from the work, see Robert Darnton, *The Forbidden Best-Sellers of Pre-Revolutionary France* (New York: W. W. Norton, 1995), 115–36 and 300–336.

be recorded.[7] Mercier converted some of his sketches of Parisian life in the *Tableau,* such as "The Buyer of Annuities," into dramatic dialogues, but more often he put them into short essays told from the point of view of a narrator who could boast that "I have been about so much while drawing my *Tableau de Paris* that I may be said to have drawn it with my legs."[8] The form Mercier chose reflected his experience as a journalist: he had published the first of his sketches in the pages of the *Journal des Dames,* a magazine he edited in 1775 and 1776.[9] This experience taught Mercier to be concise and colorful, and to vary his subject matter constantly. It would take the Revolution of 1789, during which he became the editor of several publications, to make Mercier adopt journalism as his principal activity, but the *Tableau* already reflected his determination to create a kind of writing that could truly represent the constantly changing life of a great city.

If the *Tableau* drew on Mercier's experience as dramatist and journalist, it also reflected his ambition to be recognized as a philosopher. Like almost all men of letters of the mid-eighteenth century, Mercier took it for granted that a writer should not just observe the world but should extract meaning from it. His philosophy was not the rationalism of the Enlightenment, however. Like the other writers of the pre-Romantic generation, Mercier had a keen sense of the limits of reason. Imagination was, he thought, a more powerful tool for reaching the essence of things, and he was easily attracted to illuminist speculations about reincarnation, spirits, and truths beyond the reach of science.[10] He might gently mock some of the excesses of irrationalism in his article "Love of the Marvellous," but he sympathized with the instinct to look beyond

7. In 1989, on the occasion of the bicentenary of the French Revolution, a Paris theater company successfully staged scenes from the *Tableau de Paris.*

8. "My Legs," in Louis-Sébastien Mercier, *The Picture of Paris Before and After the Revolution,* trans. Wilfrid and Emilie Jackson (London: George Routledge, 1929), 170.

9. Nina Gelbart, *Feminine and Opposition Journalism in Old Regime France: "Le Journal des Dames"* (Berkeley and Los Angeles: University of California Press, 1987), 202–38.

10. On this aspect of Mercier's thought, see Henry F. Majewski, *The Preromantic Imagination of L.-S. Mercier* (New York: Humanities Press, 1971), especially chap. 2, "Visions of a Mysterious Universe." Majewski's stimulating work is the most extensive discussion of Mercier available in English.

the visible world. Just as he rejected the French tradition of classical tragedy because it was too distant from everyday life, Mercier rejected the abstract psychological and philosophical moralizing of the *grand siècle* in favor of a concrete approach, rooted in evidence from visible life. Rather than generalizing about human nature, Mercier insisted that "my contemporary, my compatriot . . . is the person I really need to understand, because I need to communicate with him, and as a result, every nuance of his character takes on a special importance for me" ("Preface").

Although he admired Rousseau, Mercier did not share his mentor's uncompromising moral standpoint. Mercier's morality was a relativistic one, reflecting his ambivalence toward the spectacle of urban life, both fascinating and horrible. Rousseau had condemned city life as inherently degraded; Mercier insisted that "Parisian life is not necessarily any more unnatural than the nomadic existence of African and American savages." To be sure, the portrait he drew was not a pretty one. Paris was, he admitted, a mass of corruption and abuses, which "can't all be thrown out over night, because the city and its vices are too intermingled" ("Preface"). Social life was distorted by the prevalence of extreme poverty, on the one hand, and excessive and irresponsible wealth, on the other, leaving no place for the families like the one from which Mercier had come—honest, hardworking, economically independent but not rich enough to waste money on luxuries, the social group he considered to be the happiest in his chapter on "The Eight Social Classes." At times Mercier indulged in fantasies of how the city's vices or some natural tragedy might lead to its destruction, and the lessons that philosophers might draw from its ruins. But he could not keep up this tone of moral condemnation for long. Like Balzac half a century later, he was too fascinated by the spectacle of how the Parisians coped with their uniquely complex environment to focus consistently on their shortcomings.

Mercier claimed that his *Tableau* took in the entire city, but Paris was too vast even for his gigantic text. Large parts of the city's life escaped even his skillful eye. Despite his evocation of the "infinite number of arts, of trades, of jobs, of different occupations" in the city in his opening, "General Overview," he had little interest in the densely populated working-class *faubourgs* on the eastern side of the city or in the productive activities that went on in their workshops, and almost equally little interest in the doings of great nobles and the royal court. In contrast to the *Mémoires secrets,* another multivolume best-seller published in the same years as his *Tableau,* Mercier deliberately chose not to write about identifiable individuals and rarely mentioned specific events; his articles on the two Crébillons, acquaintances who had promoted his career, and on the balloon ascension of December 1, 1783, were exceptions to his regular rules.[11] Nor, unlike the *Mémoires secrets,* did he claim to tell readers the hidden secrets of Parisian life. He wrote instead about the publicly observable interactions between the city's inhabitants, in its streets, its marketplaces, its salons, its churches. It was those socially scripted encounters, Mercier was convinced, and not the characteristics of its inhabitants studied in isolation or the structure of its built environment, that truly defined the unique quality of Parisian life. Mercier's interest was in the city as a system, and his vision was a sociological one, emphasizing the structures and norms of urban life instead of specific and idiosyncratic events. He conceived of Paris as a gigantic hive, an all-encompassing structure whose identity persisted even as its individual elements changed. Nowhere was this conception of the city expressed more clearly than in the article "How the Day Goes," where Mercier imagined the consequences of married couples being regularly awakened by the sound of carriages taking the wealthy home after midnight. "More than one young Parisian must owe his existence to this sudden passing rattle of wheels," Mercier mused, suggesting that the patterns of city life were literally responsible for the very existence of its inhabitants.

What struck Mercier most forcefully about Paris were the thought-provoking contradictions it generated. "What a gallery of images, so full of striking contrasts for anyone who knows how to see and understand!" he exclaimed ("General Overview"). Here the poor constantly brushed up against the rich—literally so in his chapter on "Valets of the Street," which described the brush-wielding clothes-cleaners who ran up to mud-spattered pedestrians, ancestors of the "squeegee-men" who rush into New York traffic, hoping to earn a few coins by cleaning car windshields. In

---

11. On the *Mémoires secrets,* often referred to as the *Mémoires de Bachaumont,* see Jeremy D. Popkin and Bernadette Fort, eds., *The "Mémoires secrets" and the Culture of Publicity in Eighteenth-Century France* (Oxford: Voltaire Foundation, 1998).

"How the Day Goes," one of his finest sketches, Mercier showed how the same street might be filled with workers early in the morning and with elegant theatergoers in the evening. Equally fascinating to Mercier were the sharp contrasts between splendor and squalor, cleanliness and filth, virtue and vice. Elegantly coiffed heads emerged from the barber's shop, "the abyss of all uncleanness, repository of filth unimaginable" ("Barber's Shop"), decent women and prostitutes crossed paths in the Palais-Royal, advertisements for performances of Racine's classical tragedies went up on walls next to posters for vulgar farces ("Advertisements"), workmen hammered and swore in the midst of services in Notre Dame ("Mausoleum"). Above all, the traffic in the streets mixed everyone together, poor pedestrians and wealthy carriage-owners, dogs and dignitaries traveling in sedan-chairs. But the streets were also a place where these hierarchies might be suddenly overturned. Let the sedan-chair collide with "a herd of cattle, wild, driven creatures and no respecters of persons" and its inhabitant might find himself trapped in his overturned conveyance ("Sedan Chairs"), a metaphor for the constant instability Mercier considered one of Paris's main characteristics.

The city's endless variety and sharp contrasts seemed to rule out any simple generalizations, but certain common themes tie Mercier's thousands of disparate observations together. Mercier's Paris of the 1780s is already Balzac's Paris of the 1830s, simultaneously a universal marketplace, in which everything had its price, a theater of appearances, in which nothing was what it seemed, and a crucible of desire, its inhabitants driven ceaselessly by lust and ambition. Mercier excelled in portraying the haggling of what he understood as a completely commercialized society, whether he was writing about women searching for bargains in used clothing at the weekly "fair of the Holy Ghost" in the Place de Grève ("Second-Hand Clothes"), a preacher shopping for a prefabricated text appropriate to the next religious holiday ("Sermons"), or the respectable lady trying to convert her annuity into ready cash ("The Buyer of Annuities"). Buying and selling kept the city fed: Mercier was fascinated by the central market, Les Halles, where "the food of the whole city is shifted and sorted in high-piled baskets . . ." ("How the Day Goes"), even though he sniffed suspiciously at the half-rotten produce offered for sale ("Markets"). Lodging was also a

These two plates from Louis Bretez, *Plan de Paris, Commencé l'Année* 1734, commonly known as the *Plan Turgot*, show the center of the city a half-century prior to the publication of Mercier's *Tableau*. This masterpiece of eighteenth-century map-making showed the city as a rational and comprehensible ensemble. Mercier, who included no maps in his work, emphasized instead its mysteries and irregularities. (Courtesy The Lilly Library, Indiana University, Bloomington, Indiana)

commodity, and in his article "Rent Day" Mercier described how the market worked, forcing thousands of poor families to "shift from garret to garret" to avoid the collector and driving poor women to expedients such as renting a young daughter to apprentice hairdressers, who, "burning her ears with their inexpert tongs . . . inflict upon her a twelve hours' martyrdom at twenty sous the day."

It was not only the poor whose lives were determined by the rules of the market. Even women of the better classes had to bid for husbands, offering "cash down" in the form of dowries, and, Mercier contended, many of them had come to prefer putting their money in investments and remaining single, rejecting "a woman's natural state" out of mercenary considerations ("Marriageable"). To be sure, potential husbands had good economic reasons to be wary of tying the knot, lest they have to bankrupt themselves buying luxuries such as feathered hats for their wives ("Plumage"). The poor might have to flee the rent-collector, but the rich could take advantage of the law that said that a townhouse with a separate porter's lodge at the gate was immune to bailiffs ("Doorways"). A theme close to Mercier's heart—it reflected his own struggle to get his plays performed—was his claim that the selfish interests of the Comédie française's actors prevented true art from flourishing ("Private Boxes"). Wherever he looked, Mercier saw the influence of money and exchange.

Like so many social critics, Mercier was aware that money was the great equalizer. In the second-hand clothes market, "a grand dress worn by the dead wife of a judge" could wind up in the hands of his clerk's wife. "The buyer neither knows nor cares whence come the corsets she sells. . . . Virtue, or rather vice, goes out of them when they change hands; nothing cleanses like money" ("Second-Hand Clothes"). Nowhere was the effect of money clearer than in the hierarchy of prostitutes, a subject that Mercier was drawn to as strongly as his nineteenth-century successors. In his article "Madams," Mercier classified these women, from the great courtesans who served the needs of financiers to "the great mass of common prostitutes" who "may be hired like hackney carriages at so much an hour." The difference, Mercier claimed, was only "whether chance accords them protectors with more money or less."[12]

12. On Mercier's treatment of women, a major theme in the *Tableau*, see John

Money was linked to Mercier's concern with fashion and appearances, because wealth allowed its possessor to acquire the outward signs of status. Mercier's Paris was not so much a site of production and accumulation as it was a society obsessed with consumption and display. His book, Mercier remarked, was a "catalogue of futile expenses" ("Economy"). In "Running Footmen, Running Hounds," Mercier described how the wealthy had previously marked their special status by having liveried servants running ahead of their coaches; in his own time, the footmen had given way to equally expensive purebred greyhounds. And consumption was driven above all by the irrational force of constantly changing fashion. "Fashion changes like a weathervane," Mercier wrote; "I don't criticize different fashions, one has to obey custom" (Chapter DCCCLXX, "On porte ses cheveux," not included in this translation). After listing the recent styles of women's adornment that had already disappeared, Mercier called for "a journal in which these things and others of equal importance should be treated;" a publication devoted to these ephemeral matters "would certainly enjoy a far greater circulation than the *Journal des Savants*" ("Dress"), France's contribution to the advancement of science.

In his *Nouvelle Héloïse*, Mercier's idol, Rousseau, had captured hearts with his depiction of perfect, impossible love. Mercier's Paris was an earthier place. In "Marriage à la Mode," a bourgeois father explains the ways of the world to his daughter, who acquiesces in a practical match; "six weeks later she has the satisfaction of receiving her lover in her own drawing-room, and the last person to know of it is the husband." In "Passing the Collection Plate," Mercier suggests that it is no accident that churches so often employed pretty young ladies to pass the hat at services: not only did their presence inspire greater donations, but the clergy had the pleasure of their company. No stratagem of desire was too subtle to escape his notice. He understood why a dashing young man might lavish his public attention on a middle-aged mother: "you buss the mother heartily, and so acquire the right to lay your cheek against the daughter's" ("Kisses, Greeting"). A young man

Lough, "Women in Mercier's *Tableau de Paris*," in Eva Jacobs et al., eds., *Woman and Society in Eighteenth-Century France: Essays in Honour of John Stephenson Spink* (London: Athlone, 1979), 110–22.

would also be well advised to purchase a carriage that he could then lend to women whose "husbands, that unciv il race, eternally and senselessly busy, monopolize the conjugal vehicle" ("Pedestrian").

Money, vanity, and lust might explain much of Parisian life, but not all of it. Mercier's Parisians were, like their city, creatures of contrasts, capable on occasion of rising above their selfish interests. Mercier found it amusing that the pious Capuchin monks, who also devoted themselves to putting out fires, had found themselves obliged to rescue plaster figures of pagan gods and goddesses when the Opera's warehouse went up in flames, but he did not deny their bravery ("Hôtel des Menus Plaisirs"). He was deeply moved by the behavior of the crowd that watched the first balloon ascent in 1783. "I believe there was no single heart in that great assemblage that was not touched by the courage of the two aeronauts, men like themselves. . . . Pity, interest with no touch of self; tenderheartedness; such were the virtues I saw around me, while in the skies courage, and invention, and daring drove above the clouds" ("December 1st, 1783"). Parisian life was less stifled by preoccupations with rank and ritual than the provinces ("Commentary"), and its intensity made for greater creativity. "Ideas come more easily to birth," Mercier wrote in his article on the Palais-Royal, "and are themselves more fruitful here; they must be strong enough to withstand the buffetings of criticism, and remain firm in contact with the thousand different and changing individualities which crowd the townsman's life."

It was the inextricably mixed character of Paris and the Parisians that gave Mercier hope, in spite of his many complaints about the city and its inhabitants. Parisians might be credulous and easily taken in by charlatans ("Love of the Marvellous"), but they were not entirely ineducable, and Mercier could make a list of "Silly Customs Done Away With." Professionally trained specialists were replacing uneducated midwives and making births safer ("Male Midwives"—Mercier's article unduly depreciated women's contributions to reducing infant mortality), municipal regulations had done away with the dangerous shop signs that had once hung across the streets, threatening to fall during high winds ("Signs"), and philanthropists had improved conditions for the patients in the city's venereal-disease hospital ("Bicêtre"). Even though he frequently criticized the government of the Old Regime—the *Tableau de Paris* is often cited as the first book to use the word "bureaucracy," to which Mercier devoted a chapter—he gave due credit to the city's royally appointed administrators for their efforts to improve the city's sanitation and combat crime. The *Tableau de Paris* was no revolutionary tract, and Mercier claimed to believe that "the Parisian's instinct seems to have taught him that the little more liberty he might obtain is not worth fighting for; any such struggle would imply long effort, stern thinking, and these are not in his line" ("Political Character of the Parisian"). But Mercier left open the possibility that, "if the pressure should ever become too great," the Paris population might rise up, as it had at the time of the religious wars in the sixteenth century and during the Fronde in the 1640s.

Mercier's style was as varied as his subject matter. In the space of a single article, such as "A Closed Cemetery," he could go from sober scientific discussion of the health hazards posed by poor burial practices to lurid evocations of torch-lit tombs by night. His "General Overview" depicted the city as an enormous alchemist's laboratory, in which everything was constantly being transmuted into something else. His writing had the same character, moving with quicksilver speed from subject to subject. Mercier frequently addressed his "dear readers" directly, and never withheld his own opinions on the spectacle he described. His language was vivid and direct. He appealed to all the senses, evoking not just the look of the city but the sounds of the streets, the smells of the markets and the gutters, the taste of the food at noble banquet tables and in dimly lit popular eating places, and the feel of being jammed together with other theatergoers in an overcrowded pit.

Mercier devoted most of his chapters to portraying the anonymous social types who populated the city, but out of his thousands of pages emerged one clear, individual portrait: that of the author himself, the tireless observer of the constantly changing urban scene. More than half a century before Baudelaire defined the *flâneur,* Mercier exemplified the concept. Mercier the narrator was at home everywhere in Paris, but his progress from place to place followed no plan and served no purpose other than to allow him to discover, record, and philosophize about ever more aspects of the city. Mercier engaged himself in the life he described, dodging carriage wheels in the streets and dining in cheap restaurants, but at the same time he remained aloof from it, casting his critical gaze on the doings of his fellow citizens. Mercier's self-portrait, as it emerges between the lines of his hundreds of mini-essays, is that of the quintessential modern urbanite: an anonymous individual, with no special ties to anyone else around him, but at the same time proud of belonging to a uniquely complicated community.

The tone of the *Tableau* gives the reader the impression that Mercier composed his chapters in the midst of the urban tumult he so constantly evoked. Mercier had indeed accumulated much of his material during the 1770s, and published fragments of it in the *Journal des Dames* during his editorship. He was still in Paris in 1781 when a foreign publisher, Samuel Fauche, issued a two-volume edition, apparently without Mercier's authorization. The royal authorities, stung by the work's critical tone, immediately tried to suppress it, and Mercier decided that he would be wise to leave the capital. He took refuge in the Swiss city of Neuchâtel, home of one of the period's most active French-language publishing houses, the Société Typographique de Neuchâtel, whose presses printed the first four volumes of the text as Mercier intended it in 1782 and volumes five through eight in 1783.[13] For Mercier, then, most of the final work on the manuscript took place in exile; the Paris of words that he created was a substitute for the living reality of the city.

Reviewers were generally critical of the work, citing its lack of organization, but it was an immediate success with the public and was promptly translated into English and German. Mercier, who had returned to Paris in late 1785 or early 1786, added four additional volumes to the *Tableau* in 1788. Had the Revolution not intervened a year later, the work might have continued to grow indefinitely: Mercier ended the final chapter of volume 12 with the comment, "I have hardly ever known boredom since I started composing books." Instead, he plunged into the maelstrom of revolutionary journalism and politics. Together with Jean-Louis Carra,

13. This publishing house, whose archives are one of our richest sources for understanding the publishing world of the period, has been described in Robert Darnton, *The Business of Enlightenment* (Cambridge, Mass.: Harvard University Press, 1979).

an outspoken prerevolutionary pamphleteer, he founded the *An-nales patriotiques,* which quickly became one of the most important Paris dailies of the early revolutionary years. Carra's more militant personality dominated the paper, but Mercier was prominent enough to be elected as a deputy to the National Convention in September 1792. His basic moderation led him to oppose the ris-ing tide of radicalism that was leading to the Reign of Terror. He voted against the execution of Louis XVI in January 1793, and was one of seventy-three deputies who signed a protest against the ar-rest of the Girondin opponents of the radical Montagnards after the *journée* of May 31–June 2, 1793.

In October 1793, the victorious Montagnards imprisoned Mer-cier and the rest of the "73"; they were only released after Robes-pierre's overthrow on 9 thermidor Year II (27 July 1794). Mercier resumed his seat in the Convention and his journalism; in 1795, he was also appointed to the newly established Institut de France, the intellectual institution intended to replace the abolished acad-emies of the Old Regime, and he lectured on history at another of the revolutionary regime's creations, the *école centrale* or teacher-training college. Mercier's distaste for received wisdom, already evident in the prerevolutionary years, resurfaced during the Direc-tory. He denounced the posthumous honors conferred on Des-cartes and Voltaire, and campaigned to have painters and sculptors, whose productions he had always regarded as inferior, subjected to the tax levied on regular artisans. When he accepted a position administering the national lottery, an institution he had condemned in the *Tableau de Paris,* his critics had a field day point-ing out his inconsistencies. His collection of articles about the city during the Revolution, *Le Nouveau Paris,* appeared in 1798, just in time to be rendered out of date when Napoleon seized power the following year. Mercier remained active during the early years of the Napoleonic regime, and published his *Néologie,* a compilation of new words that had entered the language during the Revolu-tion, in 1801. But the stifling conformity Napoleon's authoritarian regime imposed was not to his liking, and his public role dimin-ished. By the time Mercier died in April 1814, just weeks after Na-poleon's abdication, both the man and his works were already largely forgotten.

Of Mercier's various publications, the *Tableau de Paris* was the only one that exerted a continuing influence throughout the nineteenth century. Balzac was familiar with it: he was among the contributors to a multi-authored imitation, the *Nouveau Tableau de Paris,* published in 1834–35.[14] Many of his novels read like expanded versions of Mercier's chapters: the plot of *César Birotteau,* for example, could have been extrapolated from the *Tableau's* essay "Bankruptcies." Baudelaire and Victor Hugo drew on the *Tableau,* and there were at least three abridged editions published in the course of the century. The very success of the tradition of urban literature that he had inaugurated tended to overshadow Mercier's pioneering work, however. To Mercier's acute observations of the surface of Parisian life, Balzac and his successors added the drama and psychological depth that came from the creation of fully rounded individual characters. Furthermore, as literature about Paris came to adopt an increasingly nostalgic tone, lamenting the "improvements" that culminated in Haussmann's reconstruction under the Second Empire, Mercier's more forward-looking vision fell out of favor. He gradually sank to the status of a periodically rediscovered "forgotten" author. In 1903, the first volume of Léon Béclard's biography made a forceful case for his originality and his importance in the history of French literature. The fact that Béclard's work remained unfinished may account in part for its relative lack of impact. The republication in 1994 of the full texts of Mercier's two books on Paris should finally assure a real recognition of his contribution. No selection from Mercier's *Tableau de Paris* has been available to English-speaking readers for more than sixty years. This volume will at least allow them a taste of the great banquet he spread before his readers.

A Note on the Translation

With the exception of seven newly translated chapters, the translations of the selections from the *Tableau de Paris* in this volume are based on Helen De Guerry Simpson's abridged version of Mercier's book, published in 1933 under the title *The Waiting City.* Born in Australia in 1897, Helen Simpson was descended from a French aristocratic family and received her education in France.

14. *Nouveau Tableau de Paris,* 6 vols. (Paris: Mme. Charles-Béchet, 1834–35).

She later moved to England, where she pursued a successful career as a playwright and mystery novelist. Her career was cut short when she was killed in the Blitz of 1940. Simpson translated less than ten percent of Mercier's original text. Her selection is not entirely representative of Mercier's main themes: she omitted, for example, the articles in which he complained of Paris's excessive influence on French life, and many of those in which he insisted most strongly on its urban problems. In the current volume, I have added newly translated versions of Mercier's "Preface" and of six other articles illustrative of aspects of Mercier's thought that are not well represented in her work.[15]

Simpson's translation is a spirited but free one, more concerned to capture something of the style of the eighteenth century than to achieve literal accuracy. She did not hesitate to modify punctuation and sentence structure, omit passages that referred to obscure events or chapters she had decided not to include in her abridgment, and add words and sometimes whole lines to clarify or emphasize points. Rather than putting the *Tableau de Paris* into twentieth-century English, she strove to re-create the effect of eighteenth-century prose, sprinkling her pages with words such as "featly" and "linkmen." Her work is nevertheless both more accurate and more readable than a rival volume of translated selections from Mercier published a few years earlier, *The Picture of Paris before and after the Revolution,* by Wilfred and Emilie Jackson, although the Jackson volume does have the advantage of containing some selections from Mercier's *Nouveau Paris.*[16]

15. Mercier's "Preface," Chapter 2, "General Overview," Chapter 3, "Unhealthy Size of the Capital," Chapter 75, "Bureaucracy," Chapter 76, "Mixture of Individuals," Chapter 78, "A Closed Cemetery," and Chapter 92, "The Eight Social Classes." One selection from *The Waiting City,* "Mushrooms," has been omitted.

16. The full text of Mercier's *Tableau de Paris* has never been translated into English. In addition to the Simpson and Jackson volumes, there are two older partial translations. The first, including 55 articles, appeared in 1782, under the title of *Paris in Miniature;* the anonymous translator boasted that "I have taken some liberties with my author, which I am vain enough to think will be approved of by those who may take the trouble of comparing." *Paris: Including a Description of the Principal Edifices and Curiosities of that Metropolis . . . ,* a more extensive and accurately translated selection of 223 of Mercier's chapters, was published in 1817 as a guide for English tourists. Its anonymous compiler explained that he had omitted articles about "buildings which have been destroyed, or customs which have been abolished since the revolution."

In preparing this new abridged edition of Mercier's *Tableau de Paris* in English, I have carefully compared Simpson's translation to the text of the French critical edition published in 1994. Wherever her work seemed to me to depart too far from the original, or to use language too obscure to be understood by present-day readers, I have not hesitated to modify it. Ellipses have been added to indicate where Simpson omitted material from the French original. I have also noted the cases in which Simpson combined and rearranged material from two of Mercier's chapters to create a single one in English. For the most part, Mercier's vignettes of Paris life speak for themselves. A few explanatory notes have been provided to identify historical personages and events referred to in the text. Fascinated by the contrast between the two great cities, Helen Simpson included excerpts from a variety of works on eighteenth-century London at the end of her chapters; these have been omitted from this volume. In *The Waiting City,* Mercier's chapters were printed in a seemingly random order; in this edition, I have rearranged them according to their place in the definitive French edition, and I have provided references so that readers can easily look up the original texts.

Mercier's *Tableau de Paris* originally appeared without illustrations or maps. This was no accident. Mercier considered painting an inferior art because it froze the ever-changing flux of life into a fixed form, whereas prose could suggest the constant succession of impressions that was the essence of the urban experience. Mercier was particularly unhappy with the 96 engravings inspired by his work that a German artist, Balthasar Anton Dunker, published in 1787, under the title *Costumes des Moeurs de l'Esprit françois.* Most modern editions of the *Tableau de Paris* have nevertheless included some period illustrations, and, with apologies to Mercier, I have done likewise. Unless otherwise indicated, the illustrations are taken from Dunker's collection.

Mercier's *Tableau de Paris*

1. Preface

(Préface, 1:13–21)

Translated by Jeremy D. Popkin

I am going to speak of Paris: not of its buildings, its churches, its monuments, its curiosities, etc., since enough has been written about them. I will describe public and private behavior, dominant ideas, the public mood, and everything that has struck me in this odd assemblage of silly and sensible, but constantly changing, customs. And I will speak of its limitless grandeur, its monstrous wealth, its scandalous luxury. Paris sucks up money and people; it devours the other cities, like a beast looking for something to swallow.

I have studied every class of citizen, and I have not forgotten those farthest removed from haughty opulence. These contrasts allow one to better define this gigantic capital's moral physiognomy.

Many of its inhabitants are like outsiders in their own city. Perhaps this book will teach them something, or at least give them a clear and precise view of scenes that they have seen so often that they no longer notice them. The things we see every day are not those we understand the best.

Anyone who expects to find in this work a *topographic* description of public squares and streets, or a history of the city's past, will be disappointed. I have concentrated on customs and their rapidly changing nuances. Moutard, the Queen's book-publisher, sells a dictionary in four enormous volumes, approved by the censors and with a privilege from the king, in which one will find the story of every castle, college, and alleyway. If the monarch ever thinks of selling his capital, this fat dictionary would serve, I think, as a catalogue or inventory.

I have made no *inventory* or *catalogue*. I have sketched what I saw; I have varied my *Tableau* as much as possible. I have depicted the subject from many points of view, and here it is, drawn just as it came out of my pen, as my eyes and my power of understanding have put it together.

Readers can make corrections wherever the writer has seen poorly, or described badly. The comparison will perhaps stimulate in the reader a secret desire to see the object described again to see how it really appears.

There is much more to say than I have said, and many more observations to make than I have made, but only a fool or a knave would allow himself to write everything he knows or everything he has discovered.

Even if I had the hundred mouths, the hundred tongues, and the resounding voice of which Homer and Virgil speak, it would obviously have been impossible for me to present all the contrasting aspects of the great city, contrasts that stand out all the more because everything is so crowded together. Calling it *the world in miniature* is not enough; one has to see it, explore it, examine its contents, study the wisdom and folly of its inhabitants, their weaknesses and their all-conquering chatter. And then one has to consider the whole collection of these little customs of today and yesterday that constitute its special laws, but that are in constant contradiction to those that prevail in most other places.

If a thousand people followed the same route, if each one were observant, each would write a different book on this subject, and there would still be true and interesting things for someone coming after them to say.

I have stated my views on many abuses. Today, more than ever, efforts at reform are under way. To denounce these problems is to prepare their abolition. Indeed, some of them were ended as I was writing. I am happy to acknowledge this, but these changes are so recent that what I had to say is still worth reading.

In spite of all our ardent hopes to see all remaining vestiges of barbarism changed and purified, so that good, the tardy fruit of enlightenment, finally takes the place of this long deluge of so many mistakes, this city still holds on to all the unworthy and short-sighted ideas that centuries of ignorance have piled up. They can't all be thrown out overnight, because the city and its vices are too intermingled.

It is easier to shape and perfect a city just being established under the control of a farsighted government than these old cities with their faulty and complicated laws, their religious customs that seem laughable, and their civic ordinances that are often ignored. Too many abuses persist because the small group who hold the wealth that gives power proscribe new and reasonable ideas, princi-

DCXI.

Mercier's *Tableau de Paris* saved from the deluge. In some of his chapters, Mercier imagined the destruction of Paris, and suggested that his *Tableau* might furnish the only surviving record of the great city. (Courtesy Library of Congress)

ples of reform, and close their ears to the public cry. Attacks on this structure of falsehoods are vain: it is solidly held together. Reconstructing it is a much harder task than it would be to start from scratch. A few modifications are made, but they are out of harmony with the overall pattern, which is still defective. One can inscribe the most elegant reasoning in books, but the least practical application encounters insurmountable obstacles. Every petty private interest, reinforced by costly and unjustified possession, opposes the general good, which often has only a single defender. Happy those cities and individuals who have not already acquired a definitive character! They are the only ones that can aspire to coherent, well-thought-out and sensible laws.

I give fair warning that all I have done in this work is wield the painter's brush, and that I have indulged very little in philosophical reflection. I could easily have made this *Tableau* into a satire, but I have strictly limited myself. Each chapter could have designated a specific individual; I have refused to do so each time. Satire directed at particular individuals is always bad, because it doesn't make anyone change, it irritates, makes people stubborn, and doesn't lead them back to the straight path. My pictures are generalizations, and even devotion to the public welfare hasn't made me stray.

I sketched this *Tableau* from living models. Enough others have dwelt on the centuries of the past; I have concerned myself with those alive today and with the appearance of my century, because it interests me much more than the little we know of the Phoenicians or the Egyptians. I owe special attention to what is going on around me. I have to live among other people like myself, rather than taking myself off to Sparta, Rome, and Athens. To be sure, the celebrated figures of antiquity offer handsome models to depict, but they are nothing more than mere curiosities to me. My contemporary, my compatriot, that is the person I really need to understand, because I need to communicate with him, and as a result, every nuance of his character takes on a special importance for me.

If, toward the end of each century, a sensible writer had made a general portrayal of conditions around him, if he had described customs and usages as he had seen them practiced, this series would now form a fascinating gallery of comparative observations.

We would have learned of a thousand things that we don't know; it might have improved morals and legislation. But people usually undervalue what is before their eyes; they go back to the dead past; they want to figure out useless information, ways of doing things that have disappeared, about which they will never come to solid conclusions, and they lose themselves in useless and sterile debates.

I dare to believe that in a hundred years people will still turn to my *Tableau,* not because of the merit of the work, but because my observations, such as they are, will be linked to those of the century about to be born, which will profit from our foolishness and our good sense. An understanding of the people among whom he lives will always be the most important thing to any writer who aims to set down a few useful truths, capable of correcting the prevailing errors, and I can say that that is the only glory to which I aspire.

If, in looking in all directions for material for my sketches, I have more frequently found within the walls of the capital hideous poverty than respectable wealth, and suffering and anxiety rather than the happiness and gaiety for which Parisians were formerly noted, let me not be blamed for the sad colors that dominate here: my brush had to be honest. Perhaps it will lend new energy to the intelligence of modern administrators, and stimulate the generous compassion of some active and admirable spirits. I have written every line with this comforting conviction, and if I had to abandon it, I would stop writing.

I like to think that in every public-spirited idea there is an invisible seed, like the seed of a plant, which, although trampled underfoot for a long time, eventually grows, sprouts and flourishes.

I know that good sometimes comes out of evil, that there are abuses that cannot be prevented, that a heavily populated city where corruption is widespread should consider itself lucky if, in place of virtues, it gives rise to a relatively small number of serious crimes. In the midst of such a concentration of conflicting internal passions, an appearance of tranquillity is not to be discounted. I repeat, I have only wanted to *depict,* and not to *judge.*

What I have learned from my personal observations is that man is an animal capable of behaving in the most varied and astonishing ways. Parisian life is not necessarily any more unnatural than the nomadic existence of African and American savages. A hunting expedition that extends over four hundred miles and an arietta in a comic opera are equally simple and natural forms of behavior. There is no contradiction in what humans do, because they deploy the power of their intelligence and of their caprice at both ends of their range. Hence this infinite number of behaviors that truly change the individual into something different according to places, circumstances, and times. There is no more reason to be shocked by the refinements of luxury in the palaces of our millionaires than by the red and blue lines that savages cut into their skin.

At the same time, however, if it is true, as I have no reason to doubt, that comparing ourselves to others usually destroys happiness, I would also confess that it is almost impossible to be content in Paris, because the ostentatious pleasures of the rich are too visible to the indigent. The poor have reason to sigh, as they watch the reckless spending of the rich, which never makes its way down to them. From the point of view of happiness, the poor Parisian is worse off than a peasant; of all people on earth, he is the worst cared for. He is afraid to give into his natural inclination, and, if he does, he raises children who have to live in a bare attic room. Isn't there a clear contradiction between *being born* and *being without property* in this case? His faculties are wasted, and his life is precarious. Entertainment, the arts, pleasant leisure-time activities, enjoyment of the view of the sky and the countryside are not for him. There is no balance or proportion between the different conditions of life. In Paris, one is either plunged into the whirl of pleasure or the torments of despair.

Do you have an honest mediocrity for a fortune? You would be wealthy anywhere else, but in Paris, you will still be poor. Passions exist in Paris that are never seen elsewhere. The sight of pleasures makes others want to share them. The many actors playing their roles on this grand and constantly changing stage force you to become an actor yourself. Tranquillity is lost; desires become more intense; luxuries become necessities; and the needs that nature gives us are far less tyrannical than those that social pressure inspires.

Really, the man who does not want to feel poverty and the even more painful humiliation that results from it, the man who feels a just resentment when the disdainful eye of the insolent rich falls on him, should flee and never set foot in the capital.

2. General Overview

(I, Coup d'Oeil général, 1:23–29)

Translated by Jeremy D. Popkin

Anyone in Paris who knows how to understand things has no need to leave the limits of its walls to learn about people from other parts of the world. He can acquire knowledge about the entire human race by studying the individuals who swarm in this immense capital. One can find Asiatics lying all day long on heaps of tiles and Laplanders vegetating in tiny cubicles; Japanese, who slit their stomachs over the slightest quarrel; Eskimos, who have no idea how long they have been alive; Negroes whose skin is not black, and Quakers carrying swords. One encounters the customs, the habits and character of the peoples who differ the most from one another: the chemist who worships fire; the curious idol-worshipper, purchaser of statues; the wandering Arab, who walks along the city walls every day, while the idle Hottentot and Indian are in the shops, in the streets, in the cafés. Here you find the charitable Persian, who gives free remedies to the poor, and, on the same apartment-house landing, a devouring loan-shark. Brahmins and fakirs, practicing their demanding daily rituals, are not rare, nor are the Greenlanders, who have neither temples nor altars. The rituals said to have been practiced in the pleasure-loving Babylon of antiquity are followed every evening in a temple dedicated to harmony.

It has been said that one has to breathe the air of Paris to achieve perfection of any sort. Indeed, those who have never visited the capital have rarely excelled in their craft. If I am not mistaken, Paris air must have something special in it. How many materials come together in such a small place! Paris can be thought of as a large melting pot, in which meats, fruits, oils, wines, pepper, cinnamon, sugar, coffee, the most exotic products arrive to be mixed together; people's stomachs are the furnaces that decompose these ingredients. The most volatile elements must evaporate and become mixed with the air one breathes: So much smoke! So many flames! What an inundation of vapors and fumes! The soil must be saturated with all the chemicals that nature has distributed in the four parts of the world! How could all the essences brought together and distilled in the liquids that are consumed in great quan-

tities in every household, that fill certain whole streets, such as the
rue des Lombards, not put something into the atmosphere that
stimulates fibers in one place rather than another?

This perhaps explains the lively and unserious outlook that distinguishes the Parisians, this distractedness, this turn of mind that
is unique to them. Or, if it is not these living particles that set
their minds vibrating and thus give rise to ideas, surely their eyes,
perpetually struck by this infinite number of arts, of trades, of jobs,
of different occupations, cannot avoid being opened at an early
age, and learning to see the meaning of things at an age when
elsewhere people have not begun to reflect on such matters. All
the senses are constantly stimulated: things are broken, filed down,
polished, fashioned; metals are tortured into all sorts of shapes.
The tireless hammer, the cauldron always kept boiling, the ever-
active file, flatten, melt, tear things apart, put them together, re-
combine them. How can one's mind remain cold and inactive,
when, every time one passes in front of a shop, the sound of some
craft that alters nature stimulates it and wakes it from its lethargy?
Everywhere science calls out to you and says, "Look." Fire, water,
air are at work in the shops of blacksmiths, tanners, bakers; coal,
sulfur, and saltpeter change the appearances and names of things;
and all these different procedures, invented products of the
human mind, make even the stupidest heads think about things.

If you are too impatient to learn these skills, do you want to
understand theoretical matters? Professors in every line of knowledge are at the lecterns, waiting for you, from the one who dissects
human bodies at the Academy of Surgery to one who analyzes Virgil's verse at the Royal College.* Are you interested in moral questions? The theaters deal with every aspect of human life. Are you
more attracted by the miracles of harmony? If you can't make it to
the Opera, the bells in the air wake musical ears. Are you a painter?
The varied costumes of the population and the diversity of physi-
ognomies, the range of possible models, all still around, tempt
your brush. Are you more interested in frivolous things? Admire
the skilled hand of this designer, who very seriously dresses up a
doll, which will show off the current fashions all over northern
Europe and as far away as America. Do you like commercial specu-

*The Royal College is now known as the Collège de France.

lation? Here is a diamond cutter who sells 150,000 livres' worth in a morning, while his neighbor the retail grocer does 300 livres of business in a day, selling small amounts that rarely get above three or four *sous*. They are both in the business of buying and selling, and their usefulness to society is indeed different.

No, it is impossible for anyone with eyes not to think, regardless of what else he or she does. The baptism that crosses paths with a burial; the priest who is called to give courage to a dying person just when he is summoned to marry a young couple, to whom the notary has talked about preparing wills on the very day of their happy union; the way farsighted laws look out for two hearts in love that take no thought for the future; the welfare of their children assured even before they are born, and the gaiety of the assembly in the midst of reminders of serious matters: everything should interest the attentive observer.

You stop to let a vehicle go by, lest you find yourself laid out flat on the pavement: you see a ragged beggar stretching out his hand to a gilded carriage, in which is settled a heavyset man who, barricaded behind his mirrored glass, seems to be blind and deaf. Apoplexy stalks him, and in ten days he will be buried, leaving two or three million to selfish heirs who will make fun of his death, whereas he wouldn't give the slightest help to the victim of misfortune who implored him with halting voice.

How many eloquent scenes that strike the eye at every street-crossing, and what a gallery of images, so full of striking contrasts for anyone who knows how to see and understand!

The prodigious consumption of eight hundred thousand people crowded together and living in the same place, among whom are two hundred thousand who are self-indulgent or wasteful, leads to a first political reflection. The duke pays no more for his bread than the porter who carries heavy loads through the streets, and who eats three times as much of it. How can one not be astonished by the unbelievable tranquillity that prevails in the midst of such great confusion? This shows what wise laws can do, how long it has taken to formulate them, what a complicated and yet simple machine this ever-vigilant administration is; and one discovers at the same time how to perfect it, without limiting this respectable and precious liberty, the thing every citizen values most.

If one likes to travel, one can voyage a long way in imagination even while dining in a good house. China and Japan have furnished the porcelain in which the aromatic tea boils; with a spoon made from the ore of Peruvian mines, one takes the sugar that unfortunate Negroes, transplanted from Africa, have raised in America; one sits on brilliant Indian fabrics, from that land over which three great powers have fought a long and cruel war. If one wants to know the details of this struggle, one has only to take in hand the latest sheet that gives the constantly changing history of the four parts of the world; in it, there is talk of a conclave and a battle, of a vizir newly strangled and an academician newly appointed. Everything, up to and including the host's monkey and parakeet, reminds you of the miracle of navigation and the devoted efforts of humankind.

By putting one's head out the window, one can contemplate the man who makes shoes to earn enough for bread, and the man who makes a coat to earn enough for shoes, and the man who, having shoes and coats, drives himself to earn enough for a painting. One sees the baker and the druggist, the obstetrician and the gravedigger, the blacksmith and the jeweler, all working so they can afford the baker, the druggist, the obstetrician, and the wineseller.

3. Unhealthy Size of the Capital

(III, Grandeur démesurée de la capitale 1:32–33)

Translated by Jeremy D. Popkin

From the political point of view, Paris is too large. It is a head too big for the body of the country, but it would be more dangerous now to cut out the growth than to let it alone. There are evils that are impossible to do away with once they have taken root.

Arbitrary governments like big cities. They do everything possible to attract people to them. The appeal of luxury and pleasure lures the wealthy; the common people are herded in, like sheep into a pasture, so that the guard dogs' throats don't have to work so hard to make themselves heard and they can keep them under control more easily. Thus Paris is a sinkhole into which the whole human species falls. There they are kept under lock and key; no one gets in or out except through carefully guarded gates. Barriers of pinewood, better respected than walls of stone lined with cannon would be, stop the arrival of vital necessities and impose a tax paid on them only by the poor. The poor are excused from all pleasures, but they have to eat. It is up to the ruler if he wishes to starve the city. He has his good and loyal subjects in a cage, and if he is unhappy with them, he can cut off their food. Before they could break through the barriers, three quarters of them would have eaten each other, or died of hunger.

Everyone has to live somehow; survival is the basic law. I see this city flourishing, but at the expense of the nation as a whole. These crowded six-story apartment houses suck up the grain and wine from the countryside a hundred miles around. These lackeys, these street entertainers, these abbés, these people who run around the streets do nothing useful for the state or for society, but they all have to eat, as the first chapter of a book I might write on legislation would say: I would call it "Of the human stomach." There are political evils that have to be tolerated, if there is no sure way of remedying them. The overgrown state of the capital is one of them: one cannot send those who live in rented rooms and attics back to the countryside. They have nothing, not even arms to work with, since they have become run down. Would you stop those who arrive at the gates? Keep this great wen, then, since there is no way of getting rid of it without endangering the political organism; in any event. . . . But let us not anticipate what we are going to say about this city, which will always be the apple of the eye in a system of government whose head is as overgrown as the city is in relation to the kingdom.

4. Political Character of the Parisian

(xxv, Caractère politique des vrais Parisiens, 1:75–76)

The citizen of the capital has never given a thought to his political importance. His kings rule as they please, their caprices rouse him only to occasional and childish outbreaks against their authority; he is neither altogether free, nor wholly a slave. The people make songs on the cannon brought up to quell them; royalty in its place with epigrams, punish the King with their silence, and his reward is in their voices and clapped hands as he passes. The feeling of the crowd at the central market is always just; the market is the place where rulers are judged, and the philosopher, taking his time, making his notes, wakes up one day to find that his considered verdict does no more than confirm its judgment.

The Parisian's instinct seems to have taught him that the little more liberty he might obtain is not worth fighting for; any such struggle would imply long effort and stern thinking. He has a short memory for trouble, chalks up no score of his miseries, and has confidence enough in his own strength not to dread too absolute a despotism. In the recent rivalry* between the laws and the throne he showed fortitude, patience, and great courage; a town besieged could not have borne itself more bravely.

He is a kindly, civil personage enough, and as a rule easily led, but it does not do to mistake his docility for weakness; the Parisian, with a wink, allows himself to be deceived; but I believe that I know him well enough to fear him, if the pressure should ever become too great; the League and the Fronde† are sufficient witness to his obstinacy. While his life is bearable it will be borne, he will still set his grievances to music and his tongue, though he holds it in public, will run freely indoors.

Paris lives in darkest ignorance of its place in history; has forgotten that three centuries back it had an English governor; and that it is less than a hundred years since Marlborough,‡ having broken Villars' line at Bouchain, found the way to the capital open, and Paris dependent upon the hazard of a single battle. As for London, the Parisian knows less of it than he does about Beijing.

---

*Mercier's reference to "the recent rivalry between the laws and throne" refers to the effort of René-Nicholas Maupeou, chancellor of France under Louis XV, to strengthen royal authority by undermining the powers of the *parlements,* the king-

dom's principal law courts, in January 1771. Maupeou's "coup" was overturned
when Louis XV died unexpectedly in May 1774.
†The League was a movement of Catholic zealots who seized control of Paris in
1588. The Fronde (1648–53) was a revolt against the unpopular minister Mazarin.
‡The Duke of Marlborough (1650–1722) was the main British commander during
the War of the Spanish Succession. He defeated the French forces under the Maréchal de Villars at Bouchain (in present-day Belgium) in 1711 and could have advanced on Paris.

5. Furnished Rooms
(XLVII, Chambres garnies, 1:129–31)

You may find a Russian prince in a garret near the Palais-Royal,
another in a dirty basement, a Swiss paying for half a sordid
room the weight of its furniture in gold. All furnished rooms are
dirty. The foreigner shudders at our uncleanly beds, ill-fitting windows, tattered hangings and staircases filthier than all the rest. Parisians fail to notice these things, they are used to them, and no
allowance is made for the foreigner's taste and standards of living.
An Englishman and a Dutchman, both men of nations whose delight is cleanliness, find themselves sharing a bed with certain vora-
cious insects, and at the mercy of a window which refuses to shut.
Thereupon they depart from a town which has used most of their
senses so ill, taking with them the good money which, with a better
welcome, they might have stayed to spend.

But these places are the debtor's refuge; a man with no goods
to be seized, no fixed address, and no money at his banker's, can
afford to snap his fingers at bailiffs. He walks in and out of his
furnished room free as air, repeating, if his tastes run to Latin, the
words of Bias*: "Omnia mecum porto."

As a denizen of furnished rooms you pay tax direct, but the landlord pays, and the landlord takes it out of you; your name is inscribed on a register, which goes to the police, who have their own
use for such things. Arrests are easily made, and arouse little interest among this floating population. The policeman answers all
questions with the one cry—"Thieving, the fellow's a thief"; and

since nobody knows the victim nobody interferes, by nightfall he
is forgotten, and twenty-four hours sees the end of him.

At one time foreigners living in Paris totalled over a hundred
thousand, all lodged like this, in rooms; now the number has
fallen. Prices vary enormously; for instance, four rooms near the
Palais-Royal will cost you six times as much as the same accommodation near the Luxembourg.

The wretched women who accost you after the play, and follow
you along the street, live in rooms. They pay twice the ordinary
rent, and the price is constantly rising, driving them ever deeper
into misery; they can never escape from their trade save by some
very exceptional stroke of luck. There is an official prohibition
against letting to prostitutes, yet but for them half the rooms would
be empty. Hairdressers and wine-sellers are the landlords, usually,
of these disgusting dens, and do very well out of them, exacting
payment in advance, plaguing their miserable tenants with threats
of the police, and getting money from the police for keeping an
eye on the tenants.

*Bias was one of the legendary seven sages of ancient Greece. When the population
of his native city had to flee, most tried to take their most precious belongings. Bias
took nothing, saying that since he had his knowledge and virtue, "I carry everything
with me."

6. Spies
(LIX, Espions, 1:156–58)

T he Parisian, they say, neither tells the truth himself nor cares
what the truth may be; but the fact is, that if he were not a
liar born, he must become one in self-defence. Spies are all about
him. Two citizens cannot whisper, without a third craning his neck
to hear what the conference is about. The Lieutenant of Police
commands a regiment of ears, differing from a regiment of soldiers only in that each private changes his uniform daily and completely; in the twinkling of an eye he can and does metamorphose
himself. One will strut abroad all day, sword on hip, and be sub-

dued at night to a gown and bands, from a limb of the devil to a limb of the law; tomorrow, swinging a gold-headed cane, he will seem a banker with only ciphers in his head; all this at the taxpayer's expense. His day's range of impersonations may include a military officer, a hairdresser's assistant, a tonsured abbot and a scullery boy. The best houses know him, and the worst hells. Now he sports a diamond ring, now a greasy wig, and dons his personality with his coat; Preville, our best actor, might learn something of his art from this fellow. He is all eyes, all ears, all feet and legs as well, for he seems, however he contrives it, to be in all the sixteen quarters of Paris at once. You may see in some *café* a solid sleepy man, snoring away the hour before supper, and pay no need to him; but he in his corner is by no means so oblivious of you. Or it may be an orator voicing some project, criticizing the Government, who claims your support, and urges you to indiscretion; if you succeed in holding your tongue, your expression is print to him; whether you speak or not, he deciphers your opinion.

For this is the rod whereby the secrets of Paris are divined; and it is on these men's reports rather than the exigencies of a situation or the demands of policy that ministerial decisions are founded. Friendship, confidence—the spy system has made such amenities too dangerous; and so we talk surface stuff for the reassuring of the Government, which thus is the actual dictator of all those imbecilities that go the nightly round in *cafés* and clubs. In some vital matter, a death, say, that you want to conceal, you have only to give it out in a whisper, with the caution—"But no talking, understand, yet awhile"—and your confidant will be mute as the grave. Our people have lost, utterly, all idea of how the administration gets its business done; and if such a state of things were not so deplorable, it might even be amusing to hear the man in the street declaiming his opinion that Versailles and Paris should give the law and set the pace for all Europe, and so for the world. Prejudice, like some unclean growth, clings about people's minds in this old town; prejudice, modified only a little by crass and incurable stupidity. Good reason why; for these unfortunates have only the *Gazette de France** to read, and take their opinions from it, such as they are.

---

*The *Gazette de France*, founded in 1631, was the French monarchy's official newspaper.

7. Hawkers

(LX, Les Colporteurs, 1:158–60)

These take up a good deal of the spies' time; they undertake the distribution of the only books an intelligent person cares to read, which naturally are not printed in France. They have a hard time of it, the police are for ever on their heels, for what seems to them no reason, since they never read their own wares, but would smuggle Bibles if Bibles happened to be banned by the police. They go to the Bastille and even to the pillory for selling some absurd pamphlet which is forgotten next day; thus avenging the printed slight put upon some important person whose pride of place gives birth to the very comments it punishes. No minister as yet has had the courage to ignore these squibs, to forestall criticism by frankness; or to reflect that unless the voice of the people may make itself heard in complaint, approbation too must be dumb. Let him punish his flatterers, who do more harm to a man than a good round truth or two, and remember that the public has a mind of its own, and that an unjust satire falls of itself, if facts speak against it.

Often the secret police, after gathering in these pamphlets, sell them to chosen buyers, and the money goes into their own pockets; thus one spy earns more than thirty hawkers.

All that is printed in Paris concerning politics and history is either satire or falsehood. Foreigners know it, and pity us. The worst of it is, that pressure exercised upon such subjects as these, reacts upon others; fear of the censorship shows itself even in the lightest, most ephemeral written stuff. Our printers must get a living as best they can turning out playbills, invitations to weddings and funerals; almanacs are already under suspicion, some Government department is already at work pruning them of treasonable matter.

The official *imprimatur* in any book is enough. You may bet, without looking inside, that it contains some travesty of political morality. It is within the King's province to say: "This scrap of paper shall be worth a thousand francs"; but when he says: "This lie shall be truth," or worse still: "This truth shall be disbelieved," he goes beyond his own powers. He can say what he pleases, but he cannot make people believe it.

What we admire about printed productions is that the great works which do honor to the human mind cannot be produced on command or for pay. They spring from the natural freedom of a broadminded spirit, which develops in spite of dangers, and creates a gift for humanity, in spite of tyrants. This is why authors deserve respect, and why future generations will be grateful to them.

And thus our unhappy hawkers, who distribute masterpieces without knowing A from B, bear the full brunt of ministerial displeasure, and save the liberty of the Press for a mere crust of bread. The author goes scot-free, they dare not attack him; that would turn public opinion against the Government, and show its firmness in a very ugly light.

8. The Police Force

(LXI, Hommes de la police, 1:161–64)

Wholly corrupt, it is divided into two classes: spies, or 'noses,' who smell out crime, and those who do the work of arrest and pursuit. Their Lieutenant launches these latter against thieves and pickpockets much as a huntsman throws his hounds after the fox.

The 'noses,' those unsavoury parasites, have lesser fleas to bite 'em; in other words, satellite spies, who report on them and make sure their work is done. These functionaries denounce each other, and wrangle over their sordid gains; thus public order is maintained. But they get short shrift from magistrates, when they bring their contradictions into court. Such is our admirable system which preserves intact the moral order.

A suspect is followed so closely that he can take no step unobserved, and they may arrest him when they please. He is described by these men to their superiors in such astonishing detail, that the greatest descriptive writer on earth could find nothing to add to the picture.

They go out by night to take thieves and such malefactors; much as though tigers and wolves had been tamed to serve man's purposes.

There are spies of all sorts, Court spies, town spies, bed, street, and brothel spies, spies upon talkers and wits; but the whole genus has the one name, *mouchard,* which was that of the first official spy of the Court of France. Among them are men of quality, who lend to those plebeian syllables their titles of baron, count, or marquis.

There was a time, under Louis XV, when espionage became so general as to affect even private and friendly gatherings. Every *salon* had its watcher, every cabinet its listening ear; the apprehensions of ministers punished even confidences of relations and friends, spoken privately and intended never to be repeated or recalled. This hateful tyranny so poisoned all social life, with all its divided innocent pleasures, and so divided the whole structure of society, that now any man known to be in the espionage service, no matter how high his capacity or his claims, is forbidden entry to polite society.

One servant in every four is a spy, by whose means the most carefully hidden family secrets find their way into unscrupulous hands.

Ministers have personal spies, who work apart from the police. These are the most dangerous of all, since they carry no signs of their trade, and are hard to recognize. By their means ministers know what the world says of them, and then are none the wiser, for they employ their information only to ruin personal enemies or checkmate rivals, and never examine criticisms or complaints to discover how wrongs may be redressed. Ministers, like other less distinguished listeners, hear no good of themselves; indeed only the King and his immediate relatives are spared by the Parisians' tongues.

Court secrets leak out in other ways, through men whom no spy would suspect; and take their interest, particularly here in France, from the quite remarkable secrecy which as a rule obscures all discussion on matters of policy. Hidden, like forbidden, fruit is tempting; certain men will always want to know more than their fellows, and take pride and interest in the machine in proportion as they know just by what power, and in what order, the wheels go round. The difficulty of attaining this knowledge is what gives it its chief value.

But Time reveals the secrets of all things. What a man has seen,

that sooner or later he will tell; even, he may tell that which he
never saw at all, but only suspected.

9. Street Lighting

(LXV, Réverbères, 1:175–76)

Lanterns went out sixteen years ago, and since then we have
had oil reflectors for our streets, which give better light, and
are more easily tended. In the old days eight thousand lanterns,
their candles askew, or guttering, or blown out by the wind, nightly
adorned the city, a feeble and wavering illumination broken by
patches of treacherously shifting darkness. Now twelve hundred of
these oil-lamps suffice, and the light they throw is steady, clear, and
lasting.

But why should this excellent innovation be marred by misdi-
rected economy? Our lighting goes by calendar; when that an-
nounces Full Moon, no reflectors are lit. Before it rises the town
lies in darkness, and when at last it does show above the horizon,
shadows of tall houses invade the streets, which thus are no better
off than before; then the moon sets, and Paris is plunged in gloom
again. . . .

Every twenty years each householder is faced with a demand for
the lighting and cleaning of his street; the tax is far greater than
the amount of the whole twenty years' expense; one more straw to
the load already on his back.

The mud of Paris is necessarily filthy, black with grit and metal
fragments detached by the eternal traffic; but it is the domestic
waste running into it which chiefly accounts for the smell. This, no
foreign nose can abide; it is sulphurous, with a tang of nitric acid.
A spot of this mud left on a coat will eat away the cloth.

Carts come at intervals to take up the mud and other ordure and
transport it into the near-by country, where it is dumped. These
depositories are places to avoid. It is all done by contract, as
cheaply as possible.

Street Lamps. The street lamps Mercier described served
to illuminate all kinds of activities, including prostitution.
(Courtesy Library of Congress)

After snow, besides the snow itself to clear away, there is ice in the gutters, and with all the other filth frozen as hard as so much stone, which must be broken up, it becomes no easy task to keep the streets wholesome. Three days' neglect is enough to maroon us all in our houses; but the police are vigilant and the service is maintained. Some quarters are so well looked after, that the total neglect of certain others is a matter for astonishment, and to be deplored.

But in a later chapter, also titled "Réverbères" (DCCIX, 2:600–601), Mercier writes:

> These street lamps are badly hung; they make, in Milton's words, darkness itself be visible. They should be fixed close to the wall, not swung out above the street on great brackets. At a distance they dazzle, close to they give little light, and standing underneath you can hardly see your hand before you. It is the business of the police, and they should see to it that public order and public convenience are better served. Another thing; they might well keep some sort of watch on the lamplighters. These fill the lamps, as they call it, nightly; actually they allow so little oil that by nine or ten o'clock half are already out; only an occasional and distant glimmer reminds you of how the streets ought to look, and of the sharp practices of public employees.
>
> Some years ago houses in Paris began to be numbered; like so many other projects, this was never carried through, but it would have served a very useful purpose, especially in the longer streets; the unhappy pedestrian would have been saved many a false direction, and many a half-hour's blind wandering. What numbers there are now are too small, half hidden, and quite impossible to find at night. No middle-class householder knows the number of his own house, or even if it has a number, so invisible are the figures, and so obscurely placed.

10. Signs

(LXVI, Enseignes, 1:177–78)

N owadays tradesmen's signs lie flat, fixed to the walls above their shops and houses; time was when they hung out above the street on long iron rods, and when a high wind swung them, threatened to clatter down upon passing heads, rods and all. Any wind, even the lightest, would set this whole rabble of signs squealing and clashing upon one another, making a plaintive and discordant *carillon*, quite indescribable; and at night they made great shadows, against which the poor light of the street lamps strove in vain.

Mostly they were of iron, colossal, and cast in relief, thus offering a world of giants' appurtenances to the eyes of the most stunted people in Europe. You saw a sword-guard six feet high, a boot the size of a hogshead, a spur that might serve for a carriage-wheel, gloves where a three-year-old child might hide in each finger, monstrous heads, and armed hands flourishing blades as long as the width of the street.

Now that these unsightly growths of metal are gone, the town has taken on a civil, pleasant, smooth-shaven look, all of which it owes to Monsieur Antoine-Raimond-Jean-Gualbert-Gabriel de Sartine,* Minister of Police; who having been perfectly successful as such, is now given the Navy.

---

*Antoine-R.-J.-G. Gabriel de Sartine (1729–1801) was appointed lieutenant général de police in 1759 and later served as minister of the navy.

11. Markets

(LXVIII, Marchés, 1:181–82)

P aris markets are dirty, Paris markets are disgusting; all the stuff for sale is piled pell-mell, and a shelter or so here and there is quite insufficient to protect our food from the caprices of the seasons; on wet days, down comes the rain through their roofs on to the baskets of eggs or vegetables, and soaks the fruit and butter or whatever the commodity may be.

The markets are ill-placed, there is no getting to or from them, with their narrow alleys, and no room for vehicles to stand. You make your purchases under the menace of encroaching wheels, and when the gutters overflow, as they sometimes do, good food is swept away; you may see fish, new-come from the sea, floating in these runnels of muddy water.

The noise, too, is stunning; so appalling that only the most superhuman voice can pierce it. The Tower of Babel was nothing to our confusion of tongues.

Twenty-five years ago the Government built a granary which a little relieved the congestion of the central markets; but the granary itself is inadequate, it cannot hold the prodigious quantities needed to feed the capital, though it might do very well for a third-rate town in the provinces; and there, too, the sacks of flour are exposed to all weathers. There is something in our modern way of building, something niggardly, that prevents anything better taking its place.

The fish-stalls are unspeakable. In ancient Greece vendors of fresh fish might not sit down until their wares were sold; it was a law, and a wise one, to ensure that this kind of food should be both cheap and fresh. But our modern fishwives will not part with a scale or a fin until it begins to stink. They sit, and as long as they please, sure of custom; for the Parisian, unlike any other civilized creature, will not take his nose for a guide. When you ask him why it is, and scold him, he answers: "What else is there, one must cook something for supper." So he sups of spoiled fish, and his stomach pays for it.

12. Department of Rivers and Forests
(CXIV, Tribunal des Eaux et Forêts, 1:277–78)

T he function of this tribunal, still known by its old name of the 'captaincy,' is to send to the galleys persons convicted of feloniously slaying partridges and hares.* A hare may eat a peasant's cabbages, pigeons may descend in swarms upon his ripening corn; in the river bordering his field fish may swim in shoals; but he may not interfere with the hare or the pigeon's proclivities, nor set a line for the fish. As for a stag, if he kills one he hangs, and that is the end of him; but this crime is so hideous, so barbarous, that it is almost unheard of; it is far more rare than parricide.

Strange that we should owe to Henry IV, that best of kings, the first law against poaching with the death penalty attached to it.

The statutes which this tribunal administers are something apart, something totally unrelated to our time, and to the main body of our laws. We have plenty of these, all savage; the ordinary citizen, do what he may, and unknown to himself, is continually breaking some one or other of them.

*Certain criminals were sentenced to a term rowing in the French navy's fleet of galleys in the Mediterranean.

13. Longchamp
(CXXII, Longchamp, 1:293–95)

Wednesday, Thursday and Friday of Holy Week are the days when all the world goes out of town, ostensibly to hear the office of *Tenebræ** sung in the village church of Longchamp, four miles out of Paris, but in reality to show off carriages, horses, and liveries, all magnificent, and most of them new.

Women choose this expedition to display their jewels, for women, in Paris at any rate, only live to be looked at. However, on these three days you may see all sorts and conditions driving back and forth along the dusty or muddy alleys of the Bois de Boulogne.

You may know the courtesan easily enough, by the luxury of her equipage; one of these has the horse's harness set with rose-diamonds. Men of rank advertise the last word in saddlery, some-times even handling the reins themselves. But all the men, on foot or horseback, crowded, jostled as they are, find time to ogle all the women. As for the poorer people, they get drunk; churches are empty, and *cabarets* full; thus the capital laments the Passion of Jesus Christ.

Once upon a time music was supposed to be the chief attraction, and the archbishop by putting his veto upon all organs thought to scotch the scandal; but no, the indomitable excursionists drove out as before, with this difference, that they never even made a pretence of going under the church.

Yet the brief journey has its meaning; it is, this expedition under clear skies, through the green of leaves unfolding, a visit made to Nature in her own temple; a thank-offering to her for remembering us once more, and for the gift of spring.

Women, for all their concern with their jewels and finery, take second place; horses, carriages and all their concomitants come first and take the eye. The dilapidated *fiacre* has its use; a new elegant carriage looks more elegant beside it. Our modern carriages are better built, more light, and less ornamented than the old; and naturally, being lighter, are faster than the older vehicles.

The working-man like everyone else joins the throng in his best clothes, and eyes the women with his betters; it is his hands, dirty and calloused, that give him away.

Some, while others walk, and take the clean spring air, actually go into the church, and there listen to voices singing the interminable jeremiads that punctuate this ceremony; which ends, however, in the wildest kind of uproar, a moment which schoolboys, and others for that matter, impatiently await.

*Catholics held a special service called *Tenebrae* as part of the observance of Good Friday. It was dropped from the Catholic liturgy by the Vatican II Council in 1962–65. The Franciscan abbey at Longchamp was noted for its choir.

14. Barriers

(CXXIII, Barrières, 1:295–97)

A re made of pine, occasionally of iron; if the amount they earn had been employed in their building they might be wrought of pure gold. [There are sixty of them closing in Paris by way of the suburbs, and two barred waterways, with custom-houses.]

At the barrier a greencoated clerk, whose wages are a miserable hundred pistoles* a year, never absent, quite incorruptible, keeps watch; not a mouse slips by him unobserved. He comes to the door of each vehicle, abruptly opens it, puts his question, "Anything to declare?" The correct answer is, "See for yourself." In steps the clerk, searches, gets down, shuts the door. His victims mutter abuse behind his back; he hears, and cares exactly nothing. When he finds something dutiable which has not been declared, then you receive a summons, signed by one Nicholas Salzard, to whom you pay your fine; he is the collector and representative of the Farmer-General,† and if the farming of taxes ever at some future date becomes a hanging matter, it is Nicholas who will adorn the gibbet.

No vehicle is exempt, save only the royal carriage and those of ministers of the Crown; Nicholas Salzard respects these; but his clerk may and does investigate every other wheeled thing, even the coaches of his master, and other potentates of taxation.

Every day persons of the most unquestioned probity may be heard lying at the barriers. Morality never disapproves a lie told to the customs; success is amusing; all of us do it, and boast afterwards of our exploits.

A bulging pocket takes the clerk's eye at once; in goes his hand. Parcels must all be untied. There are certain days when cattle come in to the slaughter-houses, and these have right of way; the main gate is shut, and a smaller one, which admits only one beast at a time, is unlocked; Mr Clerk must count the whole herd; it takes a couple of hours, and when that is over you may get on with your journey.

Manufacturer, are you? or commercial traveller? Your bale of goods goes into the *douane,*‡ and there, while your customers wait, you do your best to satisfy officials, with their: "Open this, unpack that, this must be investigated, that must be weighed"; and the whole pays its tax.

Payment involves a visit to ten offices, and the procuring of twenty signatures for each solitary bale or bag. If your luggage includes a book or two, that means another little journey to the Rue du Foin, where yet another inspector approves or condemns your taste in literature.

You argue, you protest, you declare and prove incontestably that the whole business is a preposterous folly, political delirium, that you impoverish the State by harassing its trade; Mr Clerk in his

greatcoat and his satellites of the customs care nothing fo
ment. Their attitude is, "All that we search is ours, at the barrier
all rights of property are forfeit"; and when at last they let you go
with your own, they seem to require your thanks for their selfless-
ness in parting with it.

*"pistoles": a pistole was equal to ten livres.
†Farmer-General: French taxes were collected by private entrepreneurs known as
tax farmers. The Farmer-General was the head of the tax-collection company.
‡The *douane* was the customs office, where goods were examined.

15. Our Latest Great Fire
(CXXIV, Nouvel incendie, 1:298–300)

On June 8th, 1781, the Opera House, which, with all its faults,
was spacious and gracious, went up in flames. A rope at the
front of the stage took fire from a hanging lamp, which set the
curtain alight; thence flames spread to the proscenium and the
stage boxes, and the whole theatre was gutted. One bucket of water
would have settled the original outbreak; there were pumps and
hoses attached to a special water-tank, a whole apparatus all ready
for just such an emergency; the tank, however, was empty. Members of the administrative staff were at loggerheads, and while they
wrangled precautions were neglected. Fourteen persons were reduced to ashes, and the city firemen, when they arrived, could only
succeed in saving the façade on the Rue Saint-Honoré. It was a
most horrible yet singular sight, this immense pyramidal flame
shooting up through the dome, changing colour according to
whether the paint of the scenery fed it, or the gilding of the boxes.

But by October 25th of the same year, a temporary Opera
House, well built, and as large as its predecessor, opened its doors
upon the Boulevard, equipped with all the old magnificence, offering a livelihood to the many and a diversion to the few. A hospital
thus destroyed might have waited four years, not four months,
while new plans for it were debated. But opera is another thing.
We cannot do without opera, too many people live by it, singers,

dancers, musicians, decorators, scene-painters, scene-shifters, and tailors; a microcosm. Through these channels, trade flows. Costumes must be rich and varied, and shops must keep a stock of the silks and muslins and ribbons which go to make them. Then the performances employ all the decorative arts, and the performers, by arts no less subtle, lead foreigners captive, and keep their money here in the Kingdom.

So that opera, when it dies, leaves unemployment behind it, and dulls the life of the town; besides being in itself a great and reputable art, wherein music and dancing have each their place, and by which their practitioners are assured of a living commensurate with their talents. Paris without the opera! It would be a kind of Lenten calamity for the capital. This theatre is one which offers all the arts their chance, and spectators their choice of sensation; it cannot suffer interruption. . . .

But it seems the fate of such theatres to perish by fire; disasters at Rome, Amsterdam, Milan, Saragossa and Paris, are within all our memories; and the moral of it is, I suppose, that we must isolate these buildings, and use in their construction as little wood as we can.

An English lord has recently invented a process, quite simple and not too expensive, whereby the rafters and woodwork generally may be treated with a kind of varnish, which is absolutely proof against fire. In a town, any town, this process would be invaluable; for while their fellow-citizens sleep, bakers are at work, heating their ovens to a degree which, if the cement holds none too well, may affect neighbouring walls; and once a chance spark finds fuel, there is no escaping.

If to a pump holding fifty or sixty buckets of water, eight or ten pounds of salt or potash be added, the resulting solution would hold the most furious blaze in check; it is astonishing what it can do.

16. Foresight

(CXXV, Prévoyance, 1:301)

In the old days the victim of accident, with his fracture, disloca-
tion or any other injury, found his way to shelter in some impro-
vised manner, on a ladder, or a chance-found plank, which added
considerably to his sufferings; but recently (since we are all reform-
ers nowadays) a litter or stretcher has been placed in every guard-
house, equipped with a comfortable mattress, so that transport to
hospital or home is less painful than of old. Besides this, in the
chief police-post of every quarter quantities of bandages, com-
presses, and lint are kept ready to hand, for the use of those who,
stepping out of their houses in excellent fettle, are brought home
with a couple of limbs broken, the result of adventuring into the
Paris streets; which to tread for a whole day long, on business, is
much like taking part in a full-dress assault at arms. This foresight
of our moderns is excellent, but only serves to prove, not that we
are more humane than our fathers, but that accidents nowadays
are more frequent; it is easier to think out such palliatives than to
set a limit to the infernal excess of our wheeled traffic. But then,
what can you expect? Our lawmakers all get around by carriage.

17. Bankers

(CXXVII, Banquiers, 1:304–8)

During the last half-century the transfer of bills and their with-
drawal, loans, and all the tricks of the banker's trade, have
taken the place of prudent, sane, and statesmanlike legislation.
Accountants and brokers are the nation's chief servants, the administration is become an enterprise whose stocks are bought and
sold, and which is in perpetual flux. Bankers are the rulers of
France; money comes and goes at their bidding; they call it from
the ends of the earth, and then, flick! it is gone. Dangerous magi-
cians these, citizens of no country and restrained by no loyalty; no
man can guess what will be the end of their swift and terrifying
game, their passes which turn gold to quicksilver, and bring the
treasure of a state in an instant to nothing.

he remedy is no more comprehensible than the disease; however, this present circulation of money gives at least the appearance of health, and may do more, if it lasts; but there are signs that the end is not far off. There is some talk of circulating what are called 'black notes,' the symbols of a system not unlike that of Law;* if we are to come to this, then for God's sake let them make haste, and not wait till we are *in extremis*! It might have been a good thing to begin with something of the sort modelled on the London banks and their methods. But the wealth of the nation is not in question; it is how to get money for the King, that is the problem; the King, who represents the nation and should unite it.

The bankers handle all matters such as the floating of our huge recent loans; it is become too easy to lend and borrow, and the result is that people embark upon extravagances without counting the cost, and sacrifice the present to a future which, to say the least, is doubtful. They have sucked money even from the capillary veins of the body politic; but the capillary veins need life-blood as the arteries do. This eternal pouring of money into the King's hands! What of his people? What of trade, and industry, and art? Why should their whole purchasing power flow to and through him?

True political science should regard the present; our legislators in their folly look always forward, towards the better time coming. No one, not the greatest genius of us all, can foretell the future, or calculate the strange twists of Fate's wheel. War is always a horrible evil; whatever good may result from it is always uncertain and distant.

I do not mean that a national debt is necessarily a bad thing to have; borrowing is not an evil in itself. But that the borrowed money should dribble away in a war, sink like water into battlefields, or be expended on sterile magnificence such as buildings, or shows of one sort or another; there lies the evil.

They are terrifying, the sums that are raised in this kingdom, and sunk God knows how or where. What are the money-makers at? They use all their endeavours, they toil ingeniously and on a vast scale; and at the end of it all, the goal of their achievement seems impossible to discover. Why all this mystery? To us, in the darkness of non-comprehension, success and failure look alike.

But it may be that there is no radical cure; that palliatives are all that can be applied to an old civilization, rotten with old vices, incapable of ever regaining soundness and health. Our past errors stand in the way of wise planning, and the nation itself will permit no interference, will not have it that the State is sick. The current maxim runs: Victory to him who holds the last coin; a silly saying, but accepted. How after this, can a man give over gambling with borrowed money?

Sully,[†] an economist in the stricter sense, a frugal statesman who planned both for today and tomorrow, would have nothing to do with bankers and their credits. Borrowing he regarded as a danger- ous practice, and discounted the appearance of wealth it brought. He would seem very strait-laced and pedagogic today; the Fau- bourg Saint-Honoré (where the bankers live) would hoot him as one man. The ministers who succeeded him, Villeroy and Jeannin, undid all the good of his rule; but then, they were financiers, and he was only a statesman.

I have no wish to give my random reflections a bitter sound, or to satirize these money-manipulators; time will show whether or not banking in its present form is to prove the sheet-anchor of the State, and the guiding principle of its energies. The ordinary man, the speculator, condemns certain methods; it may be that he is wrong, and that these expedients in the circumstances, and all things considered, are the right ones. I must beg leave to doubt; but it would be rash to prophesy either salvation or disaster. The bankers hold the tiller of our vessel; let us leave them to it, to manœuvre us as their judgment directs; the voyage is half done; may they bring us all safe to harbour!

---

*John Law, a Scottish financier, had been entrusted with control of French finances during the regency that followed Louis XIV's death in 1715. His ambitious specula- tions, which included the issuing of paper currency, led to a financial collapse and resulted in a long-lasting distrust of bankers in France.
†Maximilien de Béthune, duc de Sully (1560–1641) was Henri IV's principal minis- ter. He restored government finances after the religious wars of the sixteenth cen- tury.

18. Bankruptcies

(CXXVIII, Banqueroutes, 1:308–10)

Have become so frequent as to be no disgrace; the reason is to be found in the present-day outlook of our tradesmen themselves, who have dropped the reality of their old simplicity for an unsatisfying shadow of luxury; you can no longer guess a man's profession from his dress and circumstances. Our tradesmen, like the rest of us, follow the fashion, and when fashion dictates silliness and bad faith, they obey. . . .

Failures have become part of the money game; fail and grow rich is the motto now. No more fortunes hard-won by long and difficult years of probity; a couple of balance-sheets adroitly handled, and you may retire on a competence. They reckon that a bankruptcy for a million should mean two hundred and fifty thousand in the bankrupt's pocket.

What follows? Confidence, the soul of trade, is lost; everyone is wary, everyone is suspicious, and everyone is in difficulties, where a hundred years ago they might have prospered.

When the failure is declared, come certain functionaries who take your affairs and the worry of them off your shoulders; money doctors they call them. Creditors may come and go, obey summonses, swear to this and that, sign the other, and verify their claims; the debtor sits at home in comfort, twiddling your thumbs.

But there is a difference between failures and bankruptcies; the latter are almost always fraudulent, while the former may be brought about through pressure of circumstances, unlucky speculations, or being too optimistic; they deserve more indulgence.

If the tradesman were to make public his first losses, courageously, no one would complain; but he keeps these dark until the last moment, until he is over the precipice; he may bring down with him, like a ninepin falling, a crowd of lesser men.

The laws in these matters are not sufficiently clear. Your rogue avails himself of their vagueness, and brings off a gross swindle with triumphant impunity; another man, more honest, goes under because he is ignorant of the procedure, or cannot pay his way out of trouble. Only the smallest fry of debtors are caught in the legal net. A new law, and a strong law, which should penalize all such fraudulent schemes, would put new life into trade. Severe penalties would not meet the case, for severity always tends to defeat its own

ends; but they should be sufficient to deter those who fail from
choice, and protect those who do so from necessity.

19. Passing the Collection Plate
(CXXXII, Quêteuses, 1:318–19)

T he strictest of parish priests will often display great ingenuity
in arousing the generous impulses of his flock. In the morning he has preached, let us say, against luxury in dress; an abomination and a scandal he calls it, deploring the money and time
women spend on their *toilettes*. In the evening, however, one of
those he has denounced stations herself at his request in the
church, scandalously and abominably arrayed, and takes toll of the
faithful.

She is in full dress; a nosegay of flowers at her breast veils none
of its charms; there she stands at the door of the church, or the
prison, whatever the charitable object may be, and smilingly begs
of everyone who goes by. She is sweetly urgent with the unwilling,
buttonholes them, uses all her charm of manner and voice and
smile; nobody can resist the lovely bare arm so pleadingly extended, nor the eyes upturned—wonderful what people will do for
the poor!

But she acknowledges each offering, however small, with a little
curtsey; beauty smiles on you, a soft murmur thanks you, and you
have had your money's worth even before the gift goes down on
the credit side of your ledger in heaven.

After a while she leaves the doorway, and comes down the nave,
the beadle walking before, and waking the echoes with his tapping
staff. The larger the congregation, the greater her zeal. An acquaintance, some pretty fellow, gives her his arm, and thus she
goes, bending now right, now left, her white fingers holding out
the bag towards reluctant givers until for very shame a coin is
dropped in.

Yes, she is too much even for the misers; as for the servers at the
altar, and assistants, they have some ado to attend to their duties.
When she presents her open sack, she seems to be collecting

hearts. Everyone gives; as for the priest who walks behind her, he can hardly press his way through the throng. He shares her triumph, for triumphal this progress is, and as a trifle of fatigue heightens her beauty—fatigue most laudably her due—who can blame her if she seeks fresh energy in the looks which commend her figure and features so whole-heartedly? The Church will forgive her, and the swelling purse she proffers in the presbytery more than atones for these few moments' vanity.

Now comes refreshment after toil; the priest and his friends have prepared a collation, and all the bigwigs of the parish are gathered to congratulate her. One after another the clergy major and minor come up to salute her hand; the chief mute "unknits his unkind threatening brow," and ventures, not too confidently, on a madrigal; it is not well done, but the will to please, after all, is there; and there is plenty to drink, and sugar cakes to eat; and if the whole atmosphere is perhaps rather worldly, why that is a tribute to the money which has been withdrawn from worldly uses.

20. Doctors

(cxxxv, Médecins, 1:324–28)

Molière, come back to life, would be at a loss to recognize his doctors. Where are they now, those grave gentlemen; Guenaud,*mounted on his mule; Purgon, with his clyster; and Diafoirus?† No longer are our medical advisers severe and pallid, methodical in gait, weighty-worded, calm save when a prescription is disregarded; today's physician is a sprightly personage, intoning no jargon, wielding no thunders, white-handed and tossing a symmetrical ruffle, full of quips, with a pretty diamond adorning his little finger. He fingers pulses still, but merely as a gesture; we are in the best of health all of us; no reason that he can see why we should not live for ever. Even a deathbed cannot damp his professional hopefulness; he consoles, takes his leave, has his little joke on the stairs, and an hour after his departure, death calls for the patient.

Ten nobodies may die through his want of knowledge or want of care, without casting any shadow upon his countenance; but a man of quality that has slipped through his fingers will show in his face ten days afterwards; a kind of humble look, as if he begged the world's pardon.

The doctors have, as it were, each his own parish among the sick of the city. One makes a diagnosis which is fantastically wrong; a colleague is called in, who, lest another time the mistake should be his own, sustains the first in error. The decision is one of life or death; no matter, *esprit de corps* must come first, the original imbecility is hushed up, justified even; and the victim dies with ten of the Faculty round him, each knowing that a certain course of treatment might save him, but precluded by etiquette from saying so. And so the first doctor brings his professional murder safely to its conclusion, according to rule.

His accomplices may rely on finding similar discretion at time of need; they excuse failure by the slow progress of their art, the necessity for following precedent; but why? Why, if precedent kills, follow it? Why not take any and every opportunity to lift medicine out of its present murderous rut? Why oppose, blindly and with fury, every invention, every straight and simple view of their profession as a whole, if, as they maintain, the present homicidal doctrine is not sacred; if all their own experience goes to show, time and again, its inadequacy and its deadly consequences?

The reason is this. If medical practitioners are to continue to extort money from the laymen, if they are to go on paying visits which profit only themselves, the aura of mystery must still surround them. Thus they are set above argument and reason; and may, without fear of interruption or enquiry, proceed with their eternal disputing of theories which the Dark Ages evolved, and against which the daylight of sanity is powerless.

The distinction between the writer of the prescription and the apothecary who makes it up is another factor against the probability of cure; both medicine-men refuse all analysis of the drugs they employ, the one by proxy, the other in person; they have no very clear conception of the functions of the various poisons they so

glibly order and compound; yet out these go by the hundred-
weight to be absorbed by their patients, who thus have two dangers
to combat, the audacious prescriber of drugs and the dishonest
purveyor.

The science of medicine is to-day nothing more than a brazen
and accredited charletanism; its practitioners know its emptiness,
uncertainty and confusion, but hold to it none the less for their
pocketbooks' sake. Errors and prejudices from the dark ages stalk
abroad in the practice of to-day. Some progress has been made, no
thanks to the professors; but there is a pretty general acceptance
of, and delight in, the old tenebrous formulæ; and a general dread
lest the light of research should fall upon the bogey they guard.

Molière and others have so exposed these hooded impostors for
what they are, that at last they have yielded to reason in one matter;
they no longer bleed as they did thirty years back; a sick man recov-
ers now without the aid of twenty-five losses of blood. Ridicule is
the best weapon against them; constant use of it may perhaps drive
them to follow Hippocrates's method, who prescribed few remedies, but let nature take its course, without hindrance from him.

The doctors owe much to the empirics who waste no time in
philosophy, but set to work to observe the reactions of the human
body. These are less fruitful in argument, possibly, than the Faculty, but the cures they accomplish discredit the learned experts.

Mesmer‡ challenged our pundits to dispute or check his results;
they ignored him completely, after which, one would think, they
might have had the decency to keep silent concerning experiments which they refused to investigate, and leave the proof or
disproof of his method to time. Whatever the issue, their behaviour discredits them; for either they have remained indifferent and
hostile to a new and useful discovery, or, if Mesmer's experiments
are worthless, they have not taken the opportunity to prove them
so; public opinion demanded that they should make some enquiry,
if only to justify their own fulminations and angry invective against
the experimenter. But no; they preferred to bring all their guns to
bear against a colleague of their own, who said, honestly and humbly: "I know this man's work; let us see what he can do; let him
explore, this is undiscovered country; no rash judgments, no haste;
remember how other discoveries were treated at first," and so on.
Ten to one this man was in the right of it; animal magnetism may

be the marvellous and extraordinary contribution to human knowledge that its discoverer claims; from what I have heard of it, I am inclined to believe so. When I know more I shall have more to say, whether in this book or another, for I have set myself to do battle for truth, with such strength as I have and such intelligence to perceive it.

All this may seem to bear somewhat hardly on doctors; but I only quarrel with their philosophy, while they through their philosophy attack both our health and our lives. Desperate diseases need desperate remedies.

*"Guenaud," the doctor in "l'Amour Médecin" by Molière
†"Purgon and Diafoirus," two doctors in Molière's "Malade Imaginaire"
‡Friedrich Anton Mesmer (1733–1815) claimed to be able to cure illnesses through the use of "animal magnetism." Mercier, always sympathetic to unorthodox ideas, condemned the officially established medical authorities for refusing to give Mesmer's theories a fair hearing.

21. Clerks
(CXL, Commis, 1:340–42)

A re as the sands of the sea, and form a class by themselves. They earn very little, eight hundred, twelve, fifteen hundred francs; you may find thirty of them after the same job.

The better-paid clerks, the twelve-hundred-franc men, affect velvet coats and lace, and go without meals to buy finery. There is a proverb that describes them: "padded coat, hollow belly."

Nowadays everything is done by a stroke of the pen; the poorest tradesman must have some smack of education, and keep a ledger three feet tall, on which the single bottle and the solitary capon are entered cheek by jowl with the hogshead of wine and troops of bullocks, and you get your receipt for the one as for the other. Their sole talent, these scribes, consists of knowing how to fill out forms; outside these they know nothing, learn nothing, and have nothing in their heads. As for figures, they can add correctly enough, but that is part of their routine.

Witness the story of a gentleman returning from Egypt, who had
purchased a mummy at Bassora. The case in which it was packed
was too clumsy to go on the back of his carriage with his other
luggage, and accordingly he sent it post, by coach from Auxerre.
The packing-case on arrival was immediately opened by a swarm
of clerks, who finding in it a blackened body decided that this was
certainly a corpse that had met its death by fire. The ancient linen
shroud they took for the remains of a burnt shirt; accordingly they
prepared a report for the police and transported the mummy to
the Morgue. Apparently there was nobody in charge with authority
enough to step in and prevent these officials making fools of themselves; it was a most typical exhibition of customs intelligence.

Well! The owner arrived in his town, and went at once to claim
his genuine antique at the posting-station, when he was heard, but
with incredulity; everyone stared; the gentleman's demeanour
changed from civility to towering rage, until at last one of the
clerks gave him a hint, if he valued his life and had no wish to be
hanged, to be off out of the town. The astounded collector was
obliged to seek out the Lieutenant of Police in person, and get his
order to withdraw from the Morgue the remains of an Egyptian
prince or princess, who, after two thousand years' tranquillity in a
pyramid, was within an ace of being buried in consecrated ground
instead of standing erect in a glass-fronted cabinet. Permission was
granted, but it took three days coming and going to obtain it.

The clerks at three thousand give themselves a great many airs;
they are grandees in their own estimation. It is one whole act of a
comedy to see them throw back their laces to cut a pen, and then
solemnly try the point as though the well-being of the State were
about to flow from it. If Vaucanson* instead of a mechanical musi-
cian had made an automatic clerk, this latter would have been
more use in the world.

The hands of their watches determine with absolute exactness
the course of their day; their wives set the clock by them.

But the chief panjandrums of all the tribe are those of Versailles,
who have nothing in common with these others but the word that
describes them. They sit there at their desks, ministers in all but
name, while their nominal masters look to them for policy and
guidance; the monarchy is split up among these officials, in their
hands lies the real power. Women and ambitious young men fre-

quent and lay siege to these potentates with quite incredible assiduity. The clerk is the key which sets the works of the great machine in motion, and the question is, who shall turn the key? Everyone makes the attempt. But the full treatment of this question had better be left to that future chapter on Versailles which I may or may not write.

*Vaucanson's automaton was one of several ingenious mechanical figures that mimicked human movements constructed in the eighteenth century.

22. Men-About-Town
(CLVI, Les élégants, 1:370–72)

We have no Don Juans* nowadays, gentlemen whose mission in life it was to keep fathers alert, husbands in bad humour, and set whole families in an uproar; gentlemen who were forbidden to darken this door and that, whose names were never mentioned singly, but always coupled with that of some woman; all this is done with, dead as the dandy; but we still have our men-about-town.

This modern product uses no scent, takes up no attitudes, wastes no wit in empty compliment; he is fatuous, but decently, quietly so; he smiles instead of speaking. He will ignore a mirror; yet his eyes are always busy with himself, some detail of his dress or bearing. His visits last a quarter of an hour, and no longer. There is no more obvious snobbery, my friend the duke of this, the darling duchess of that, parties in great houses. No, he talks of his study, of chemistry which takes up all his time, of how he loathes the social round.

He is a bad listener; there is always a faint mocking smile, and an air of abstraction; he slips out of the room without taking leave, and writes you a note ten minutes later as if he had not seen you for weeks.

Women, too, are less extravagant in talk; you no longer hear the words 'delicious,' 'astounding,' 'incredible' in every sentence, instead there is a sort of affected simplicity, which admits no ex-

tremes, whether of admiration or displeasure; disasters and triviali-
ties are greeted with the same exclamation; chemistry and gossip
are all their conversational stock-in-trade.

Men's dress has become simpler; there are no more high-piled
wigs, for instance, which is a good thing, for they were preposterous. And there is no more, among the women, this absurd talk of
looking too plain for words, of having nothing to wear, of being in
rags, and so on; provincial ladies, who imagine this way of talking
to be still the fashion, please copy. A woman insisting on perfumed
playing-cards and ambrosial chambermaids would be laughed at
now in Paris. . . .

The difficulty of a writer in these times is not to talk science
with the learned, tactics with generals, dogs and horses with the
aristocracy; but to talk about nothing at all with several women at
once, after the inspiriting example of our men-about-town.

*Don Juan: a notorious seducer, as in Molière's play of that name.

23. Dress
(CLXVIII, Parures, 1:395–99)

A new-found diamond has its own beauty; but not till it has been
cut, and polished, and set, is its full brilliance declared. So
with women. Dress is their distraction and their joy; it repairs, to
some extent, the ravages of Time; and if they take delight in that
which gives back something of the lost freshness, the lost contours
of youth, who shall blame them?

History tells of the five hundred she-asses which furnished the
Empress Poppæa* with her baths of milk. Cleopatra, too, was a
woman of taste, who made the most of her charms, and by their
aid took captive those two great Romans, Cæsar and Antony. Berenice had amazing hair, from which one of our constellations
takes its name. Semiramis quelled a revolt by appearing before her
people half naked, like a woman in despair. Helen of Troy, that
adorable cause of so long warfare, so many jealousies and passions,

is familiar too; we know, after thirty centuries, that she was lovely. Jezebel,[†] it appears from the Bible, wore rouge before she was torn by dogs. But the ancients, though lavish enough with their descriptions, are unreliable as concerns the fashions in which their heroines appeared.

A Bacchante,[‡] with her hair about her shoulders, thyrsus in hand, ivy-crowned, might please as well as a marquise with her hair elaborately done up. Roman tunics were, for aught I know, as gracious as our modern dresses, and Roman sandals as elegant as the high-heeled shoes of to-day; but why have we no description of any of these things? There is nothing in ancient literature to give any idea of how hair was worn, how fashions changed, or what ornaments were most in favour. And why? It would have been of interest to know how their antique jewels were set, where the ladies of fashion wore their topazes and pearls, and how they secured and garlanded their wreaths of flowers . . .

Yet now that I come to set such matters down, I find myself at a loss. I may talk of a toque trimmed with two large 'attentions,' a Gertrude bonnet, a Henry IV hat; a turnip bonnet, a cherry bonnet, or one *à la fanfan,* meaning a bonnet too utterly sweet; I may talk at will of pleated 'sentiments,' of 'broken chains' or again of a diamond scraper, a jewelled comb or a girdle in the style called 'unknown as yet'; and after all, who is the wiser? These are but words; and Homer himself chose rather to describe the shield of Achilles than Helen's filleted locks. . . .

At the beginning of this century it was the fashion for women to hang upon their breasts, which low-cut gowns exposed, a little diamond cross, or a diamond dove to represent the Holy Ghost. A priest denounced these from the pulpit; What a place, he reproved the women, to hang the Cross, antithesis of worldly pleasure, and the Spirit of God, whence only thoughts of heaven should flow!

The colour most in fashion as I write is puce, which translated stands for flea; Flea's Back and Flea's Belly are the two shades of it. (My book is already out of date; Paris Mud, and Goose-droppings are the two which have succeeded these. I had meant to speak of that *coiffure* known as the 'porcupine,' but it was gone before I could set it down, and the 'baby's cap' reigns in its stead. Feathers are quite out. How impossible it is to fix a likeness of anything so fleeting!) As for the headdresses, the chief styles re-

Seconde Toilette
CHAP. CCCC XCVII.

Hairdressing. The subject of women's hairstyles provided
Mercier with one of his best illustrations of the constantly
changing nature of fashion and the excesses of the
wealthy. (Courtesy Library of Congress)

cently have been the English Park, the Windmill, and the Grove; other names such as Rivulet, Flocks, Shepherds and Shepherdesses, the Huntsman in the Hedge, have also had their brief day. But since, with these erections on their heads, our women found it impossible to get in or out of any reasonably sized vehicle, necessity gave birth to the strangest and most tasteful invention of all, a kind of spring whereby these triumphs of millinery could be lowered or raised at will.

Our historians of the Academy of Literature who delve with such pertinacity into the past for the purpose of discovering what necklaces the Roman ladies wore, might well turn their attentions to present-day fashions. Why not? These too are slipping into the past; the Pomegranate is gone; gone, too, are the Boston, the Philadelphia, the Blind-man's Buff; even the Periwinkle is in its decline. But it shall be my task to speak of the skirts, puffed, panniered, crinolined, which lend a pleasing likeness of flesh to women who are naught but bones. I dream of a journal in which these things and others of equal importance should be treated; it might be called *Feather and Furbelow,* and would certainly enjoy a far greater circulation than the *Journal des Savants.* . . .[§]

---

*Poppæa, Cleopatra, Berenice, Semiramis, and Helen of Troy were famous female figures from ancient history and mythology.
†Jezebel, wife of the Old Testament king Ahab, was killed for her immoral behavior and her body was thrown to the dogs.
‡In Greek mythology, Bacchantes were female followers of the wine god, Bacchus.
§The *Journal des Savants,* founded in 1665, was France's oldest and most important scientific journal.

24. Economy
(CLXIX, Économie, 1:400–401)

And now, after this catalogue of futile expenses, where does economy come in? The answer is, nowhere. Avarice or prodigality, but no mean course; thus pride dictates. Our fathers, even men about the Court, had their old coats turned, their worn shoes resoled. But breathe no word to-day of cobbling shoes; every Mrs Nobody would faint with dismay at the notion.

There are certain rich houses where a man might as well go naked as lack velvet and gold lace. True, M. de Buffon* lays it down that the love of finery is inborn in humanity; the historian of nature seems to consider this no bad thing. How, then, is a woman to blame who shuts her door in the face of those who appear at it unadorned with ruffles?

And so, laces at the wrists you must have; they may be dirty, yellow with age, no matter, they are your passport. A dust of white powder will hide their sins; if it should come off in the course of your visit, exposing the original hue, who cares? Cleanliness no one expects, but it is only decent to seem well-to-do.

A warning; never, in company, pull from your pocket a coloured handkerchief, unless you wish to see in the eyes of the women about you a chill disdain for your ignorance of the proprieties. On the other hand, the handkerchief must not be of muslin, for which there are various names, such as mazulipatan and paliacate; this at once stamps you as a clerk in the East India Company.†

There is a good story of a poor but ingenious person who, having only one lace ruffle, displayed it with assurance before the eyes of a porter, as giving him undoubted right to the *entrée;* the other hand (adorned, alas, with a mere muslin frill) kept close beneath his coat-tails the while. But in the abandon of conversation, forgetting prudence in gesticulation, he had the ill-luck to withdraw this obscene wrist from its obscurity and flourish it before the scandalized eyes of a whole drawing-room. The mistress of the house, justly indignant, sent there and then for the porter, and trounced him before them all for his lack of proper vigilance. The poor, bewildered Swiss could make nothing of the whole tirade, since the original sinner, when pointed out to him, had once more tucked the unclean muslin out of sight, and was gesticulating freely with his lace.

Next day the porter's inflexibility was such that an officer who had lost one arm in action found himself under suspicion; the Swiss demanding to see both sleeves, swearing that it was as much as his place was worth to let one unaccompanied ruffle ascend madame's stairs; even if the *Gazette* [*de France*]‡ announced the officer's loss to all of Europe.

*Georges-Louis Leclerc Buffon (1707–88), the leading French naturalist of the eighteenth century. His books described animal species and geology.

†East India Company: a privileged trading company with a monopoly on commerce with India.

‡The *Gazette de France,* founded in 1631, had an official monopoly on news about foreign affairs and the Court.

25. Mentors of Manners
(CLXXIV, Maîtres d'agréments, 1:412–14)

You may well stare, sir, coming new to it all from your own country, but the fact remains; we in Paris have schools of civility, and men who teach polite behaviour to others for hire. For this is an art, and a curious one; nothing must be left to chance, as it is in places like Russia. We are not barbarians, we know that the little things count most; important matters can take care of themselves.

And so we have these gentlemen who instruct their pupils before the mirror, teaching them to smile fashionably, take snuff gracefully, use the eyes subtly, and bow elegantly. They teach them to talk at the back of the throat, like our actors, who must be imitated but never copied; to show their teeth when they laugh just enough and not too much. They practise these invaluable airs and graces, pupil and master together, two or three hours at a time.

Consider the young man of fashion, whom his watches and seals announce by a pretty tinkling. He goes to the right hairdresser, that is evident and necessary; the well-dressed head despises the head less exquisitely piled, and bears in its arrangement of curls the trade-mark of the artist. A woman will ask—"And who may that creature be?" of a man taking the weight of a nation on his shoulders; he is not freshly curled, and therefore, socially, is naught.

These youngsters are well drilled only to show emotion or anger over trifles. They keep themselves in hand, never stamp, never swear, save only when their horses are two minutes late being brought round; then they let themselves go.

The next thing they learn is the art of dress, all the variations of breeches, shirts, and scarves must be carefully studied. And this is generally the topic of their morning visits, made about midday; when they discuss with their hostess, negligently, such burning questions as rings, snuff-boxes, and the newest mode in bracelets. Sometimes they grow petulant, and then they keep their morning dress on all day, and loudly refuse invitations to supper.

In this class of masters in behaviour may be included certain doctors, those whose practice lies among imaginary invalids. Such a man need know nothing of medicine, providing he is handsome, with pretty manners, and a fund of amusing stories, and calls every day.

It is altogether correct to be mad for novelty, new dishes, new fashions, new books, to say nothing of a new actress or opera; and as for a new way of dressing the hair, it is enough to set the whole crew of fashionables raving. The novelty, whatever it may be, spreads in the wink of an eye, as though all these empty heads were electrified. It is the same with people; some man, of whom nobody has previously taken the least notice, suddenly becomes the rage, and lasts six months; after which they drop him, and start some other hare.

By the rules of politeness it is agreed that one must be amusing; this, both masters and pupils agree, is the one vital thing; it is divine, it is sublime. And so it happens that a young man who is, by women, universally considered a prodigy, the most satisfactory personage ever bestowed by nature upon an undeserving world, sings rather small in any other society; men of sense laugh at him, but by no means as he likes it, and his conversation reveals him the sheerest fool.

Yet he has paid to learn to be an imbecile!

26. Commentary

Helen Simpson's translation combined selected paragraphs from Mercier's two chapters of short observations, CLXXVII, Remarques, 1:418–24, and CCCXXIV, Légères observations, 1:852–60. The source of each paragraph is indicated at the end as (R) and (LO), respectively

O ur Parisian women are thin; at thirty they have lost all round-ness, but they prefer this, it is the fashion; at the first sign of fat, they set about reducing, and drink vinegar to bring them back to elegance. Our men last till forty, but then are quite done for. (LO)

What with nurses, governesses, tutors, colleges and convents, a woman has no excuse for remembering she is a mother. (R)

Children are brought up more sensibly nowadays; cold baths and light clothing are the rule, and a good one. (R)

Demoiselle is the name for all girls just out of the school-room. These are old enough to go out without their mothers. (LO)

Women do more sewing for practical use, and have forgotten how to knit; they make lace; or do embroidery on a frame. (LO)

In all the great houses the mode lets you wear your sword at table; then at the end of the meal you slip away, or try to; but it is thought more civil if the hostess, seeing your departure, calls out some vague invitation to remain, which you answer briefly and ig-nore; but you must call on her within eight days, that is the eti-quette. If you have neglected a hostess for any length of time, you must be reintroduced, and some friend must make your apologies; you have been out of town, or travelling abroad; she, who has seen you nightly at the opera, pretends to believe you, and all goes on as before. (R)

We are all tired of ceremony; life grows easier—save in the prov-inces—every day. Of all our absurd old customs the only one with any life in it is that of saying God bless you when a man sneezes. (LO)

The rich eat much less than they used, for one reason or an-other; you may see your host, at the head of his magnificent table, dismally sipping a glass of milk. Thin soups and fruit juice are the whole duty of a modern cook. No house in Paris offers both dinner

to its guests. Lawyers dine, financiers eat supper. The
͟ ͟ͅɑ̀ĸes its chief meal at three-thirty. (R)

Eating has degenerated; there is little or no drinking; one clean
plate replaces another, as we let the guest on our left know, in a
whisper, the faults of our right-hand neighbour; over all is a curtain of chill dignity, instead of the old gaiety that came with wine.
(R)

Our rich men have money for luxuries, none for necessities. (R)

Women begin their dinner at the sweet course; and *à propos* of
dining, I warn every man to take his footman with him, if he has
one, when he sits at table with the rich. There is no drink procur-
able save through the offices of a servant; all wine is kept on the
buffet; at your timid signal the fellow turns, and brings liquor, but
not for you. Soon, as you grow more parched, your voice becomes
inaudible, and the language of the eyes is quite useless save in love.
Your throat is dry, you have no palate left for the dishes; you endure until at the very end of the meal merciful custom accords you
a glass of water. All this is deliberate. Your rich man is protecting
his table against the assaults of beggars, for such, if you have no
footman, he may rightly assume you to be. (LO)

However, fashion now permits boasting of a good digestion, an
impossibility in our fathers' day. The servants remain in the room
all the time, even through dessert, and this makes for a certain
constraint. There is no talking freely; and so the meal itself tends
to become shorter, and with our present-day continence in food
and drink, less gay. (LO)

To be ruined, and loudly tell your company so, is very much the
thing. (LO)

The greatest expense nowadays is in furnishings, which must be
changed every six years to keep up with the fashion. Beds above all
must be ornate, and walls panelled in precious woods with a touch
or two of gilding. Marble is not always what it seems; they imitate
it now in stucco, painted, quite amazingly well. The latest ban is
upon necessary woodwork, such as beams, which it is indecent to
have exposed. All walls now are pierced for bell-wires, very skilfully;
it is quite an art. Some women will summon a servant to pick up a
dropped handkerchief. (LO)

Our inventories would astonish a visitor from classic times returning to this world. The vocabulary of a sheriff's officer, for ex-

ample, who must know the names of all these fashionable superfluities, is a very large one, very specialized, and would be unintelligible to a labourer. (LO)

Only persons with no feeling for the proprieties spend their summer in Paris. You may hear on the Pont-Royal all the right people saying: "But I abhor town, I simply live in the country." (LO)

Strangely enough, chemistry is the science in which people are taking most interest. (LO)

Women of very high rank sometimes cheat at the card-table with the calmest effrontery; they borrow money to gamble with, and when they win, tranquilly inform their temporary banker that they had made no bet, thus pocketing the table's money and his into the bargain. This has been known to happen even playing with royalty, where, of course, there is no accusation or scandal possible. All that can be done is to spread the story next day throughout Paris; but they pretend not to be aware of what is said. (LO)

27. Second-Hand Clothes
(CLXXXII, Piliers des Halles, 1:447–50)

The markets rise on a strange foundation; nothing less than the house in which our glorious Molière was born, and which still exists in part. There along the arches are ranged the used clothing stalls, ill-lit on purpose, that stains may be less noticeable, and colours deceive the eye; thus the suit of solemn black, bought and paid for, is transformed before your eyes, by the mere light of day, to purple or green, and spotted at that.

These stalls all have their touts, who call your attention, none too civilly, to their wares; yield to the wiles of one, and you will have all the rest of them at your heels. The stallholder's wife, child, assistant, and dog, all bellow in your ear at once; and the din continues till you are well out of their clutches, and out of the gloomy precincts of their chosen trade.

Sometimes these fellows will seize on some innocent passerby, and drag him into their shops willy-nilly; it is one of their stock

jokes. A few blows with your cane will free you, but nothing, it
seems, can altogether cure them of this senseless trick. . . .

On Mondays the wives, sisters, aunts, and cousins of these huck-
sters hold a kind of sale of their own, called Fair of the Holy Ghost,
in the Place de Grève;* there are no executions that day. They sell
only women's and children's clothes, and all who must make their
money go a long way, shopkeeper's wives and such, get their bon-
nets, linen, cloaks and even shoes there, ready-made. The police
'noses' hang about there too, waiting for pickpockets, who dispose
in this way of the odds and ends they have stolen; and the honest
thieves who come there to seek fences, like their colleagues who
put in a little active practice among the crowds, find themselves
in the end before the magistrate. The site itself should serve as a
deterrent, but these people have no imagination.

The fair itself is an amazing sight; a whole province might have
been unfrocked to clothe its stalls, or a whole people of Amazons
despoiled. Skirts, panniers, loose gowns are there in piles, from
which you may choose. Here, a grand dress worn by the dead wife
of a judge, for which the wife of his clerk is haggling; there, a
young working girl tries on the lace cap of a great lady's lady-in-
waiting. They all change in public, but so far only the upper gar-
ments; no doubt it will get down to petticoats soon.

The buyer neither knows nor cares whence come the corsets she
sells; a poor honest girl will clasp about her, under her mother's
very eye, some garment that a kept dancer of the Opéra has dis-
carded, only the night before. Virtue, or rather vice, goes out of
them when they change hands.

Since both buyers and sellers are women, the bargaining power
is about equal on both sides; they make noise enough about it; you
may hear the chaffering, shrill, noisy, discordant, half a mile off.
Close to, the scene is more curious still. A women pricing and cov-
eting clothes has an unmistakable expression; the term 'fair sex'
at such moments is a misnomer.

By nightfall the whole mass of clothing is gone, magicked away,
not one poor scrap left; but the fair itself is inexhaustible, and
reappears without fail the following Monday morning.

*The Place de Grève, in front of the Hôtel de Ville, was the site of public execu-
tions.

28. Rag-and-Bone Man

(CLXXXIV, Le chiffonnier, 1:452–53)

An ignoble title; I beg my reader's pardon for setting it down. But see the man himself, with his forked stick; watch how he lifts God knows what from the muck on it, and stows the trophy away in his basket. Don't turn your head away; this is no moment for false delicacy, or snobbery either. These vile rags, his gleanings, are primal matter, which later and under another form will adorn our bookshelves, and set forth the treasures of the spirit of man. Montesquieu, Buffon, Rousseau—this abomination is their fore-runner.

Without that basket of his, reader, my work could not exist for you. No great loss, you say; perhaps; but neither could any other book exist, for this is the raw material of all paper, this rubbish that the rag-and-bone man gathers. Rags, pounded to a pulp, make that substance by whose aid the fiery periods of the orator, the thoughts of wise men, the records of virtue and of courage are preserved to us.

Ideas by this means are brought to birth as soon almost as conceived. All the images the mind engenders by this means are set down and take form, and remain indissolubly upon the printed page; so that what was one man's hoard is distributed about the world, to last and give pleasure while the world lasts—the rag-and-bone man's monument!

29. Love of the Marvellous

(CXCI, Amour du merveilleux, 1:471–75)

The following was advertised not long ago in London; that on a certain day, at a given hour, in full view of the public, a grown man would creep into a bottle. How in the world did this piece of effrontery take anyone in? The English are not a specially credulous nation, but they love something to gape at, as, for that matter, do the citizens of Paris, Madrid and Vienna. Every man of them must have said to himself, "Well, but this fellow can't hope

Rag-Picker. Of the many artists who depicted the poor of Paris during the eighteenth century, Jean Duplessi-Berteaux was among the most effective. For Mercier, the rag-picker served primarily as pretext for philosophizing about the interconnectedness of urban life; Duplessi-Berteaux's engraving shows an isolated figure, ragged and miserable. (Courtesy The Lilly Library, Indiana University, Bloomington, Indiana)

to defraud a whole town; he makes his claim publicly, the walls are covered with bills proclaiming his powers and promising marvels; there must be something in it. Numbers of respectable people are coming to see him; he may really have some secret that no one has yet discovered."

If the performer had gone to each individual separately and said: "I will now stow myself away in a pint bottle" he would have been laughed at for a madman; but there were the posters stuck up for all to see, there was the assembled crowd, there was the clink of real money dropping into the impostor's purse; and so each said to himself once more: "It must be genuine, there are so many of us, and all so respectable." There you have the weakness of popular enthusiasm: they think, "How can we possibly be fooled if enough of us are gathered together?" The notion that a man, after all these preliminaries, should quietly decamp with the money leaving his bottle still empty behind him seems to have occurred to no one. You have only to promise loud enough and boldly for people to believe you, especially in money matters. The loans France has subscribed during this past hundred years!

Since the magician of the bottle, another miracle-monger, this time in Paris, and with not the least intent to deceive, contrived to acquire a prodigious following; but for the police, they would have made a god of him. [It was ten years ago, in, I think, the Rue des Ciseaux, which was filled from end to end with a crowd of some thirty thousand people, all declaring that he was a prophet and healer, who could do cures with the touch of his hand.

The street was blocked with cripples and blind men; there was a general hysteria. The most curious thing, however, was the complete absence of any violence or disorder; over all was a sort of calm and happy confidence, very unlike the usual manifestations of popular enthusiasm. Their conviction was absolute; they approached his house with devotion, and in silence. The healer was a man of humble and simple appearance; none more startled than he to find himself set up as a prophet. The police, however, soon had him out of the town with his wife, and the people, finding him gone, began to murmur and to call down blessings on him wherever he might be; and at last dispersed, still without the least sign of disorder.]

There have been other marvels since; a child which could see

underground, whose feats were credited by academicians and recorded in the gazettes. And the other day a canon of Étampes set
out to borrow a hundred thousand francs for the perfecting of a
flying machine, and got them; they are now in his notary's hands.
. . . Then there are what they call the convulsionists who really do
perform the most incredible contortions, better than anything of
that kind to be seen at a fair. Few have the trick of it, and so these
performances are legitimately surprising, and may well seem, to
certain minds, to have something of the supernatural about them;
although, as we all know, fanaticism and self-deception are responsible for most miracles. . . .

A new sect* has arisen in Paris among the younger generation,
. . . which encourages its members in that strange yielding, that
sickness of the soul which is this century's stamp; we look too much
inward, and thence comes the desire, the demand for signs and
marvels. They believe, these young men, that man is a degraded
being, through whom evil has come into the world; that he has left
the centre, which is truth; God in His mercy retains him within the
circumference of the universe's plan, when He might have allowed
mankind to be exiled into infinity; man has still, therefore, the
right to hope, and may regain the centre by coming at it from a
tangent.

Accordingly these empty-minded sectaries do what they can to
travel along the tangent; live in rigorous continence, fast until they
drop, build ecstasies from their own bodily weakness, and endeav-
our to dissociate themselves from things of earth; only thus, they
say, can a soul be free to pass into the centre, which is truth.

Activity of the human spirit, impatient of its own ignorance;
strong will of that spirit to penetrate the sense of things by its own
powers of comprehension; vague half-knowledge deep in each
human soul, that it is the repository of high secrets; these are the
forces that set man exploring the invisible. As it withdraws, he follows, demanding miracles, confident of mystery, until to the seeker
this world of the spirit becomes real as our outward world of things
and time.

*The "new sect" Mercier refers to was the Martinists, followers of the mystical
religious writer Louis-Claude de Saint-Martin (1743–1803).

30. Private Boxes
(CXCVI, Petites Loges, 1:486–90)

S igns of the times; our present toleration of indecency allows them. The performance and the convenience of a whole audience must be sacrificed to the imperious sensibility of two or three hundred idle women; and part of the pit goes to make room; so that an equal number of their fellow-citizens, too poor to afford such luxuries as privacy, must forgo their evening's pleasure.

But the arrangement is good for the management. Box-rents are paid at the beginning of the season, and once sure of their money the actors see no reason to exert their full powers. New *rôles* are too much trouble, and so they continue to please themselves, and disdain their paymasters. The art of acting is dying from this very lack of discipline and order. But no, our actors may work for six months of the year, laze the rest, and still be seventeen or eighteen thousand francs in pocket; which money is subscribed by the general public, paid to such and such a performer for the privilege of seeing him on the stage.

The simplest remedy, of course, for this state of things would be to pay each actor so much a performance. Then he might put some life into his part, for fear of being passed over; good acting would have to meet competition, and become better in self-defence. If a man must put forth his best or go hungry, there is little enough doubt which he will choose.

Another argument against the box system is this; against all reason and, for aught I know, all legal obligation, actors refuse to account to the author for the sum the boxes bring in; the money was paid before ever his piece came on, they tell him, and so the pit goes on losing ground to the boxes, and nobody has a word to say, except the public, which grumbles, naturally enough; but let one of our fashionables put her side of the question. (I disown her, quoting from a pamphlet called *Vues simples d'un bon homme* by J.-H. Marchand, 1776).

Why should I sit through a whole play, when I am rich enough to listen to just one act of it? What have I done, that people should interfere? Can't a rich woman please herself? All this talk of liberty—and yet, just because for once I come to a public theatre, instead of having the actors at home, I am

expected to dress for it, and turn up in time! Why shouldn't I
come in an hour late? And why should anyone object to my
being comfortable? I bring my dog, and my own candles, of
course, my chamber-pot, and various other bedroom necessities; why not? And if I like to have people coming in and out
to keep me amused, and then go away if the play bores me,
where's the harm in that? I don't see what's the good of having money and taste if one isn't free to make use of them.

And so our pretty ladies keep their boxes, in which they recline
with a spaniel or two, cushions, a footwarmer, and a small pet imbecile with a spyglass, who tells them who's who in the audience,
and the names of the actors. But set in the fan which the pretty
hand sways is a little round of glass, through which my lady continues to see, unseen.

Outside, money in hand, disappointed playgoers are turned
away from the ticket office; there is no room for them. The boxes
may be empty, often are, but they are paid for by the year and must
be kept sacred; so the playgoer wanders off, wondering when he is
ever to see the inside of his national theatre again.

There ought to be two companies at the Français.* The interest
of author, public, and even the actors themselves imperatively demands it. But who cares for the public? Our gentleman-in-waiting
have the last word. To art they say, "No farther"; to the public,
"Take it or leave it"; to the authors, "We call the tune"; thus offering the interesting prospect of an art, a public, and an otherwise
vocal section of society, the authors, all quiescent under the
thumbs of a set of Court lackeys.

How did their lordships acquire this inexplicable supremacy?
How do they come to treat on equal terms with genius? And how
did they compass the total subjection of an art in which the dignity
and pleasure of a whole nation are centred? What have these Court
dignitaries to do with the stage? Who sets them in judgment upon
an author? Nobody knows; least of all themselves. But they enjoy
their tyranny, and exercise it without questioning whence it comes;
and since passion ennobles even the pettiest struggle, our princes
and princesses of the boards cling to power as though their very
existence as functionaries were in question.

As for authors, without whom no theatre could exist, and no

actor, their rights are so unsure and so unprotected, so exposed to the attacks of infidelity and caprice that their opinions very rightly go for nothing in any discussion on reform. Three years ago they entered into some sort of association to protect themselves against exploitation, of which M. de Beaumarchais† was to be the spokesman. . . . It remains to be seen what they make of it; for all the members are men of intelligence, and might even show courage and character in their own cause. A curious experiment; it may solve another little problem in morals, which observers in other spheres have been meditating this long while in secret.

*The Comédie française was the only theater officially licensed to perform serious plays in French.
†Pierre-Augustin Caron de Beaumarchais (1732–1799), author of "The Barber of Seville" and "The Marriage of Figaro," led a movement to give playwrights a greater share of the profits from the production of their works.

31. Quack Medicines
(cci, Annonces des spécifiques, 1:501–3)

There is a certain disease,* the price of pleasure, which by a very curious and secret poison brings a man to his death; it is so widespread now that for very familiarity it has ceased to be regarded as shameful; more's the pity.

At one time it was thought that the first discoverers brought it from the New World, but nowadays the opinion is that it has always existed in Europe, changing character slightly from time to time. It is what the Jews and Arabs mean by their word for leprosy. If it be true that when it is widely distributed it becomes less deadly, the small change as it were of disease, then Paris should never suffer, where there is hardly a creature untouched by it; you have only to watch the faces in the streets, the pallor, the look of suffering on most of them, to realize that.

There is something arising out of it, worse even than the malady itself, and that is the swarm of decoctions that are advertised as cures, anti-venereal compounds to be taken internally, each one worse than the last, and all with the Government stamp.

For this, venereal disease, offers the charlatan his widest scope. Printed papers with specious promises are thrust into your hand; these specifics—disguised in some sort with resounding adjectives—are topics of common discussion; mercury is quite gone out, at least for external use; you swallow it instead, disguised as chocolate, or syrup, or sweetmeats, or elixir; soon there will be cream puffs and bread-rolls impregnated with the stuff. And people buy, though the specifics they trust to are discredited every day. These various methods, publicly described and offered, are quite sure, and perfectly agreeable and harmless, according to their inventors; the cure is quick, easy, and lasting. So persistent are these claims that young men have come at last to think that the disease cannot matter, since the remedy is certain; and continue so, until increasing pain sets them thinking differently.

But how can they tell which is the quack remedy and which the true, since both come out with the approbation of the Faculty of Medicine, and the Government stamp?

*Venereal disease: the reference is to syphilis, long believed (wrongly) to have been brought back to Europe by sailors after the discovery of the Americas.

32. Orders to the Coachman

(ccx, Langue du maître aux cochers, 1:527–28)

It is easy enough to tell the station of an employer by the look of his coachman, to know a judge's carriage from a courtesan's, or a duke's from a banker's; but to discover the destinations of these various vehicles after the play, listen what the owner says to the footman, who repeats it to the coachman on the box. "Home," says Mr Nobody-very-much, and you may know that he lives in the Île-Saint-Louis. "Back to the house," says Mr, or possibly Lord, Rather-more, whose address is Faubourg Saint-Germain; while the final, the superb order is "Let's go," and that means nothing less than the Faubourg Saint-Honoré. No need to comment on this last, its grandeur is amply evident from its simplicity.

Every theatre keeps a kind of porter with a prodigious voice who bawls: "My Lord Marquis's carriage!" "My Lady This's carriage!" "Mr Justice That's carriage!" His thunders penetrate even the tavern noises, disturbing lackeys at their wine and coachmen quarrelling over their billiards; the air of a whole quarter trembles, and all other noises, the tumult of horses, the voices of men, fade before his roaring. At his summons lackeys and coachmen quit their pint pots and cues and run to the horses' heads, the carriage-door.

Stentor attributes these superhuman powers to his entire abnegation of wine; he spurns it, and drinks only brandy. He is perpetually hoarse, but this very hoarseness gives a terrifying and raucous tone, a tocsin* quality, to his roar. Such fellows never last long. Others step into their shoes, vociferate, drink, and at last die, like their predecessors, from a superfluity of cheap liquor.

[Mercier's comment on the first of these three addresses is as follows:

> The Île-Saint-Louis seems to have escaped the general corruption of manners. No prostitute can find a lodging there; as soon as her way of life becomes known, out she must go. Here the middle class is its own police; every man's way of living is an open book; as for the women, no girl guilty of an indiscretion (and these things are always found out) need ever hope to find a husband in that quarter. This neighbourhood is the nearest thing to a third-rate provincial town that Paris can show . . . [CLXXXVIII, L'île Saint-Louis, 1:457–58]

He gives no special notice to the Faubourgs of Saint-Germain and Saint-Honoré; but the former was sacred to the nobility, and the latter the quarter favoured by bankers, farmers-general, and other financial interests.] (Note by Helen Simpson)

*"tocsin": a loud alarm, rung by the bells in the city's churches.

33. Coliseum

(CCXIV, Colisée, 1:536–37)

We are not Romans; our amphitheatre will hardly bear witness to us eighteen centuries hence. Nor have we built to accommodate two hundred thousand spectators; that would have put too great a strain on our police. We have borrowed nothing but the name of one of the proudest monuments of Rome, and even there we have deformed the spelling; for the original was the Colosseum, as befitted its grandeur. Our imitation has lasted a bare ten years. It is in the hands of creditors now, who cannot come to any agreement as to what should be done with it, and so the place is closed. Small loss, for its only charm lay in its situation, which was the happiest choice imaginable. Inside, the place was dreary; a wretched orchestra, childish or incompetent dancing; sports on a dirty muddy lake; uninspired fireworks; the discomfort of too great a crowd, or the weariness of no crowd at all; this was the best it could do in the way of entertainment.

The Chinese Assembly Room has replaced it; a strange new temple of idleness which draws the public away from the contemplation of noble actions as offered by our various theatres. Here the spectators are the play; pallid Adonis, Narcissus adoring his reflection in the long glasses, Mr So-and-so from the Opéra humming a tune, the long-haired fool and the arrogant young women, here crowd each other, and the walks.

Compare this Vaux-Hall* with the enchanting London pleasure gardens, and at once it becomes evident that the Frenchman's sole pleasure lies in seeing and being seen. The English taste is more for variety, gaiety; it demands amusements less vapid, more substantial than this eternal parade of all the vanities forever pacing its unchanging circle, making its own spectacle and desiring none other. The difference of government under which the two peoples live is well exemplified in the conduct of their pleasures; our coldly elegant assemblies contrast oddly with the varied and piquant amusements England has to offer.

True, the Englishman pays down his guinea,† while we disburse a mere shabby thirty sous. But then, our pleasures are not our own, are not free, that is to say, from the shackles of Government guidance. They are under authority, which sees to it that they shall be innocuous, and frowns on all change.

*The Vauxhall was a popular London amusement park of the period.
†A guinea was the equivalent of twenty-one shillings. Thirty sous equaled one and a half French livres, which was worth about one English shilling.

34. The Italian Comedy
(CCXVI, Comédiens-Italiens, 1:540–42)

They keep the name, but not the tradition; you never see an Italian play there, nor yet one of those blank canvases, as it were, on which Carlin's* art once painted such naïve and delicious pieces. This company of actors has the right, conferred by licence, of presenting moral and interesting plays; a right, let me say at once, which they by no means abuse. But the fact is, that since vaudevilles have become the fashion, they have followed public opinion, are indefatigable in search of novelty, and take all possible pains to please. This disinterestedness is singular. They spend lavishly on costumes and scenery, and give their performances all the splendour they can. They have a feeling, too, for music of the lighter, more expressive kind; their taste in plays is not quite so sure, but that will follow.

Vaudeville,† then, has been the chief concern of this theatre during the past eighteen months. Success and excess are two ends of the same measure, and so it is possible that this excellent troupe may find itself caught in the net of double meanings and other modish indecencies. Why bring a blush to the cheeks of the Graces?

Such trifles are pretty, unpretentious, and amusing enough; but they are like field-flowers springing up in a rich soil, which may choke the golden life-giving grain. The playwrights had hoped to make this theatre a rival to the Comédie française; they left out of their calculations the fact that singing will always prevail over speech, and that true drama goes too deep to alternate with empty little sketches on this stage. Vaudeville and the song of the moment will always command more hearers than Marivaux‡ and his successors, whoever these may be.

*"Carlin" (Carlo Antonio Bertinazzi (1713–83) was the last of the great Italian
actors who specialized in playing the comic role of Harlequin on the French stage.
†"vaudeville": a light, often comical theatrical piece frequently combining panto-
mine, dialogue, dancing, and song.
‡Pierre Carlet de Chamblain de Marivaux (1688–1763) was France's leading comic
playwright in the first half of the eighteenth century.

35. Marriageable
(CCCIV, Filles Nubiles, 1:796-98)

U ncounted numbers of our women have not married. True,
there are difficulties, not religious so much as civil; their dif-
fidence, which would accept the eternal nature of the knot, baulks
at the necessary couple of notaries and the payment of cash down.
Plain women with only youth to offer have no chance of a husband, and even the beauties must do battle. It might be no bad
thing to revive here in Paris the Babylonian custom, whereby all
young women were assembled in the market-place for the bache-
lors of the city to choose from; naturally enough, the best-looking
fetched the best prices, and this money went to provide dowries
and thus husbands for their plainer sisters.

Marriage nowadays is a yoke, and a heavy one; people avoid it as
long as they can. No wonder, for the appeal of the single state is
strong, with its promise of security, tranquillity, and reasonable
self-indulgence, and that men should prefer not to marry is under-
standable. The strange thing is, that nowadays women too reject
all idea of it, at least in the middle classes, where girls join with
sisters or friends to live together, and with the money that might
have acquired them husbands, buy annuities. This voluntary refusal to adopt what is, after all, a woman's natural state, this anti-
conjugal outlook, is surely one of the most curious comments on
our time.

Each year in Lacedæmon* unmarried persons were publicly
whipped in the temple of Venus by women. I should like to hear
Lycurgus's opinion of our younger generation, living singly from

choice, and proud of it; living like men, in freedom such as no other nation in the world permits to their sex.

And the result of all this? The middle class, those with sufficient incomes, who either marry late or not at all, have hardly any children; the poor marry early and rashly and have children in dozens; so that money tends to become concentrated more and more in the hands of a few, while the largest class, and that which has most need of money, gets least.

Every social circle has its old maids, women who have refused the duties of their sex, and have no corner of a hearth they can call their own. Marriage with its pains and pleasures they have passed by, and therefore should be allowed to usurp none of the consideration and respect due to those who have accepted the responsibility of life. These women are barren vines, whom the sun has never warmed to fruitfulness; their rare and withered leaves make but poor showing. They are more malicious than their married neighbours, quarrelsome, with sharper tongues and quicker tempers; and they are apt to have an ugly passion for money.

These celibates, men and women alike, should be taxed. I would raise the age of consent for religious vows, which are taken sometimes under compulsion and sometimes too impulsively; the army should be allowed to marry, which would mean as many girls husbanded as there are soldiers; moreover a man with a family makes a better patriot, he has more to defend. Finally there should be a revival of our ancestors' custom of the left-handed marriage;[†] this alone would solve many of our present difficulties. A mistress, in the old days, was not too different from an honest woman.

It does not do to attack man's social freedom; he finds his liberty elsewhere. Here is a case where it may truly be said that the law has made the crime.

---

*Lacedæmon, also known as Sparta, was one of the principal city-states of ancient Greece. The legislator Lycurgus had laid down its severe law code.

†A left-handed marriage, also known as a morganitic marriage, was one in which a nobleman married a woman of lower status, with the understanding that their children would not inherit his title.

36. Advertisements

(CCCVII, Les affiches, 1:802–6)

E ach morning early the bills of the three great theatres are set
out; the boulevard theatres* and the fairs advertise, too. On
the same hoarding you may see *Athalie* cheek by jowl with *Fun in a
Laundry; Castor and Pollux* and the latest devil-dance; the theatres
cater for all tastes. Why not, after all, provided the plays give no
offence? And there would be no risk of that if the police, and not
the actors, held the censorship. (Yes, the actors; for they decide
whether or no a play shall be presented. When the responsibilities
of the theatres are considered, and how easily they can impose an
undesirable code of morals, it seems fantastic that this function of
government should be left in such hands.)

There are many poor devils who read these posters, though they
never go to a play; they know the names of the pieces and the
players, and feel the richer for it, and see themselves in dreams
applauding from a box with countesses and lords.

It is the Lieutenant of Police† who issues licences for bill-posting;
if you lose a dog or a diamond, you must have his signature before
you can advertise for it. True, this signature is all ready stamped;
there are piles of blank forms in his office waiting to summon back
to their owners lost spaniels and macaws, lost muffs and gilded
canes.

There are, in all Paris, only two documents which may be
printed without leave from the police, the wedding invitation and
the funeral card; so far these are free, but such a state of affairs
can hardly be permitted to continue; what are our police doing?
Why should these only be scattered broad-cast, without leave from
the Lord Chancellor, or the Lord Chamberlain, or some other person whose duty it is to preserve public morals? Why should bride-
grooms and bodies alone have the right thus brazenly to rush into
print, without proper authority?

Certain other private and rascally persons have the impudence
to set down, without *imprimatur,* their names and titles on small
sinister scraps of pasteboard, announcing themselves as counts or
marquises, esquires and even advocates. Why? They may have no
right to these titles. There should be appointed, and without delay,
a royal censor to approve and examine the host of unscrutinized
visiting cards which find their way in at doors. What unhallowed

taint distinguishes paper from pasteboard? No printer should set one word of type without approbation from on high. God knows what errors may creep into society, borne on these cards . . .

Even the bill-sticker must have his copper license disc somewhere about his person before he can begin to slap up announcements of plays, new books, sales of property and the like. These functionaries—there are forty, as in the *Academie française*‡—both cry and sell broadsheets of all the hangings, and are glad of an execution since it brings them in a little extra money.

All these announcements, are torn down next morning, to give place to new ones; if they were not, the notice-boards would thicken with the horrid mass of sacred and profane advertisements until they obstructed the streets; for there, superimposed pell-mell, would lie police orders, quacks' nostrums, decrees, Orders in Council cancelling these same decrees, notices of sales by order of executors, sales in bankruptcy, lost dogs, church services, marionette shows, preachers, expositions of the Blessed Sacrament, recruiting posters, and eulogies of elastic stockings; in short, all the rubbish that afflicts the public view but is never by any chance read, and whose sole apparent purpose is to cover the nakedness of walls. If it were possible by some means to insist on posters being read, such perusal might do much to improve the general standard of orthography; but as things are the Parisian goes his way, in happy ignorance alike of the caprices of his own language, and of advertisers' wiles.

Sometimes a royal decree is posted up, very imposing, some six feet of paper by three, covered with the most minute printing; sheer waste of paper, since nobody dreams of reading it, although everyone halts a moment to regard the production with awe. The matter in question may be only a decision whereby one of two litigants secures, at the cost of his entire fortune, the inalienable right to plaster up some dirty ruinous wall; this example of Gothic prose may have cost him anything up to sixty thousand francs. Judges' clerks and those who live on litigants' fees are always grateful for a royal decree.

The names of notaries, attorneys, sheriffs' officers and the like are writ large at every street-corner; the gentlemen in question, however, remaining none the less perfectly obscure. They are perpetually in the public eye, which never knows one of them by sight.

Street Signs. Painters preparing advertising signs to be put up in the streets. Mercier was a keen observer of the growing commercialization of Parisian life at the end of the Old Regime. (Courtesy Library of Congress)

But though fame may not come their way, money does; a fat inventory will often bring in as much or more than an elegant book.

The theatre bills are always in colour, but too high up. There will be six or seven of them, one above the other like the steps of a ladder, grand opera coming first in glory, with tight-rope walkers bringing up the rear. But often the announcements of boulevard distractions hold modestly aloof from those of the three theatres. See what a sense of order, and proper respect for authority, can do!

---

*The boulevard theatres, which offered more popular forms of entertainment than the Comédie française, the Comédie italienne, and the Opéra, were located on the broad avenues that had been constructed on the outskirts of Paris during the eighteenth century.

†The Lieutenant of Police was the royal official in charge of maintaining order in Paris.

‡The Académie française, established by Cardinal Richelieu in 1635, had forty members, supposedly the outstanding writers of their time. Mercier was not a member.

37. Doorways

(CCCXVI, Portes cochères, 1:834–36)

The well-to-do and well-born have a way, when anyone in their houses is ill, of strewing straw—and straw mixed with manure at that—in front of their doors and some way along the street, so as to dull the noise of the traffic. This undeserved privilege turns the street into an awful sewer whenever it rains. Everyone has to walk through the black and stinking muck, which comes halfway up your leg. Besides, it is dangerous, for you can no longer hear carriages coming. Thus, to spare one sick man's sensibilities, thirty thousand pedestrians perhaps have to suffer. Carriage-folk, naturally, make nothing of it; but the rest of us can perceive no reason why we should breathe our last under muffled wheels, because M. le Marquis has a touch of fever or some difficulty with his digestion.

Socrates went on foot, as did Horace, and J.-J. Rousseau. By all means let Mr Nobody keep his berlin, and build his doorway to shelter it; let him splash mud all over us, we can get ourselves brushed down; but let him leave us our lives. After all, a man is not a criminal because he likes to take his time, and use his legs, and do his thinking as he goes; he has not deserved for this to be broken on the wheel.

Often, from these shelters, a carriage will swing out without warning, cutting across the street diagonally, and at speed; the danger is upon you too soon, you can do nothing save jump for your life, and that at random, since you cannot guess whether the coachman will turn left or right. It ought to be possible for the porter to warn passing pedestrians; a whistle would serve, of some distinctive note; that would save a good many accidents. Home-going vehicles are less dangerous, because the lackey runs before and bangs on the knocker, so that you have time to take the hint, and look about you.

It is almost squalid not to have one of these erections before your door; no matter how jerry-built, it looks better than merely opening on to the street. As for those entrances where you go up a path to the house, they are out of the question, no matter how clean they may be kept, or what sort of house they lead to. Your carriage shelter may be dark, narrow, clotted with vehicles, wherein you blunder about until a blow in the stomach from some unseen shaft or wheel-hub doubles you up; all the same, it is better than any mere gate with a covered way. The smart world does not visit those who live thus vulgarly, up an alley.

They are useful, another important point, to debtors. The porter's lodge is the limit beyond which no warrant for debt may go, no bailiffs pass; and thus, when it comes to a rich man being sold up, all his creditors get is the miserable stuff out of the lodge. It is not so when the house has only a gate, and a mere covered way; there the bailiff can go up to the seventh floor if there is one, and seize anything he likes; but behind its porter's lodge any dwelling is sacred. It is an odd custom, but none the less popular for that; and, indeed, you can hardly wonder.

But the real annoyance is quite other. The fact is, such places are used by any and every passer-by as public toilets; you drive up to your door to find a gentleman attending to some call of nature,

who sees no reason why he should budge or hurry for you. Nowhere else would such a thing be tolerated, but the public seems
to have established a kind of right to relieve itself in these shelters;
which is a disgusting trick, and most embarrassing for women.

38. Silly Customs Now Done Away With
(CCCXXIII, Sots usages abolis, 1:850–52)

T he little *bourgeois* now is the only person left who goes in for
any great parade of civility; stupid protests, foolish urgings
which to his mind still stand for true politeness, but which the man
of the world finds intolerably tedious.

And so there are no more of those excuses: "I'm afraid we've
given you such a bad dinner"; no more being pressed to drink; no
more tormenting of the guests to make them circulate when they
are happy talking, just to show that the hostess knows how these
things should be done; no imploring of unfortunates to sing. All
this sort of thing, ridiculous as it seems now, was the mark of good
breeding in our grandfathers' day, which we have slavishly and un-
thinkingly imitated.

The table then was an arena, round which dishes made their way
like chariots, passed around out of politeness, never resting, until
two slammed into each other going contrary ways. Not one moment's peace could the truly polite enjoy; the meal itself was a
continuation of those duels of civility which had begun in the anteroom, wherein the most ceremonious was the most applauded.

Young ladies, bolt upright, silent, immobile, rigidly corseted, sat
with never-lifted eyes; and touched no morsel that was set upon
their plates, not they, though their neighbours implored them; for
eating is gross, and these young persons set up for examples of
temperance and modesty.

When dessert came in they opened their mouths, but only to
sing; and then the difficulty was to sing without making faces, and

to give civil answers to compliments after the performance without catching anyone's eye.

Nowadays girls are not afraid to eat, seldom sing, enjoy all reasonable freedom, look about them, talk, but a trifle less than their mothers; they smile rather than laugh. Otherwise they are allowed to be natural, with only the little trace of schoolgirl decorum which is so charming at their age.

True politeness has conquered the false; the old ceremonious practices are done with. Our modern manners are the outcome of common sense, neither embarrassing nor embarrassed. We have no set rules, but behave as circumstances dictate without undue stressing of this point or that, without tactless candour or intolerable concealment; we are adequate, I think, to all occasions, because our behaviour depends, not on preposterous set rules, but on a natural and reasoned inclination to please.

In fact, without knowing much of the world, you may do very well so far as manners go. After all, it is only the intention to offend that offends, conceit and pretentiousness are the only social crimes. These two will always be with us, but nowadays they dare not show their heads; punishment is swift and salutary, and the offender in a moment is brought into line with the conventions of his fellows.

39. How the Day Goes

(cccxxx, Les heures du jour, 1:873–81)

It is curious to see how, amid what seems perpetual life and movement, certain hours keep their own characteristics, whether of bustle or of leisure. Every round of the clock-hand sets another scene in motion, each different from the last, though all about equal in length.

Seven o'clock in the morning sees all the gardeners, mounted on their nags and with their baskets empty, heading back out of town again. No carriages are about, and not a presentable soul, except a few neat clerks hurrying to their offices.

Nine o'clock sets all the barbers in motion, covered from head to foot with flour—hence their soubriquet of 'whitings'—wig in one hand, tongs in the other. Waiters from the lemonade-shops are busy with trays of coffee and rolls, breakfast for those who live in furnished rooms; while along the boulevards trot would-be horsemen learning to sit on, with a lackey riding behind; it is the passer-by, often, who suffers most from their inexperience.

An hour later the Law comes into action; a black cloud of legal practitioners and hangers-on descend upon the Châtelet,* and the other courts; a procession of wigs and gowns and brief-bags, with plaintiffs and defendants at their heels. [*Mercier's note:* The saying goes, you should always take three bags into court; one for your money, one for your brief, and one to stow your patience in.]

Midday is the stockbrokers' hour, and the idlers'; the former hurry off to the Exchange, the latter to the Palais-Royal.† The Saint-Honoré‡ quarter, where all the financiers live, is at its busiest now, its streets are crowded with the customers and clients of the great.

At two o'clock those who have invitations to dine set out, dressed in their best, powdered, adjusted, and walking on tiptoe not to soil their stockings. All the cabs are engaged, not one is to be found on the rank; there is a good deal of competition for these vehicles, and you may see two would-be passengers jumping into a cab together from different sides, and furiously disputing which was first; on which the cabman whips up and drives them both off to the Commissary of Police, who takes the burden of decision off his shoulders.

Three o'clock and the streets are not so full; everyone is at dinner; there is a momentary calm, soon to be broken, for at five fifteen the din is as though the gates of hell were opened, the streets are impassable with traffic going all ways at once, towards the playhouses or the public gardens. *Cafe's* are at their busiest.

Towards seven the din dies down, everywhere and all at once. You can hear the cab-horses' hoofs pawing the stones as they wait—in vain. It is as though the whole town were gagged and bound, suddenly, by an invisible hand. This is the most dangerous time of the whole day for thieves and such, especially towards autumn, when the days begin to draw in; for the watch is not yet about, and violence takes its opportunity. [*Mercier's note:* A man was

a Neuf heures du matin
CHAP. CCCXXX.

9 am. Balthasar Anton Dunker's illustration for one of
Mercier's finest chapters, "How the Day Goes."
(Courtesy Library of Congress)

arrested in 1769, who had killed three persons in six days at this season of the year, mid-October, before he was caught. His weapon was a kind of sling.]

Night falls; and, while scene-shifters set to work at the playhouses, swarms of other workmen, carpenters, masons and the like, make their way towards the poorer quarters. They leave white footprints from the plaster on their shoes, a trail that any eye can follow. They are off home, and to bed, at the hour which finds elegant ladies sitting down to their dressing-tables to prepare for the business of the night.

At nine this begins; they all set off for the play. Houses tremble as the coaches rattle by, but soon the noise ceases; all the fine ladies are making their evening visits, short ones, before supper. Now the prostitutes begin their night parade, breasts uncovered, heads tossing, colour high on their cheeks, and eyes as bold as their hands. These creatures, careless of the light from shopwindows and street lamps, follow and accost you, trailing through the mud in their silk stockings and low shoes, with words and gestures well matched for obscenity. This sort of thing keeps the pure women safe, that is the cant, the excuse; without these creatures there would be more assaults, and the innocent would suffer. Certainly, whether or no this is the reason, rape and assault have become much rarer. But it remains a scandal for all that, and one unthinkable in a provincial town, that these women should ply their trade at the very doors of decent folk, and that honest wives and young girls should be obliged to see them at their business; for it is impossible not to see them, and worse, not to overhear what they say. . . .

By eleven, renewed silence. People are at supper, private people, that is; for the *cafe's* begin at this hour to turn out their patrons, and to send the various idlers and workless and poets back to their garrets for the night. A few prostitutes still linger, but they have to use more circumspection, for the watch is about, patrolling the streets, and this is the hour when they 'gather 'em in'; that is the traditional expression.

A quarter after midnight, a few carriages make their way home, taking the non-card-players back to bed. These lend the town a sort of transitory life; the tradesman wakes out of his first sleep at the sound of them, and turns to his wife, by no means unwilling.

More than one young Parisian must owe his existence to this sudden passing rattle of wheels. Thunder sends up the birth-rate here too, as it does everywhere else.

At one in the morning six thousand peasants arrive, bringing the town's provision of vegetables and fruits and flowers, and make straight for the Halles;§ their beasts have come some eighteen leagues perhaps, and are weary. As for the market itself, it never sleeps. Morpheus never shakes his poppy-seed there. Perpetual noise, perpetual motion, the curtain never rings down on this enormous stage; first come the fishmongers, and after these the egg-dealers, and after these the retail buyers; for the Halles keep all the other markets of Paris going; they are the warehouse whence these draw their supplies. The food of the whole city is shifted and sorted in high-piled baskets; you may see eggs, pyramids of eggs, moved here and there, up steps and down, in and out of the throngs, miraculously; not one is ever broken.

Then the brandy starts to flow across tavern counters; poor stuff, half water, but laced with raw spirit. Porters and peasants toss down this liquor, the soberer of them drink wine. The noise of voices never stops, there is hardly a light to be seen; most of the deals are done in the dark, as though these were people of a different race, hiding in their caverns from the light of the sun. The fish salesmen, who are the first comers, apparently never see daylight, and go home as the street lamps start to flicker, just before dawn; but if eyes are no use, ears take their place; everyone bawls his loudest, and you must know their jargon, to be able to catch what your own vendor shouts in this bedlam of sound. On the Quai de la Vallée,** it is the same story; but there hares and poultry take the place of herrings and cuts of salmon.

This impenetrable din contrasts oddly with the sleeping streets, for at that hour none but thieves and poets are awake.

Twice a week, at six, those distributors of the staff of life, the bakers of Gonesse,†† bring in an enormous quantity of loaves to the town, and may take none back through the barriers. And at this same hour workmen take up their tools, and trudge off to their day's labour. Coffee with milk is, unbelievably, the favoured drink among these stalwarts nowadays.

At street-corners, where the pale light from a street lamp falls,

the coffee women stand, carrying their tin urns on their backs;
they sell their coffee in earthenware cups, two sous a cup, one
penny, and not too well sugared at that; but our workmen find it
very much to their taste. Incredible as it may sound, the company
of *café*-keepers, incorporated by statute and all the rest of it, has
put every possible obstacle in the way of this perfectly legitimate
trade. They, in their mirrored halls, sell this same coffee at two
and a half times the price; but workmen have neither time nor
inclination to be looking at themselves in mirrors while they drink.

So coffee-drinking has become a habit, and one so deep-rooted
that the working classes will start the day on nothing else. It is not
costly, and has more flavour to it, and more nourishment too, than
anything else they can afford to drink; so they consume immense
quantities, and say that if a man can only have coffee for breakfast
it will keep him going till nightfall. They take only two meals in
the twenty-four hours; that at midday and the evening snack of
supper, what they call the *persillade*.

Now that it is full morning you may see the prostitutes' clients
emerging, white-faced, their clothes in disorder; and as for their
expression, it is rather that of apprehension than of remorse; the
lees of pleasure taste bitter by day, but pleasure is a habit for all
that, a tyrant who will not let them go; they will creep back again
to-morrow, and so on till the end.

And what of the gamblers? Out they come, from the exclusive
club, or the filthy den, paler even than the prostitutes' victims;
some striking their foreheads, cursing their luck, others with bulging pockets, which the next night's play will empty.

Laws are powerless against this devouring passion; the desire for
gain is at the root of it, a desire that runs through all classes alike.
The Government itself panders to it; what else are lotteries but
gambling under another name? Public gambling is licensed, private gambling is illegal; that is how the law at present stands.

If the sybarites of Paris, those who like to lie abed till noon, had
their way, there would be no smiths in the city, no horses shod,
and no pots and pans mended; all such noise would be banished
without the walls, together with those street criers who, it must be
admitted, make day hideous with their performances, and against
whose voices neither shut windows nor thick walls avail. These, the

lie-abeds, would have a dozen trades suppressed or exiled, that they might sleep till noon behind the drawn curtains of their alcoves.

Their complaint is well founded; but if their remedy were followed, and carried to extremes, there would be no hats made in Paris, because of the stink of the felt; no leather tanned, no varnish nor perfume made for the same reason, although they themselves make use of these commodities; nor could they permit the tobacconist to ply his trade, by reason of the snuff that gets in their noses as they pass his door. Privilege would allow no shop-windows, but only porticoes to shelter carriages; would strew straw in the streets from midnight till midday, when Privilege does the world the honour of waking; would forbid church bells, and would have soldiers, as they march to the changing of the guard, muffle their drums till that hour; for only Privilege may be privileged to fill the streets with the clatter of wheels and hoofs and to keep others from sleeping.

On the tenth, twentieth, and thirtieth days of the month, from ten o'clock till midday, you may see messengers bent double under the weight of the sacks they carry, and which are full of money; they run as if an enemy army were at the gates of Paris; and it is a sign of our financial backwardness that we have been able to devise no equivalent for these mounds of metal, some paper token which might represent the transfer, instead of shifting actual cash from one strong-room to another. . . .

Nearly every year, towards the middle of November, influenza and catarrh begin their rounds; the reason is, the sudden drop in temperature, and the fogs which result from it, and which check perspiration. There are always a good many deaths from these two causes; the Parisian, who takes nothing seriously, calls these really dangerous afflictions by pet names, the *grippe,* the *coquette;* and three days later is himself gripped, and coquetted with, and, like as not, buried.

People court danger by going straight out into the night air from some hot room or other; perspiration is suddenly checked; and though this present fashion is a good one, of wearing great cloaks, they are not always donned soon enough to be of use. Women often have to wait while their carriages are called; and these delicate creatures, shivering under a portico or at the top of a flight of steps, would do well not to trust altogether to their cloaks to preserve them from illness.

*Châtelet: the main criminal court of Paris.
†Palais-Royal: the garden surrounded by arcades with shops and cafés constructed by the Duke of Orleans. See Chapter 88.
‡Saint-Honoré quarter: the neighbourhood around the rue Saint-Honoré, between the Palais-Royal and the Place Vendôme; a fashionable quarter for the wealthy.
§Les Halles: the city's central wholesale food market.
**Quai de la Vallée: now the quai des Grands Augustins, on the Left Bank facing the Ile de la Cité.
††Gonesse: a suburb of Paris, famous for the excellent bread baked there.

40. Balcony
(CCCXXXVIII, Balcons, 1:916–18)

O ne of the more curious sights of Paris may be seen without trouble; you have only to lean over your balcony and look down into the street below, upon carriages crossing and blocking each other's way, and pedestrians, like game that flees before the menace of the gun, dodging in and out among the wheels of stationary juggernauts; one leaps the gutter to escape a shower of mud, miscalculates an inch, and finds himself in mud up to the eyes, while another, more lucky, goes mincing along unscathed, parasol under arm.

In a gilded chariot, velvet-lined, with glass windows and a pair of horses exquisitely bred and matched, a duchess in all her regalia reclines; and there she remains, unable to get forward or back by reason of an old filthy cab, with boards on straps instead of glass, which is blocking the way. One of the horses is blind, and the other lame; the cabman whips up both impartially, and quite ineffectually; but blind and halt though his pair may be, they contrive without difficulty to hold up any number of thoroughbreds until the whole procession reaches a cross-roads where there is room to pass; then the gilded equipage flashes by, striking sparks from the stones as it goes. Compare this vehicle and its pace with the huge market wagons that lumber slowly along, taking up the whole street, leaving no room for the pedestrian, who goes in terror of one of their great hubs catching him amidships and plastering him into a wall.

A poorly paid lawyer in his cab at twenty-four sous the hour may hold up the Lord Chancellor; a marshal of France must wait while the recruiting sergeant's party drags its slow length along, and a call girl yields no ground to an archbishop. All these different interests in motion, perched up behind coachmen whose vocabulary respects neither ducal, nor clerical, nor legal ears; and the porters at the street-corners, giving in their own lingo as good as they get; what a sight, what a blend of splendour, and poverty, and riches, and wretchedness.

Listen to Madame la Marquise; she is in a hurry, and her shrill little voice sings soprano to the bass of the wagoner calling on all the powers of heaven and hell. But this moving picture is full of such oddities, what with berlins, and sulkies, and cabriolets and whiskies, and carriages jobbed by the week; there is always something queer, or strange, or laughable for the observer to ponder.

You see, for instance, the woman of birth in her coach, ugly as sin, but covered with diamonds, and rouge, and her face shining with some fashionable concoction; compare her with the little fresh, plump nobody in her simple dress. Then the bishop, leaning back upon his cushions, empty-headed but magnificent, a jewelled cross upon his breast, and some grey-headed magistrate in a shabby berlin, reading the affidavits in some case or other. A young fashionable thrusts his head out of the carriage-window, and bawls till his throat aches: "Well, you pack of rascals, have I got to wait here all day?" Nobody heeds him. He makes some poor attempt at swearing, but his meagre voice has about as much effect as the buzzing of a fly upon the hardened tympanums of carters. A neighbouring doctor eyes him solicitously, but the plethoric double-chinned financier on the other side takes no notice of him, or of his surroundings, or the waste of time.

Confusion becomes worse confounded; six hundred vehicles are involved by this time, and there is no help for it, they all must wait until somehow or other they are disentangled. Now, what can have been the preoccupation of that elegant youngster who could not make himself heard? Meeting a lady, perhaps? Not a bit of it. The

CHAP XLVIII

Carriage Collision. The constant confusion and danger in the capital's streets served Mercier repeatedly as an illustration of the city's irrational character and the need for reform. (Courtesy Library of Congress)

trouble was, he wished to be seen that night at all three theatres, the Comédie française, the Opéra, and the italienne.

41. False Hair

(CCCXXXIX, Faux cheveux, 1:918–21)

A woman's head delights you; above her delicious face the tresses are piled high, on her shoulders they lie curling; colour, contour, elegance, you adore them all.

Undeceive yourself. Her hair is false. The head on which it grew is mouldering, like as not, in a grave to which some loathsome sickness has brought it; a malady unnameable in her presence who displays that which was its pride, and now is hers. She discounts any risk of infection that may remain; yet the fashion of bracelets and chains of plaited hair, so popular once, went out for this very reason, the skin diseases that it caused.

Women will dare the chance of such inconveniences rather than disobey their hairdressers. If the skin under the lofty mass is irritable, they use a little instrument called a scraper, to ease it. The heat of the great contrivance sends the blood to their heads and reddens their eyes; no matter, the sacred edifice stands firm.

And this is not all; for besides false hair; the *coiffure* demands a prodigious cushion stuffed with horsehair, and a forest of pins seven or eight inches long, which pierce this and secure it to the scalp below, whose nerves are inflamed by the eternal pomades and powders, highly scented but soon rancid. Perspiration is totally checked, a dangerous thing in itself where the head is concerned. If some considerable weight were to fall on one of these modish piles, the pins, which are of steel, and sharp, would riddle the skull and drive into the brain in a moment.

At night the whole construction is compressed by means of a sort of triple bandage which everything goes under, false hair, pins, dye, grease, until at last the head, thrice its real size, and throbbing, lies on the pillow done up like a parcel . . . so that even in sleep the *coiffeur's* handiwork is respected. The cushion, the foundation of the whole structure, sometimes is made to serve until its outer cover no longer holds together, ragged with pins, and foul with old pomade.

They cannot, however, these fashionables, well afford the time to strip their heads at night; the days are short enough as it is, with gambling and eating, to say nothing of dancing. Bed is unthinkable before three in the morning, and as soon as it is light, the same round begins again. Not unnaturally health suffers, their few remaining hairs fall out; fluxes and toothache, earache and blotches are their portion; while the village woman, who keeps her head clean, covered only with a linen cap which she washes, and who uses the very simplest preparations in the way of grease or powder, keeps her own rich locks to the end of her days; and though they turn white with the years, become thereby the more gracious.

42. Running Footmen, Running Hounds
(CCCLXVIII, Coureurs, chiens coureurs, 1:1020–21)

There was a time when running footmen used to be much more commonly seen in Paris; two men, lightly clad, keeping ahead of a pair of blood-horses. They wore flat shoes and white stockings, which never seemed to get splashed, though they ran at the gutter's very edge. A curious sight, certainly, but was it humane, decent, respectable, to treat men this way? To let a fat, rich man sit back on his cushion, while a couple of slaves thus preceded his coach; two men, fellow-creatures, whom a single false step would pitch under the wheels?

This dangerous and unseemly form of display is no longer the fashion, but those who could afford such luxuries retain them in another form. Greyhounds now race before a carriage, for the sole purpose, it would seem, of throwing people off their balance, and so under the wheels or the hoofs. Pedestrians in our narrow ways have a hard enough time of it already; there are heavy market carts to beware of, carriages, and swift cabriolets, to which now is added

this plague of dogs, which bark, and leap, and fight in the middle
of the street, to such purpose that neither the warning sound of
wheels can be heard, nor the voice of the coachman.

The well-to-do think themselves sole proprietors of the public
roads; or it would seem so, judging by the inconvenience they
cause, and the actual dangers to which their unseemly whims ex-
pose other citizens.

43. Men Midwives

(CCCLXXXI, Accoucheurs, 1:1052–55)

At the beginning of the last century such a profession was unheard of for men. Royalty alone, able in such matters to
please itself, gave an example which for sixty years was unfollowed;
an example which perhaps old custom, or prejudice, or notions of
propriety combined to set at naught.

But the women charged with these duties, being ignorant or
careless, maimed or crippled some of the children they helped
into the world, besides adding to the number of imbeciles by com-
pressing one or two heads; and the end of it was that propriety
yielded to common sense, and the race of *accoucheurs* came into
being—a change not unregretted by our women, accustomed as
they were to the supple and delicate hands of the midwives; but
the *accoucheurs* make up for their larger hands by the use of oil and
certain specially prepared ointments.

They know more about these things now, and can from an earlier diagnosis guess better how the case will go; whether the business will be brief, or painless, or difficult. There are drugs which
help the pain, fewer still-births and fewer terrified women; Caesar-
ean operations too are less often necessary; and soon no mother,
not even the least little shopkeeper's wife, will have any reason left
to prefer women to men in this office.

Southern husbands, and in particular those of Spain, are less
philosophic than the French in their acceptance of these skilled
gentlemen; and whether from jealousy, or because their wives' suf-

ferings appear to them of slighter importance, utterly refuse to countenance the *accoucheur*. The notion of admitting another man to view the territory that they have made their own is too much for them altogether; though a trifle of reflection would show them that however attractive may be the pallor and languor of a woman in child-birth, however appealing her cries for help, her appearance *au fond* is the reverse of desirable. Besides, the functions exercised by these men have a kind of sacred quality; they go about their business soberly, as if they were, so far as their patients are concerned, deaf, blind, and dumb.

Decency, then, is not affronted; and despite a book entitled *The Impropriety of Licensing Male Midwives,* published in Paris in 1708, and written by a certain Hecquet,* our women themselves, six weeks after it is all over, sit between husband and doctor at dinner, with never a blush.

This new operation, recently tried, but not yet wholly proved, called symphysis,† is perhaps too dangerous still to be popular, despite the praise which is its inventor's due. The forceps is bad enough, but less alarming in prospect; and since its use will surely become more skilled, and its shape perfected as time goes on, it seems better to trust to it, than to the rash expedient of cutting a woman in two.

There is at present in Paris a public course in midwifery where practitioners can learn; and while the smaller towns and the villages wholly lack such instruction at present, there is no lack of skill in the capital; where, indeed, it has become as easy and pleasant to bear a child as to conceive one.

---

*P. Hecquet, *De l'indécence aux hommes d'accoucher les femmes* . . . (1708), a book written to denounce the practice of male doctors and midwives assisting at births.
†"symphysis" was a procedure of separating the mother's pubic bones in difficult births, allowing more room for the baby to pass through the birth canal.

44. Dentists

(CCCLXXXII, Dentistes, 1:1055–56)

A tooth or so lacking will spoil the loveliest mouth, one such gap in Helen's smile, and farewell the wars of Troy; farewell, too, the divine *Iliad* that records them. For good teeth are the sign of health, and even the voluptuary prefers a healthy woman. A beauty lacking this one charm must rely on grimaces to hide her defect, and laugh behind her lifted fingers or a fan.

Since good teeth are necessary for health as well as beauty, there can be no excuse for neglecting them, and nowadays dentists are clever enough to try to keep our teeth in our heads instead of pulling them out on the slightest provocation; the dreaded forceps is less often seen. The most astonishing artist of them all is one Catalan, in the Rue Dauphine; not only has he a most delicate and light touch, but intelligence and observation into the bargain, so much so, that he has contrived a modern miracle. He can and will make you (so far has anatomical knowledge advanced in this line) he can make you, I repeat, an entire set of false teeth with which you can chew anything you fancy, no matter how tough. He has discovered the mechanical principle of the workings of the jaw, and imitated it so perfectly that I think it only right such enterprise and ingenuity should enjoy the publicity it deserves; here then are his name and address.

If your tooth starts to plague you in the course of a stroll through the street, look up; almost certainly you will see, somewhere near at hand, a dentist's sign; one enormous molar the size of a bushel measure, with a hand pointing, and the words "First Floor." The dentist offers a chair, throws back the lace at his wrist, grips, adroitly tweaks out the offender, and offers you a decoction to gargle; after which you pay, and continue your stroll in comfort. What could be more convenient?

45. The Fortnight Before Easter
(CCCLXXXVI, Quinzaine de Pâques, 1:1067–68)

The common people make a great to-do about their Easter duty, and it is a real problem for shopkeepers. This is the time when confession and communion are obligatory, and the head of the family lets them all know it; children, assistant, servant, he harasses them all. It is a bad moment for agnostics in the bud, who are in two minds whether to neglect their duty or perform it.

And in the churches themselves, and the convents, what a bustle! Priests, monks, all up in the air; sermons, exhortations, lectures, retreats. At home children are made to get the Passion Gospel by heart; it is a long business, there are tears, and consequent scoldings followed by more tears, followed by bread and water. All the theatres are shut, and all the brothels open; for the police it is the busiest time of the year. What with concerts instead of comedies; charity meetings; the *Tenebrae** service made tolerable to polite ears by music; advertisements of popular singers; Longchamps; and the departure of all persons of any account for the country, this is a redoubtable week of din. Footmen and maids escape from their duties to kneel in the straw of confessionals. Morning and night the Passion is sung, the churches are none of them large enough to hold the throngs; a white cloth constantly veils the altar-rails, and the ciborium† makes many a morning journey; the baker allows double the number of hosts to each mould; and the tabernacle door is for ever opening to the sesame of the *Confiteor.*

After all this appearance of devotion, at the end of the fortnight the churches once more echo to an occasional step, people take up their normal lives again, and put confession out of their minds for another year. Vegetables have already given way to meat at table; when they reappear, it is time to examine consciences again.

Poor people always speak of "the man with two shirts"— meaning their confessor.

---

*Catholics held a special service called *Tenebrae* as part of the observance of Good Friday. It has been dropped from the Catholic liturgy since the Vatican II Council in 1962–65. The Franciscan abbey at Longchamps was noted for its choir.
†The "ciborium" is a goblet-shaped vessel for holding eucharistic wafers.

46. Valets of the Street
(CDLV, Décrotteurs, 1:1255–59)

The old name for Paris was Lutetia,* Mudville; but it is not known at what period this characteristic gave birth to its corrective trade, so essential in our magnificent but filthy city; the trade of brusher-down. There is no defence against our mud; you may walk delicately, you may cultivate eyes in the back of your head—all to no purpose; sometimes, even, the too-zealous broom of a street cleaner bespatters with its gleanings the white stockings of the passer-by. This is the signal for the brusher-down, who lies in wait at the street-corner, ready for just such accidents with his officious brush; he cleans you, and fits you for the minister's anteroom or the fashionable *salon*, both of which are generous enough to overlook shabbiness and indifferent linen, but draw the line at mud, even on a poet.

The Pont-Neuf† is the heart of this industry, the brushing there is excellent, there is more room, and the constant stream of traffic never interferes with you in your backwater. Speed and skill are the watchwords of these practitioners, masters, all of them, of their art; elsewhere you risk falling into the hands of some inexpert apprentice, who, seizing the leg confided to him and taking up the blacking brush by mistake, ruins your stockings with a greasy and indelible smear, which defies all laundering. Imagine such a fate befalling the unfortunate author who has only this one pair of white silk hose, and is on his way to dine with a duchess, and read her a comic dialogue or an erotic poem.

Authors, beware; entrust yourselves only to one of the master brush-wielders of the Pont-Neuf. On a rainy day, or a broiling one, he will hand you an umbrella, and thus save from disaster your barber's handiwork, more precious to you even than your shoes.

Strange to say, this trade is not taxed. When they have bought a foot-rest and two brushes, their talent is their own, and they may ply where they will, an advantage very unusual in this city of ours.

Often a man of talent, elegant speaker and good writer, finds himself on admission to the Bar unable to make use of his natural qualities, so hedged about is this profession with the tyranny of custom. There is none of this, no lean period of waiting and devilling, in the trade of brusher-down. His comrades, older in practice, have no advantage over him; he takes up his brushes at once, and begins to earn. There are no jealousies, either, among them. You beckon to one, four or five come running, and may jostle you a little, thrusting their rests against your legs; but when you have chosen your man, there is no argument, off go his mates at once with never a protest. The strong and the weak take their turn; the clever fellow never makes mock of his clumsier colleague. How do our various illustrious academies and other gatherings compare for brotherhood with this?

Their price never alters. (Would to God one could say the same of other public functionaries!) There is no cheating, and no monopoly among these wandering Savoyards.‡ From time immemorial, in all weathers and all places, whether the price of food is low or high, no matter how the value of money shifts, the price never varies; two liards only, one halfpenny, is the charge for brushing down your stockings and shining up your shoes.

They are good citizens, these men, always the first to shout for the King; sometimes their loyal enthusiasm will start a crowd cheering that before was apathetic; and they never use English blacking, for the reason that it is called so. They prefer a mixture all their own, a blend of oil and soot, which comes off irrevocably on the light dresses of ladies by whose side their clients sit in carriages. Woman should make a stand, and, patriotism or no, insist upon the use of the English product, which does not rub off on everything it touches. . . .

Chassé, an actor at the opera, one day employed the services of one of these men (for actors go on foot; it is only their feminine counterparts that can afford horses). The job done, his hand went to his pocket, but the brusher-down would accept no payment. "And why not?" asked Chassé. "Well, sir," said the man, "I play dragons and suchlike at the opera, where you do the kings. We're two of a trade." . . .

They play other parts besides dragons; for instance, the ascending gods are always done by these fellows. When there is a trifle of flying to be done, and the chance of a highly paid actor breaking his neck, they dress up a Savoyard in the regalia, and swing him across the stage on a horizontal wire. The spectator's eye is deceived, and forth steps the singer from the wings, with no trace of the anxiety which must have been his had his fate and song both hung upon a pulley.

Finally, these artists of the brush, modest as they are, and ever ready to be of use, a while ago rendered the public a considerable service, of whose value they to this day remain unconscious. When the new Opera House was put up on the boulevard the question arose of how to test the strength of its construction. To make trial of this, all the Savoyards and brushers-up in Paris were invited to a performance. They overflowed the boxes, orchestra, and gallery; staircases and corridors echoed to the tread of their considerable feet—all this according to plan. The new building came through the test unshaken, and next night the elegant world, silked and scented and secure, filled the now proven amphitheatre.

Trying out a house is the builder's and architect's name for this procedure; and I should like to ask all you wise and prudent persons, just how you proposed to reassure the public had these excellent citizens failed you. But they love such free treats, especially when a place is new, and you take advantage of their enthusiasm and their poverty—so far, thank God, without reproach to your consciences. But what will posterity say, think you, of this expedient, the best our intelligent century has been able to devise; this artless method of ascertaining whether or no a public building is safe for public use?

*Mercier's belief that the Roman name for Paris, Lutetia, meant "city of mud" is no longer accepted.

†The Pont-Neuf, the most famous and oldest bridge in Paris, crosses the western tip of the Ile de la Cité.

‡Many of the poor who tried to make a living in the streets of Paris were immigrants from the Alpine region of Savoy, known as Savoyards.

47. Riots

(CDLX, Émeutes, 1:1273–76)

D angerous rioting has become a moral impossibility in Paris. The eternally watchful police, two regiments of Guards, Swiss and French, in barracks near at hand, the King's bodyguard, the fortress cities which ring the capital round, together with countless individuals whose interest links them to Versailles; all these factors make the chance of any serious rising seem altogether remote.

During the past fifty years there have only been two such attempts and both were quelled at once.* Paris has had more than a century of peace since the time of the Fronde; what with mounted police and troops stationed around the capital, sedition finds no rallying point; the length of time this state of things has lasted, is perhaps the best guarantee that it will not soon be changed.

There is a law against peasant gatherings, but even supposing the peasantry did assemble, where could they go? And what, no matter how desperate their grievance, could they do? They would have to reckon first with the police, then with regiments, and finally with an army or two.

If the Parisian, on the other hand—who has his moments of effervescence—were to attempt anything of the kind, he would find the door of the huge cage in which he lives promptly shut upon him; no food would be allowed to reach him; and an empty belly would soon bring him to his knees. . . .

A handful of watchmen has been known to disperse a group of five or six hundred angry men, and that without difficulty, although the demonstrators at first seemed intractable enough; but a few blows with truncheons and the securing of the ringleaders is, generally speaking, enough to cool them down.

Any attempt at sedition here would be nipped in the bud; Paris need never fear an outbreak such as Lord George Gordon† recently led in London. . . . It took a course unimaginable by Parisians; for it appears that even in disorder the crowds were under some kind of control. For instance, a thing which a Frenchman can hardly credit; the houses of certain unpopular men were fired, but their neighbours not touched; our people in the like circumstances would show no such restraint.

The Londoner, even up in arms, keeps his head and his temper, and concentrates his rage upon some definite object; while his inborn political sanity draws a line of conduct beyond which, though provoked, he will not go.

But a Parisian in the same turmoil, and flushed with some early slight successes, would get out of hand at once; it is only the thought of the police and magistrates at his back that keeps him quiet; these curbs removed, there is nothing in our people's own tradition to supply the want; and their violence would be the more cruel, since they lack in themselves all power to control it.

We are not practised rioters, we Parisians, and possibly for that very reason an outbreak (if such a thing were ever to occur) would assume alarming proportions. Still, if it should happen, and were met at the outset with prudence and moderation, above all if bloodshed could be avoided, I maintain that the people's ill-humour would evaporate of itself. Certainly this is the course adopted by the magistrates in such troubles as we have had, and their rational firmness prevented the conflagration of discontent from spreading.

This freedom of Londoners, who may in a sense please themselves in matters of revolt, is an ever-present danger to their city; and yet these stone-throwers and incendiaries make brave sailors and soldiers; they have not learned to fear. Set over them a strong police force too ready with its weapons, and they will lose their qualities as fighting men; England's loss in energy and courage would outbalance the gain of order. You cannot have a satisfactory population both ways, good fighting men and peaceful citizens; these two spring from different stock; and it is the true triumph of government to reconcile them as far as may be; to leave the citizen his freedom against authority. We have not worked out this problem as yet, nor assessed the civic values of pride *versus* insolence in a people, though we have had examples enough in our own history. Nor have we settled in our minds the difference between disturbance and revolution.

Politically speaking, each generation ought to be allowed its Saturnalia,‡ there would be no great danger in that. It may be that a few broken windows and constables' heads are necessary for our existence as a fighting race; to say nothing of an occasional rotten apple thrown at the lawyers. But what of certain other intangible, invisible onslaughts? Why leave the schooling of a people's character to an all too zealous, none too tactful, force of police; and how assess the damage, the weakening influence, of such schooling?

*Major riots had occurred in Paris in 1750, in reaction to rumors that children of the poor were being kidnapped and shipped out of the city, in 1769, in protest against high bread prices, and in 1775, during the "flour war," another episode of high prices. It is not clear which two of these Mercier was referring to.
†During the Gordon riots of 1780, an anti-Catholic crowd set fire to many buildings in central London.
‡The Saturnalia was a Roman festival, during which social hierarchies were temporarily suspended.

48. Street Singers
(CDLXIII, Chanteurs publics, 1:1283–85)

Are of two kinds, sacred and profane; the former offer hymns for sale, the latter's stock-in-trade is more secular; but you often find them not forty paces apart. One tries to sell you a medallion against the wiles of the devil, who is painted all clothed in red, with an opening in the costume for his tail; the other chants some famous victory or other, very much in the miracle vein too, so that their hearers are in two minds which of the pair to heed, and end by listening to both, one ear lent to the devil (who tempted a poor man with ill-gotten gold), and one to the history of some general or other who confronted the enemy sword in hand. The saintly singer wears his hair uncurled, and looks half-witted; the extoller of carnage has a jolly and peaceable red face, and the larger audience; a contrast which very graphically shows the relative popularity of saints and sinners.

At length the ballad-singer, having gathered all available listeners around him, leaves the medallion-seller deserted, alone on his box, displaying the horns of the enemy of mankind to empty air; his promises of salvation count for little compared with the lure of the songs of this world, so richly descriptive of good living and loving; and the end of it is that the coin, which has been hovering between psalm and ballad, goes into damnation's pocket.

Each bawls his loudest; each has a placard with—"By licence of His Lordship the Lieutenant of Police"; for all these fellows like to throw Lordships about. These placards with the Lieutenant's name at the bottom are one of the reasons why the people suppose him to be absolute master of Paris, all-powerful in all matters; his is the visible power, and all the rest goes for nothing; they cannot imagine such a thing as a minister without a horde of inspectors and spies at his orders.

All these canticles, spiritual and the reverse, are presumably submitted to the censor, and approved by him; this censor, oddly enough, is a rhymester himself, but he has never turned out anything that for spontaneity, mockery, and grace can compare with certain of these songs of the street; the censor must bow to the poet.

There are still a good many broadsheets* relating the exploits and horrid deaths of criminals; these are the most affecting and most popular of all. When by a stroke of luck some well-known personage ascends the scaffold, his death is set to music at once, and sung with violin accompaniment. Every event is song-stuff in Paris; a man unsung, be he marshal or malefactor, is a man unknown. And I maintain here and now that to the man in the street Desrues† is a more illustrious name than Voltaire.

---

*Broadsheets were sheets printed on one side, with illustrations and text purporting to tell the stories of notorious criminals and sensational events.
†Antoine-François Desrues was condemned to death in 1777 for having poisoned a Madame de la Motte and her son. His public execution was the subject of numerous broadsheets.

49. Sanctity in Mourning
(CDLXXV, Saints défigurés, 1:1308)

O ur church porches are rich, most of them, in Gothic figures; all of which saints at the moment of writing are so hideous with soot, that they have more the look of condemned sinners than of the elect in Paradise.

Noses, ears, arms—one or all of these are wanting. Angels and cherubim are docked of their wings; the archangel of the Last Judgment fills his cheeks, but lacks his trumpet; and these celestial visages, disfigured by the pox of time and weather, are of a nature to inspire terror rather than devotion in the faithful. Then why lend a final irony to their forbidding appearance by wreathing them with flowers? The contrast is unfortunate. A sooty saint grinning out from among roses looks altogether Satanic; and piety is, to my mind, no good excuse for bad taste. This practice disparages the images it would honour.

The front of Notre-Dame offers a most amazing jumble of allegory, which you can read as you will; theology, occultism, chemistry, all are represented there. One adept was good enough to assure me that the secret of the philosopher's stone was hidden among these enigmatic carvings, if only one could find the clue to it. But this last, as he had to admit, was the difficulty.

50. Horse Exercise
(CDLXXVIII, Monter à cheval, 1:1311)

A Parisian pretty soon learns to keep his balance on a slippery pavement, to dodge horses' hoofs, and to thread his way among the moving wheels and shafts of vehicles; his stomach is biddable, he can flatten it out to nothing, Gascon-fashion;* he serves his apprenticeship in gutter-leaping, seven flights of stairs are nothing to him, he can run up without taking breath, and down again without mischance in the dark; but there is one thing he never can or will learn, and that is, to sit on a horse.

The fact is, there is very little scope for it. Riding-schools are few and costly, and licensed, of course, most exclusively; they are not allowed to instruct anyone and everyone in the noble art. And the end of it all is, that you never see a horseman of the middle class; even the shortest journey is made by cab; and the Parisian continues to be, and will remain, the world's least enthusiastic horseman.

*Gascons had the reputation of having little money and thus having flat stomachs.

51. Sedan Chairs

(CDLXXIX, Chaise à porteurs, 1:312–13)

I t is not the easiest thing in the world to carry a human being through the dirty and crowded streets of the capital; therefore chairs are never seen except in the mornings, and in certain of the less crowded quarters. Dowagers always proceed in this manner to Mass, with a lackey going before, to carry the *Book of Hours* in an embroidered red velvet bag; whose splendour each old lady would have you remark, before kneeling on it to ask forgiveness for the sins of her youth. But in the more crowded streets horses have the best of it.

Two sturdy mercenaries, sweating and staggering in their great nailed shoes, carry the man who, by reason of gout and obesity, cannot walk. At the turn of a street they encounter a herd of cattle, wild, driven creatures and no respecters of persons; one horn slips under a pole, and over goes the box with its occupant who, too fat to extricate himself, must wait till the herd is safely past. Horned heads threaten him as he lies; he shrinks into the farthest corner of his shelter, for all that horns are no novelty to him, until the frail box is righted, and he can escape. Rage swells in him, the door of the contrivance is grown too small for him, but out he bursts at last, to shake his cane at the fleeing porters; forgetting, in his fury, that in the *mêlée* he has lost his wig.

Wheeled chairs are safer, they rarely meet with this sort of accident; but when they do, and the passenger is a lady, imagine the scandal! The shafts of the vehicle, and its occupant's legs, all pointing skywards! There is only one thing left for the poor creature, and that is to faint, which she does, thereby losing all consciousness of her situation, and the bystanders' comments.

52. Lampoons

(CDLXXXIII, Placards, 1:1318–21)

T here was a time when the walls along the streets were actually used by the public: when you might find pasted up here and there little broadsheets with satirical verses on the events of the day. But nowadays the police keep such an eye on the bill-posters that nothing of this kind can ever happen. Paris has no equivalent of that mutilated statue on which, in Rome, *pasquinades** are stuck for all to read who run. Critical wit and police supervision go none too well together, and the would-be critic of events thinks twice before he risks exile or prison for the sake of an epigram. There are still plenty of these latter, but they circulate by word of mouth, or in manuscript, and no longer find their way into print.

In the old days when supervision was less strict, or the powers of the police less abused than they are at present, there was one device which never failed, whereby unlicensed persons could broadcast their opinions. This was the way of it; a porter would come along with a great basket on his back, and at the corner of the street halt a moment as if to rest his shoulders, leaning the basket of course against the wall. In two seconds a small boy would pop up from his hiding-place in the load, stick his bill under the cover of the basket's two flaps, and huddle down again out of sight in no time, when the porter would resume his slow and painful march to the next convenient wall. But this is no longer done; we pass leaflets about now from hand to hand, a less laborious method of distribution.

But even if such things were not prohibited, the public would be no better off. Our people are too much taken up with sheer daily toil, and the ever-recurring problem of buying enough to eat, to have any time for politics; public events no longer affect them one way or the other; they have lost interest, and heart, and the capacity for laughter. Why should they care who stands at the tiller of the ship of State? All they know of its progress is the wake, which is all they see, and in which there can be no change.

And so satire keeps close; your financier may laugh at a turn of phrase here and there, but the meaning goes by him. Wit travels slowly; the blunder and the epigram which chastises it are often a year apart, which is as though an usher should birch a schoolboy for faults twelve months old. Punishment must come at once if it is to serve its purpose. In any case the politician, minister, whatever he may be, cares exactly nothing for these squibs,† and goes his way unperturbed by them. Why should he care? History's verdict will wait for his death, while the verdict of the governed, that clamour which nevertheless, and because of its long repression, voices truth, seldom reaches his ears in his lifetime.

So much for our rulers. What of our unhappy writers? Poor devils, they cannot make one single false step without a pack of yelling critics at their heels; sometimes, even, the critics yell when there has been no false step at all. Yet the Government permits and encourages such libels, which only hamper or quite possibly ruin one class of citizens, while it steps in at once to prevent any criticism of matters which may affect the entire nation. Admirable system!

The Popes, autocrats as they were, left a clear field to Pasquin and Marsorio,‡ and why not? These trials of wit kept the people amused and informed. Is it not surely better to stick up a lampoon on a statue, rather than leave the grievance it stands for festering in a man's mind? It is a safety-valve for popular ill-humour; free speech in the end means fewer broken heads.

*"pasquinade": Pasquin was the name of a Roman statue on which citizens posted satires or pamphlets, hence the name "pasquinades" for these writings.
†"squibs": lampoons
‡"Marsorio": another statue in Rome where pamphlets were posted.

53. Bill-Stickers
(CDLXXXIV, Afficheurs, 1:1321–22)

There are, as in the French Academy, forty of these functionaries, and the likeness between the fraternities does not end there. A bill-sticker too must be able to read and write before he is considered eligible for the post; but he need possess no other qualifications, thus completing his resemblance to certain members of that illustrious assembly created by the despot and rhymester Richelieu.*

The bill-sticker wears an apron, and a kind of copper medal, his licence, in his buttonhole; he carries in addition to these insignia a short ladder, a brush, and a pot of paste. He will advertise every-thing and anything except himself, which is more than can be said of all the Forty Immortals. He is impartiality's very emblem; sacred or profane, the solemn condemnation or the lost dog, he slaps up his bills with no change of countenance, one after the other, and reads no word of any printed paper he handles, except the magis-trate's name at the foot; on that authority, he would slap up his own death warrant.

Consider this fellow, who has known in advance the date of every new play, every opera for the past thirty years, and yet may never have set foot in a theatre. When he has set the poster up at its due street-corner and made sure that it is not upside down, he steps back, eyes its symmetry with satisfaction, and departs.

Church doors and walls, and those of any religious house, are supposed to be safe from his activities, so far as notices of plays, or novels and such profane books are concerned; however, the nature of a book is not always betrayed in its title, and walls make no protests; and so the bill-sticker may, and does, paste up pretty well what he pleases, where he chooses.

A word of warning; never stop to read any notice whatsoever, high or low, that involves standing near the curb; it is a position fraught with perils. I have known inoffensive persons obliged to leap for their lives in the very middle of some edifying sentence; a state of affairs which precludes that calm so essential to all study, even the assimilation of news. "On the curb, they feel secure," too much so to observe that the stone has been worn down by passing wheels to a height at which it no longer offers any obstruction to traffic; and thus, while you stand in meditation, some vehicle bears down upon you, and takes you in the back of the calf.

*Armand du Plessis, Cardinal de Richelieu (1585–1642), Louis XIII's principal minister and the architect of the French absolutist system of government.

54. Tapestry
(CDLXXXVI, Tapisseries, 1:1325–27)

On Corpus Christi* day the streets along which the Blessed Sacrament passes are hung with the loves of pagan gods. Ganymede borne in Jupiter's arms, Bacchus with his mad women, the Carian nymph that stole virility from men, Daphne fleeing Apollo, Venus smiling at Adonis; these are the images, hung by pious hands, that look down upon the Holy of Holies in procession. The marching priests have only to lift their eyes to read in embroidery all the metamorphoses of Ovid. A pagan, risen from the inferno to which our theology condemns him, would find his own gods doing all the honours of our mysteries. Strange that it should be so; that these pictured records of idolatry triumphant should adorn Christian walls, and that men who bear in their hands the living God should walk so meekly encompassed by the deities of a religion they condemn!

Even, they throng about the altar of repose, the tiny chapel where the Blessed Sacrament is halted, and which solid citizens vie with each other to adorn. Jupiter brandishing a thunderbolt looms there, threatening the Virgin Mary, while Apollo and his nine Muses receive with the rest the benediction of the lifted monstrance. For the decorators entrusted with such matters see nothing odd in nailing up a Bacchante or two above an altar-piece, and through the very rays of the monstrance itself the face of ravished Proserpina† shows white. . . .

Except for these public occasions, tapestries are banished; they used to dominate every room, making the queerest background for furniture. Now they are relegated to antechambers, and our walls are panelled in damask, which has a far more civilized look. The old figures, ill-drawn, heavy, and unpleasing, have become unsuited to present-day feminine taste. There are plenty of them left, but for the most part in the country, while in town they lie folded in attics to await the feast-days of the Church.

But it is a sight to see the decorators in all their glory on Corpus Christi, clambering up their ladders, sliding down them to lose no time. Every door must have its hanging. On moves the procession, and while the tail of it is still in sight you see men with hammers untacking great mythological canvases; man and canvases tumble to earth together, and at once the latter are folded and spirited away by the former to serve some other street on the route of the procession.

The miracle is, with all these ladders, planted against walls and hurried overhead, all these hammers being flourished, all these crowds surging below the decorators on their unsteady eminences, that there should on these pious occasions be so few martyrs to the cause of religious pomp and the zeal of the hammerers, who on such days are no respecters of persons, and set their feet upon devout heads with no more concern than if these were so many paving-stones.

*Corpus Christi: Catholic festival in honor of the Eucharist
†Proserpina or Persephone was the daughter of Jupiter and Demeter, abducted by Pluto to reign with him over the underworld.

55. Midnight Mass

(CDXC, Messe de Minuit, 1:1337–40)

C hurches are all full on Christmas Eve, but whether the crowds come to say their prayers is another matter. Young men stroll in towards midnight, looking about them, casting an appraising eye over the assembled women; amused to see the pretty creatures kneeling, who ordinarily would be in their beds at this hour, and busy with quite another occupation.

There was some idea that these noisy crowds came for the music, and all organists were bidden to be mute; but even without music the effect of darkness outside and lights within, the turning upside down for once of custom, would be enough to lend these hours a special charm. It is the only nocturnal ceremony the Church allows, and naturally enough, despite the holy ground, anyone bent on mischief will attempt to profit by it.

Most of our Paris ceremonies are well known; the really curious sights are to be seen in village churches a few miles outside the capital. To begin with, this is the triumphal night of the farmer's wife; it is she, or rather, her shepherd, who presents the lamb to the deputation of village girls, virgins officially, who come in procession to claim it; and very sick of its beribboned basket the poor little beast must get before the performance is over.

At midnight the bell sounds, the procession gets under way; this is the order of it.

First comes the parish beadle, carrying the Star of Bethlehem, that famous star that, had it shown itself in their lifetime, would have given Newton and the other astronomers something to think about. The three Kings in person follow it; one of them, Baltasar the Moor, with his face all sooty, and very provocative of mirth; however, nobody laughs. Next, four angels with cardboard wings, which as far as flying goes are every bit as good as M. Blanchard's balloon;* then some wise virgins with flaming lamps, followed by others less wise, with lamps extinguished. Gabriel comes next, the best-looking of the lot, eyeing Mary with a tenderness far from archangelic, while her husband Joseph—a part always given to the village idiot—vainly attempts to quiet the bleatings of the unfortunate lamb. The shepherds are muffled in great cloaks, which open now and then to show their crooks. Finally, and far more at ease than the young men, come the shepherdesses, last and most pleasing item of the procession. . . . One carries the Tree of Jesse, another Aaron's Rod (recently superseded by Bléton's hydroscope)†, while a third bears the apple, not that of Troy, but the fruit by which humanity fell, and a fourth holds fast the identical snake that caused all the confusion in Paradise. The remaining girls carry crooks, either their own, or those of their shepherd lovers.

A perambulating orchestra accompanies this assemblage; two fiddles, a clarinet, a serpent and half a dozen bagpipes. . . . Some dog that has slipped into church unseen at his master's heel sets up a lamentable howling as his contribution to the accompaniment, which changes to yelps of pain as beadle and shepherds combine to eject him. The din is unspeakable.

At length two girls advance for the purpose of singing certain spiritual canticles designed to increase reverence and favour piety, as no doubt they do, to judge from the only verse I can now recall:

> Gabriel came to Mary once
> When he had occasion,
> She a mother then became
> Without copulation.

After Mass, which these good people hear with real devotion and simplicity, comes the Christmas supper, when all the eating houses fill in defiance of the local magistrate's early closing order; and after that—who knows? There are occasions when even the wisest of virgins does well to put out her lamp.

*Blanchard's balloon: François Blanchard (1753–1809) was the first to cross the English Channel in a balloon, on January 7, 1785.
†Bléton's hydroscope: Bléton was famous for his supposed ability to detect water under ground.

56. Barber's Shop
(CDXCI, Boutique de Perruquier, 1:1340–45)

The abyss of all uncleanness, repository of filth unimaginable, to which persons come seeking to become presentable. Its window-panes, greasy with pomade, opaque with powder, intercept all light; outside in the street the constant trickle of soapy water has worn itself an unsavoury runnel among the stones. Floor and beams alike are crusted with powder, and in the corners dead spiders hang in their spectral webs, stifled by the eternal eruptions of the powder-sifter. No need to go in; better stand by me, and take your view through the broken pane.

A man is in the chair, covered from head to heels with the usual cape of waxed cloth. The barber has been curling him, first twisting up the hair in paper, then arranging it with a hot iron; a reek of burning hair fills the room. Next to him reclines a figure topped by a cloud of soapsuds, while upon a third head the assistant tries his largest and strongest comb, in vain; he dusts the matted mass with a top-dressing of powder, and sends the customer away satisfied.

There are four of these assistants, pallid featureless creatures, handling in swift succession comb, razor, and powder-puff. One is a surgeon's apprentice, new come from the practice of his other trade; with hands still reminiscent of their explorations in some poor wretch's bowels, he takes his place among the rest, for business is brisk; the Parisian corner-boy must have a trim head for Sundays, to look his best at vespers and during the subsequent walk.

There are women too, who help; these, rolling up dead hair upon their hair combs, are almost more repulsive than the men. Their body-linen is a dingy yellow as though steeped in grease, their skirts and hands are equally dirty, soap and water have never come in contact with them, and even the 'whitings,' the men barbers, never solicit their favours.

Sunday morning is the busy time. The master has his work cut out, his razors one by one grow blunt upon his patrons' chins. About sixty pounds of starch is used in such a shop on such a day, all upon the heads of artisans; puffs of white from the sifter even blow out into the street. The victims emerge with faces like ghosts, and as for the master's own coat, it must carry three times its own weight of flour, six pounds at least of the stuff, in addition to which, if he is talkative, he has probably swallowed something like four ounces more, in the course of his functions.

Yet on Sunday afternoon at four o'clock this same master-barber shakes the white dust of his shop off his feet, and ascends to an upper room, where he strips mother-naked, and washes; then, going into a further closet, he arrays himself in decent black, and goes out, clean as a counsellor-at-law, by the back door; not daring, even he, to pass through the squalor wherein his living is earned.

After this, whither? To the opera, most likely, to applaud Mlle Guimard.* In the pit he sits cheek by jowl with his customers, caring for nobody's elbows, no longer condemned by the incommodity of his trade to stand aloof from his fellows; 'whiting' no more, but a judge of music seated among his peers.

Returning, he undresses with care, folds his black coat, puts away his laced shirt, and returns to his greasy clothing for another six days, unless by the grace of God a feast-day intervenes, to set him back in the pit again, worshipping that new god of the dance, M. Vestris.†

This profession, revolting though it may seem, is sacred, I would have you know, and may not be exercised without license from the police; unauthorized performers upon the razor are hauled off to jail, there to reflect that their pretensions have drawn down upon them the thunderbolts of the law. The amateur may not plead ignorance, or lack of equipment; an old blunt razor, a pot of grease, a comb found in his possession are enough to damn him, and a severe sentence of imprisonment avenges his attack upon society.

Such are our laws; such the pretexts upon which the liberty of human action is assailed. And yet they have the impudence to quote St Louis, patron and legislator of barbers, in support of this preposterous claim. Make no mistake; the privilege of shaving a warehouseman, powdering a porter, combing a man of letters, or frizzing a lawyer's clerk, must be bought and paid for.

One other thing in this disgusting hovel fascinates while it repels the eye; a mass of false hair emerging from the oven in which it has sustained some hours' baking. Imagination shudders at its resemblance to the crust of a good Périgueux *pâté*. The mere thought is enough to turn any stomach.

Only a century ago the wig was a costly and unusual item of attire, whose price might be anything up to a couple of thousand francs. True it was an enormous structure; the spoil of half a dozen heads barely sufficed to make a covering for one. To-day you may buy a decent article for something like ten francs, not only cheaper than the older kind, but better made and more shapely, to say nothing of its more natural appearance.

Village schoolmasters, vergers, public letter-writers, and aged ushers of the law-courts care nothing for this last recommendation; they have no intent or wish to deceive. They buy their headgear second-hand on the Quai des Morfondus,‡ where there is a dealer, and go tranquilly about their business with an inch of their own hair showing between wig and brow. All the same, these old wigs are sturdy, and good value still, despite ill-usage and the ravages of time. And, taking one thing with another, heads are pretty much alike, both outside and in; such differences as do exist count for little close to, and at a distance for nothing at all.

Our schoolmaster, as might be expected, chooses his on a system, not too exacting; he casts over the tumbled heaps of hair his philosophic eye, and from the assortment selects one not too different from his own colour; if it affords reasonable comfort and shelter to that casket of bone which enshrines the jewel of his intellect, he is suited, and pays his money down. Fancy toys with the thought of his predecessor in that wig. Did he argue thus: Did his purchase become him any better? How reason upon a wig divorced

CHAP. X X II

Powdering a Wig. Mercier devoted several chapters to
barbers and wigmakers, the "whitings" who got their
name from the powder that covered their clothes.
(Courtesy Library of Congress)

from the intelligence below it? The schoolmaster at any rate is
troubled with no such speculations, but pays his thirty sous, claps
his purchase on his head, and returns to his class, to whom he
appears neither more nor less ridiculous than before.

In all Paris only one man could be found to defy the hairdressers, before whose scissors the proudest must bow. This brave vet-
eran had the courage to make public declaration of his
independence; he had, he said, no use for them or their trade.
Bareheaded, he was seen about everywhere, even at Court, and by
his fortitude earned the right to be reckoned a great man; yet,
such thin partitions do the bounds divide, the solitary addition of
a wig would have been enough to bring him down again from his
pedestal, and transform the hero to mere mortal.

*Marie-Madeleine Guimard (1743–1816) was a famous ballerina at the Opéra.
†M.-J.-A. Vestris (1760–1842) was a famous ballet dancer.
‡The Quai des Morfondus is now known as the Quai de l'Horloge du Palais, on the
north side of Ile de la Cité.

57. Window-Boxes
(CDXCIX, Pots de fleurs, 1:1367–69)

T he love of a country life and growing things, common to all
men, is not yet extinct in the Parisian, with his unvarying land-
scape of bricks and mortar. His gardens hang above the streets,
and are never more than three feet long; sometimes a single
flower-pot represents this exile's sole tribute to mother Nature. Or,
in the chink of a French window, you may see a dwarfish fruit-tree
in a tub, which the Parisian, to whom green fields now are fairy-
tales, waters morning and night. Roses and daisies dwell in the half
of a packing-case, and six inches of grass console him for the loss of
spring's green carpets, and the thick rich undergrowth of woods.

Naturally, this amateur horticulture is forbidden by the police,
but the stay-at-home citizen defies their orders and clings to his
boxes and pots, which he hides when the inspector passes, and

brings out again a moment later. But this life is uncertain; the next
moment, perhaps, a careless movement topples the whole thing
over; it goes crashing five floors down, and he who can dodge is in
luck. Flower and shrub are borne off on the gutter rivulet, and
only fragments of earthenware and lumps of mould remain to tes-
tify to the dangers from which his fortunate star has preserved the
passer-by.

Every street has its offering to the exiled goddesses Pomona*
and Flora, but especially in those quarters where artisans sit pri-
soned at their sedentary tasks. Here a housewife will set up an in-
door farmyard with four fowls, six rabbits, and eight canaries in
cages; while in her window-box a tiny plum-tree and a gooseberry-
bush recall the kitchen garden. This love of living and growing
things goes deep; it pierces even to those dens which, by reason of
the surrounding chimneys blocking all light, enjoy no more than
a single hour's sun, perhaps, in a long day. The housewife, tied to
her one room, waits for this auspicious hour; this is her happiness,
to see pinched buds open to the short-lived warmth. She runs, and
calls in a neighbour to watch with her the mystery of life unfolding.

*Pomona was the Roman goddess of fruit trees; Flora was the goddess of flowering
plants.

58. Carthusian Monks
(DX, Chartreux, 1:1401–2)

T his enclosed order has its abode in the heart of the town, near
a public garden, and not far from the Comédie française. But
these are solitaries, surely; what of their solitude in such circumstances? And how do they like it, and is it not the very reverse of
their founder's intentions? which were that his order should dwell
among the untrodden ways, and flee the vile contagious breath of
cities.

Their monastery is just by the Tuileries, and close to the Opera
House. Going about their religious duties, the monks must neces-

sarily encounter in the streets such chorus-girls and dancers as have not yet risen to a carriage of their own.

The site of their cloister is immensely valuable; it could be put to some excellent public use, and hermits, after all, are out of place in a town, especially one so closely built as Paris, which cannot afford space for contemplatives to be at ease. All these objections, which are both rational and obvious, were put to the fathers, together with the suggestion that they should be transplanted elsewhere.

An innocent proposal enough; but received by the monks with what clamour, what stern and unbending refusal even to consider shifting their ground! Seriously, the resistance made by this body of anchorites was staunch and completely effective; which looks as though they were not so detached as they pretend from the perversions and corruptions of the town, since it proves so hard to dislodge them.

There was a time when kings and princes gave money to found such places; is it not high time some potentate were to set about doing exactly the opposite?

59. Theatre Scenes
(DXIII, Portes des spectacles, 1:1406–9)

T he Parisian invariably arrives at his chosen place of entertainment to find a company of guardsmen already in possession, or drawn up outside, shouldering arms.

Before Punch and Judy can launch their quips, grenadiers in tall bearskins take command of the theatre; Racine or rubbish, promptly as the clock strikes four the soldiers deploy, and go through a number of other military evolutions, as if their countrymen in search of pleasure were an enemy army. Watching carefully, you may observe that the guns are actually loaded with ball, a reassuring circumstance which puts you nicely in the mood for comedy; you can afford to laugh at the *Bourgeois Gentilhomme** with these weapons of war, full-charged, at your back.

If the play is a success, it may cost you a broken rib even to get near the ticket-office; there you scramble, and ply your elbows and sweat, while from a balcony above the actors look down, and have their laugh of the public whose good money pays for their supper.

Once in, the grenadier packs you together tight as onions on a string; stout patrons are reproved, thin patrons taken advantage of; so many posteriors and no more must go to a bench, and any unfortunate who gasps aloud for air is peremptorily told to hold his tongue. Molière reigns on the stage, but elsewhere the moustachios of the military are supreme. Laugh too loudly, weep with too much abandon, and the impassive spectator in the bearskin will soon bring you to reason.

The sergeant in charge is a sulky untidy fellow with a weather-beaten face; he knows the actors, seeing them as he does every night, while he knows nothing of the eternally changing pit, and cares less. Take care how you hiss; the actor you abhor may be a friend of his, and in that case, man of taste, man of integrity though you may be, with nothing against your character but an inability to tolerate ranting, out you go, plucked from your bench between two verses of Corneille.

He is a great, an absolute critic, this fellow; there is no arguing with him. As for the privates, with their cartridge boxes and powder flasks, they always agree with a superior; such is discipline. This personage, this sergeant, having weighed in his own mind the degree of criminality involved in the spectator's protest, hands the wretch over to justice, in the shape of the nearest police magistrate, who as a matter of course is wholly guided by the learned sergeant's opinion, and never fails to confirm it.

The strange thing is that in London, with no grenadiers to keep order, the public never gets out of hand, whether outside the theatre or in it; Londoners are free to come and go and criticize without let or hindrance, and there is never a breath of trouble. Why? Because the keeping of order is left, as it should be, in the hands of a public which has learned to respect itself.

But that would never do in Paris. A guard is necessary here; the carriages, for one thing, would never keep in line, there is always some coachman or other ready to press forward out of his turn. The question of national character comes in; our people have been kept on a leash so long, they run wild without it.

And yet, after all, though the slight constraint is irksome, it does at least ensure the audience against senseless interruptions. The real theatre-goer, who only wants to listen in peace to Corneille, can do so with a mind at ease, knowing the soldiers are there ready to deal with any demonstration of impatience or prejudice. And if the sergeant is honest and a man of sense, this guard is, on the whole and for Paris, no bad thing, though it would be out of place in London; it is only giving up one liberty to gain another.

However, of late years there has been a tendency to take theatrical seditions less seriously; the pit is less dragooned than it was, and occasionally is allowed to speak its mind, the only privilege playgoers value. It would be better for all parties if the public were left perfectly free to express its opinion, flattering or the reverse, of stage writers and performers; better absolute licence, than any curtailment of this liberty.

Friend Sergeant, you at whose command a pair of muskets clashed and crossed, forbidding me the entrance which was my right, and to which in all innocence I made claim, for God's sake let the pit and gallery alone! Let them hiss if they choose, I and my fellow-authors will write the better for it; and you will face your country's enemies none the less valiantly lacking these customary martial exercises against fellow-citizens.[†]

Le Bourgeois Gentilhomme, one of Molière's best-known plays, mocked the pretensions of social climbers.
†The last paragraph refers to Mercier's lawsuit against the actors of the Comédie française, who refused to perform any of his plays because of his criticisms of them and their repertory. At one point, he tried to force his way into the theatre, and was physically blocked by the guard, as he describes here.

60. Lantern-Men

(DXVI, Falots, 1:1414–17)

They are numbered, and carry lanterns, with which they rove the streets after ten at night, crying "Here's your light." After supper is the best time for this cry, and these fellows go calling, and answering one another, all night long, to the great prejudice of those whose bedrooms face on the street; they are to be found in clusters at the door of any house of entertainment.

The lantern-man's light is a convenience, and a precaution well worth while for those whose business or pleasure keeps them late from home; the man lights you to your door, to your bedroom—if seven flights up, no matter—and this aid is of value when perhaps you keep no servant, and can find neither matches nor tow, nor anything lightable; a plight not rare among smart young men, most of whose money goes in coats and theatre tickets. These wandering lights are a protection, besides, against thieves; and are in themselves almost as good as a squad of watchmen.

They are, in fact, hand in glove with the police; nothing is hid from them; and certain fellows, availing themselves of the darkness to query a window-fastening with light fingers, slip their hands back into their pockets when a man with his lantern turns the corner.

They supplement the hanging lanterns. Our streets are safer since these latter were installed, you can find your way about and get your direction from them; and the lantern-men are available when these, through accident or carelessness, are out of use.

When the theatres come out, these men are in league with the cab-drivers, who respond to your hail or pass you by, according to the tip you have given the lantern-man beforehand; for tip you must, and heavily, if you hope to secure a vehicle. Then they play all manner of tricks; crossing their torches to light the lantern jaws of some poor proud Gascon, and addressing him as "Your Grace"; this is a favourite notion, to call all pedestrians by the grandest titles. "Sword-fish" is their name for a colonel, and the long-haired notary's clerk, making off at full speed not to miss dessert at his master's table, they gratify by the appellation of "My Lord Chief Justice."

They go to bed at dawn, and make their report to the police later in the day. No citizen contributes more to the keeping of

public order than the lantern-man, whose unexpected presence is
the bane of thieves; besides, he will always run to fetch the watch
at the first sign of trouble.

The worst of them is their cry, but at least they are the only
night criers, while as for those trades which bawl by day, they are
uncounted and uncountable. Our poorer classes are naturally
noisy, and shout with equal disregard for their own throats and
their listeners' ears. Cries make a Babel of our mean streets, cries
raucous, or toneless, or shrill. "Mackerel, live mackerel, new
caught!" "Fresh herrings, all a-shiver!" "Hot apples, nice apples,
all hot!" (This last is a kind of cake, and quite cold.) "Ladies, take
your pleasure!" (Almond biscuits, these.) "Sea-fresh, sea-fresh!"
means oysters. "Portugal, Portugal!" (These are oranges.)

Add to all these the voices of the old-clothes men, of the um-
brella-sellers, old-iron vendors, and water-sellers; men screaming
like women, women shouting like men. The din never ceases; no
words can give any idea of the abomination of this piteous vocal
torment when all the cries meet and mingle, as sometimes they do,
at a cross-roads.

They say that chimney-sweeps and fishwives even in sleep are not
silent; their cries have become second nature to them, and find
involuntary voice.

[But in the autumn fogs of which Mercier complains elsewhere,
these men's lights were useless. He says, in the chapter entitled
"Fogs" (Chapter CCCLXIV, 1:1014):

> I have known fogs so thick that you could not see the flame
> in their lamps; so thick that coachmen have had to get down
> from their boxes and feel their way along the walls. Passers-by,
> unwilling and unwitting, collided in the tenebrous streets; and
> you marched in at your neighbour's door under the impres-
> sion that it was your own.
>
> One year the fogs were so dense, that a new expedient was
> tried; which was, to engage blind men, pensioners, as guides.
> They got good pay, up to five louis a day, and deserved it, for
> they know Paris better than those who have made our maps;
> and this was how people contrived to get about when some
> freak of our climate turned day into night. You took hold of
> the skirt of the blind man's coat, and off he started, stepping

firmly, while you more dubiously followed, towards your desti-
nation.

61. Mausoleum

(DXXIV, Mausolées, 1:1447–50)

When a prince dies, a bishop is immediately commissioned to
preach his funeral sermon; next, an architect-decorator is
given the job of erecting a catafalque* in the middle of Notre-
Dame. For a month the sacred edifice echoes to the sound of ham-
mering; workmen shout above the sanctus bell and the drone of
canons; the choir cannot be heard for the racket of carpenters,
and the prayers of the *Magnificat* and *Orate fratres* are reduced to
mere dumb show. The serpents of the choir (a wind instrument, as
everyone knows; but to hear people saying, "There's an admirable
serpent in this or that church," has an odd sound, and odder still
is it to see advertisements in large letters: "Grand performance of
serpents in St Benedict's on such a date"), the serpents, then, and
the organ in the nave, have no chance against these workmen; it is
as though axe and saw conspired to silence the divine office. But
nobody thinks to remonstrate; the prince must have a bier fitting
his dignity.

Mr Architect-decorator next surrounds the construction with
statues (hollow), representing such various virtues as the deceased
is least likely to have possessed.

Then the orchestra assembles; all the violins and cellos of Paris
are gathered together. And ten thousand candles are lighted. And
the atmosphere generally becomes like a furnace, so much so that
usually firemen are kept standing at the ready; the relatives of the
deceased having no wish to share his fate, or to risk being burned
alive upon the architect-decorator's hastily constructed match-
board masterpiece.

The solemn masquerade lasts four hours. Honest tears are rare;
and for all the trappings and the suits of woe, grief from the heart
has no place in this celebration.

"What, will you flatter still the princely dust!"

Members of the princely family, who of course have commissioned the funeral oration, turn up in force to listen—but taking due precedence of each other, even here; pride will have its due, even in the face of death and judgment, for the dead man has been judged, not only by his Creator but by his people; and the priesthood connives at this folly.

Now and then the orator will vow that nothing but the truth shall find its way into his sermon; at once he finds himself in difficulties. The vow goes the way of other vows, Truth parts company with him at the foot of the pulpit, and up goes the preacher alone to brazen it out. He uses all the tricks of his trade to make the late idol seem an excellent man, and sweeps away his hearers on the wind of his gusty periods. His figures of rhetoric are as empty as those other cardboard figures that adorn the monument, whose painted tears are about as suited as his flights of eloquence to the expression of Court grief.

Next day, or the day after, down comes the whole affair, plaster virtues and all; the preacher's tropes dissolve, these too, into thin air; for the people, who knew to a nicety what he would say before he said it, have their laugh at his performance when it is over.

These funeral sermons crying up the princely dead ought to be done away with; however, this is only one of the lesser abuses that the curious eye may discover within our good town, or at least within that area contained by sixty-four majestic barriers of pinewood. The sham chapel with its illumination at least gives work to a good many workmen, and diverts to their hands some small part of the money which, but for the ostentation or folly of the great, would never come their way.

The total amount spent on catafalques during the past century and a half would have given the capital lasting and lovely buildings, and a new impetus to sculpture. But the only mausoleums remaining are those of the two Cardinals, Richelieu and Fleury; Marshal Saxe's fine monument now adorns the town of Strasbourg.[†]

It is not our way to set the image of any great man up beside that of his King; posterity will link their names, the sculptor may not. And for what reason? Surely all classes should be glad to know and recognize greatness. Westminster Abbey is an instance; you see people there in crowds, looking up at the monuments, reverencing the illustrious dead, and remembering what those same dead have done for their country. This is the form gratitude takes in a sensible nation, this homage paid to those whose glory, and the memory of it, is all that remains of them; the kings and princes are forgotten, while there, in the light of immortality, stands the bust of some humble commoner who in his lifetime was subject to them.

Cochin[‡] is the artist to whose tool we owe engravings of these funeral ceremonies; he delighted in them, as in the representation of Court balls; his talent for rendering effects of light and shadow found in both subjects its fullest scope. They had no other interest for him; and his engravings are all that posterity will know of these curious ceremonies, in which neither reason nor feeling found place, and whose cost in money would have been better applied to setting up bricks and mortar that served some useful purpose.

A candle vendor, no doubt, would not agree with me; but to my mind it is preposterous, and a custom for which there is nothing to be said, to set thousands of wax candles flaring in broad daylight, at the risk of fire taking hold upon old beams and paintings. Why should we of today be thus dragged at the chariot-wheels of the past?

*Catafalque: a temporary wooden scaffold erected to support a coffin during a public funeral.

[†]Armand du Plessis, Cardinal de Richelieu (1585–1642), was Louis XIII's principal minister and the architect of the French absolutist system of government. André Hercule Fleury (1653–1743) was another cardinal-minister, serving Louis XV. The Maréchal de Saxe (1696–1750) was a celebrated military commander.

[‡]Charles-Nicolas Cochin was a celebrated engraver of the period.

62. The Buyer of Annuities*
(DXXVI, Acheteurs de rentes Viagères, 1:1453–61)

A curious trade; the strangest speculation of all. For this man must have constantly before his eyes the tables of mortality, and eternally be calculating, for good or ill, the chances of his clients' lives.

A woman, let us say, comes to his office, with a document showing that her income is twelve hundred francs a year; this she wants to exchange for capital. The purchaser looks her up and down in silence for a while, and finds her appearance satisfactory—neither too fat nor ominously thin; this preliminary examination completed, with one final penetrating look for luck, the dialogue opens:

The Seller. Monsieur, I would like to sell my interest for ready cash, if it can be managed.

The Buyer. Money's hard to come by nowadays, madame.

The Seller. I know; but there's money about, for all that, and it's no good to anyone shut up in a safe; it doesn't gain if it's not in circulation.

The Buyer. How old are you, madame?

The Seller. Forty-seven, monsieur.

The Buyer. Birth certificate?

The Seller. Here it is, all correct.

The Buyer. Forty-seven, so you are. Well, that's a good thing. If you'd been forty-two I should have refused to have any dealings with you.

The Seller. I take your meaning. But I'm over the critical time now; there's plenty of life in me.

The Buyer. The life of man, madame, is as a shadow that passes away—

The Seller. But I live very regularly; no heavy suppers, no late nights; I spend six months of the year in the country.

The Buyer. So I heard, madame. That is why I agreed to see you. *(Rising.)* But you will excuse me if I make a somewhat closer examination—

The Seller. By all means, take a good look, you won't find many wrinkles.

The Buyer. It's not a question of wrinkles. Kindly let me see your
teeth.

The Seller. My teeth! By all means, quite right, good teeth are the
surest sign of health. Mine are my own, nice and white too, as
you can see for yourself, monsieur. Now, what offer will you
make me? Twelve hundred a year, and I'm in perfect health—I
forgot to tell you I've had four children, just the right number,
not too many and not too few. Women that have had children
live the longest.

The Buyer. Madame, this office is full of people coming to sell their
annuities. You'd think the end of the world was in sight; everywhere people trying to shift their annuities on to me, for cash.
But I'm not made of money; I've got to have my security; I
can't buy from everybody. For instance, I never buy from a
man; there's too much pleasure-seeking, nowadays. So I've
made a rule only to buy from the ladies. That's what they do
in Geneva, and believe me, the Swiss know what they're about;
but they, of course, have their choice of good healthy lives,
lived in good mountain air; and your home is in Paris.

The Seller. Only six months of the year, monsieur; only the winter.

The Buyer. The most dangerous season of the lot. I don't know; it
seems to me that our winter winds always carry some germ—
listen to that! They're tolling for someone. Ah, there's been a
lot of burying these past three months.

The Seller. Why, that's only an old lady of ninety they're ringing for.
I shall get as far as that, I hope, and you'll have had the use of
my money all that time.

The Buyer. Yesterday, madame, I had the offer of buying up four
thousand francs a year; but I didn't accept. Why? Because I'd
heard that the lady in question was for ever going to balls.
One night's dancing may be deadly. Might I enquire what your
occupation is?

The Seller. Housekeeping; and when that's done I read, except that
I always take the air for an hour or two every day. Now, monsieur, you see I lead a very regular existence; how much will
you give me for my twelve hundred a year?

The Buyer. Well, I'll tell you. Four thousand eight hundred.

The Seller. Never! Why, there's nothing the matter with me; what
terms would an invalid get from you, I wonder!

The Buyer. Madame, you might break your neck going down my stairs. . . . And then, what about revolutions?

The Seller. Revolutions! You don't think that! And even if there were, these annuities would get paid first of all. Why, the King guarantees them—

The Buyer. Madame, I won't argue the point. I'll give you four thousand eight hundred for that document of yours, and perhaps in a week's time the postman will hand me your funeral notice. You don't look to me at all robust. And women are delicate creatures; late nights, too much good food, too much wine— the question of diet's most important. Cards, even, are bad for the health.

The Seller. I never play, and I live most carefully. I'm only selling because I've got a case, a family matter, coming up in the courts.

The Buyer. A case in the courts? That means anxiety—

The Seller. Not for me, I've got a good case, my lawyer's just told me so this very morning; and anyhow a little uncertainty is good for us all. Come now, monsieur, be reasonable. How much will you add to your four thousand eight hundred?

The Buyer. Not a cent, madame. You may lose your case and commit suicide—

The Seller. I'm a good Christian, I know my duty too well.

The Buyer. À *propos*, what's the name of your doctor?

The Seller. I've never needed a doctor, monsieur. I've never had a day's illness in my life, except a headache now and then; twenty-four hours' pain, and then it's all over, and that's the sum and total of my troubles.

The Buyer. But you've had smallpox; I can see the marks.

The Seller. Yes, so I shan't get it again.

The Buyer. Well now, if you'll come along with me to a notary, this business will be settled in an hour, and I'll pay you the money down.

The Seller. But monsieur, four thousand eight hundred—and you'll be drawing twelve hundred for twenty-five years perhaps— come now!

The Buyer. You may well look incredulous. Nobody but a fool would pay that much for a scrap of paper on a life. Here to-day and gone to-morrow! But take my advice; move near the Luxembourg, beside the Porte d'Enfer; I've got one or two clients there, getting on nicely towards eighty. It's to your advantage as well as mine, after all.

The Seller. More mine than yours, to my way of thinking. Well, come on to this notary, since you won't give me better terms. To think of all that good money going into the lawyers' pockets! But that's the way of it; no use grumbling.

The Buyer. Wrap up well, madame. You know, I suppose, that I don't buy in my own name?

The Seller. Paul or Peter, what do I care? Well, you're a hard man; but I hope I live long enough to convince you you've had the best of the bargain.

---

*An annuity is a financial policy that guarantees the owner a fixed income every year up to his or her death. The woman in Mercier's sketch wants to exchange her annuity for a fixed sum of money; the purchaser needs to estimate whether she is likely to live long enough for him to make back his money.

63. Cows
(DXXVII, Vaches, 1:1461–63)

You see them at the barriers, all skin and bones, and with their udders shrunken and dry; a contrast, this, to the proud cows of Switzerland on their fat pastures, who care for nobody and budge for nobody, as though they knew they trod the soil of a free country, where the tax-collector ceases from troubling. Their coats are shiny, their tread majestic; these are no longer creatures to be beaten and driven, but kin to Io, the heifer-goddess; and their full flanks seem swelling symbols of their owners' prosperity.

But the beasts that troop into Paris resemble nothing less than goddesses; they are Pharaoh's lean cows* come to life; starved themselves, and driven in to feed the starving.

Their carcases are sold as beef; real beef, the great houses and the convents between them monopolize, so that there is nothing left for the poorer classes but cow. Everywhere else these two are different in price, but here true beef and this wretched stuff fetch the same; which puts up the cost out of reach of the very poor, and is a crime against the public stomach. This is a reform long overdue; for why should I pay the same for good meat as for this? And why should I be obliged to accept cow-meat when what I ask for is beef? Paris is the only city where such an abuse continues despite daily grumbling from the whole population.

Besides this, we are the world's most remarkable butchers; you never can buy a piece of meat without half the weight being bone. A cutlet means, often as not, a cut off the jawbone; and many a poor man has found to his dismay a great tooth in the steak that he fondly imagined was cut from the rump.

There was a good deal of talk about importing cows from Switzerland; we went about congratulating ourselves that soon we should all be drinking good Swiss milk. Lung-sufferers believed themselves cured already, men-about-town looked forward to a new lease of life; it seems to have occurred to nobody that the promoters of this scheme could hardly import, with the cows, their mountain pastures rich in good fresh grass. And so the fat cows dwindled on our thin French fields, gave less milk, and less nourishment with it, and at last ended up at the butchers! The enterprise was a failure, to the great astonishment of all simpletons who had expected Swiss cows to go on yielding Swiss milk for ever.

This one instance is enough to show how credulous our townspeople are, how crudely ignorant; it shows too the reasons why Paris has become a paradise for company promoters and advertising.

*"... the Pharaoh's lean cows"—an allusion to Pharaoh's dream, in Genesis 41:17–21, of lean cows eating fat cows. Joseph interpreted it as a warning that famine would strike the land of Egypt.

64. Madams

The accepted translation of a word less polite.

Madams are of different kinds. Kept women of the grander sort have their duennas who go with them everywhere. Such an attendant waits on every better-class actress or dancer; she looks out for those waifs and strays of the world of pleasure, who go from one playhouse to another in hope of adventure, in other words, supper.

They have no need to seduce girls with false promises into their service; present-day licence, love of pleasure and poverty combined—ill counsellor this last—bring girls enough to them of their own accord. Still, they do, these women matchmakers, try to get hold of pretty young creatures who already know something of the game. They keep houses for would-be prostitutes, houses of accommodation to which the small tradesman's wife and such may resort, and earn for themselves some piece of finery. The very immensity of Paris favours this kind of traffic; parents and guardians are none the wiser; the women are chaste to all appearance. Women of higher condition secretly frequent these places too, and preserve their reputation among their acquaintance, thus making the best of both worlds.

Other madams work by means of a list of addresses. They know where all their girls are to be found, and they collect them in cabs, and deliver them at the doors of various clients—old gentlemen, hypochondriacs, persons with gout, or young men who cannot take the trouble to choose for themselves.

Experience is theirs; the caprices and fancies of men are to them an open book, and they lend their *protégées* such knowledge as they can. The girl from the hat-shop, for instance, becomes a little girl fresh from the country; the needlewoman is transformed into a young provincial, fleeing to Paris from the tongue and tantrums of a mother-in-law. The *rôle* is thought out for them and taught, dress and speech correspond, and since pleasure is chiefly a matter of the imagination, the matron's male clients are content.

Now come those who have launched out, and keep women for all tastes under their own roofs. In such a house you may see, one at a time or together, such varieties as the modish girl, the languishing, silly-sweet, or smart girl; the proud, the wild, the passionate, the temptress, and a dozen more, temperament and colouring to suit all tastes; as for complexion and figures, you can suit yourself with those too; there are thin girls and plump, pale faces or ruddy; there is even one with a limp. Just as racehorses for breeding, blood-stock, have their descriptive names, so have these women.

Madams with less capital cannot afford quite such vast rooms, nor such sumptuous beds, and accordingly they run establishments on a smaller scale, with the girls living in. All the money they make must go to the madam, who takes it as her just due; for has she not gathered her flock from the wilds of the country, rescued them from barbarism, and taught them manners? She has a right to their earnings; does she not fit them out with dresses, a white *négligé* to wear at home, a cloak for summer, a thicker wrap for winter, with silk dresses to go to the play in? Who else should have the money? These girls in their native wilds would be going about in smocks and aprons, with dirty blistered hands, washing down floors and sleeping with yokels; yet they have the impudence to expect her to share her takings with them. Presents are another matter, and their own affair; if they can wheedle a new ribbon out of an admirer, let them. (Ribbons, in these people's parlance, mean any little tip given by a customer pleased with the service.)

Last of all come the *marcheuses,* the lowest rung of the vile ladder; these are creatures old and penniless, creeping out into the world from some hospital, with the scars of their past life upon their faces; for just as a soldier may have half his body carried away by shot and still live, so these women still belong to life, and that life is their trade. They must keep touch with it somehow, the habit of debauch is strong; they cling to it by instinct, and because it is the one way of living they know. And so they run errands—hence their name—for the poorer-class prostitutes, those in furnished rooms, whose only equipment is a pair of shoes and one white petticoat. This last must keep its whiteness as long as it can, and so the *marcheuse* sallies out through the mud in its stead.

It is an unwritten law that no virgin may—how shall I put it?— take service in one of these houses; the girl must have gained her experience elsewhere before a madam will admit her; and if by chance it were not so, the inspector of police would soon get to know of it and there would be trouble.

This last sentence sounds improbable; nevertheless, I am seri-

ous. The idea seems to be to make some show of honourable dealing even in these dens of dishonour; to keep certain abuses within
bounds; to protect innocence, and check the assaults of vice. And
so there are no complaints from aggrieved fathers, if their daughters go wrong the madam and her house are not to blame, and
this is something; it is certainly a point in favour of the police.

It is a painter's task, not a philosopher's, to set out symbolically
the various degrees of woman's degradation in Paris; nevertheless,
this sketch may indicate the scale in some measure.

At the top of the ladder you see the ambitious and haughty
women, who aim always at the highest; nothing less than a financier will serve their turn. They have no passions, but only calculating brains to note a weakness, and turn it to their own account.

Below these come the opera-girls, dancers, actresses, neither
wholly venal nor altogether disinterested, who bring a trifle of sentiment into their relations with men.

Then there are the half-honest wives, the women whose 'friends'
come to their houses, often as not with the husband's connivance;
these are dangerous and worthless creatures who set out adultery
in pleasant colours, and lay claim to a social respect which they
have forfeited by their conduct.

And lastly, we must reckon another immense class; servants who
are something closer to their masters; housekeeper-mistresses;
there are plenty of these, and they are the most mixed lot of all.

The base of the pyramid rests upon what may be called the ama-
teurs; milliners, dressmakers, sewing-girls, women who rent their
own room and hold themselves aloof from the prostitutes. These
have made no special study of the art of love, but they accept what
pleasure comes their way, take pains to please, and are conscien-
tious in the performance of their duties. You take them occasionally to a play, or stand them a supper, and they ask no more;
perhaps now and then they permit themselves a variant upon the
official lover, but otherwise they are honest, decent girls.

The eye travelling down this structure of disorder rests uncom-
fortably upon the great mass of common prostitutes, leaning in
doorways, leering from windows, and otherwise displaying their
charms in public places. These may be hired like hackney carriages
at so much an hour; among their number you find actresses from
the smaller theatres or the shows on the boulevards.

Now come those horrors, buried too vilely deep for the casual
eye to discover; the hideous women of the Pont-au-Bled, and the
Rue du Poirier, or the Rue Planche-Mibray. The painter who sets
these in his composition will do well to show nothing but their
heads, which are awful enough. Vice loses, in these places, even
the semblance of allure, and soon, and dreadfully, brings its own
punishment.

The changes to be observed in the hierarchy are amazing. Up
or down the women go, and take precedence or lose it, according
to whether chance accords them protectors with more money or
less. It is all pure luck; an infatuation, rightly bestowed, may mean
that some little person is lifted to the skies overnight, and leads
the mode, who before was never heard of. A fortnight later she is
in her carriage, bowling down the same boulevard which before
her elevation she patrolled with sidelong glances, seeking casual
lovers. Ex-clients, clerks at fifteen hundred francs a year, see her
in her glory, and can hardly believe their eyes.

Another, having outlived her moment, falls back into poverty,
and throws in her lot with the lackey who wore her livery six
months before.

And the causes of these spectacle vicissitudes? Who can tell? Deschamps* is dead, but in her lifetime her toilet-seat was hung with
English point lace and her horses tossed their heads in harness set
with rose-diamonds. How? Why?

Another who has just died, an opera-girl, left quantities of furniture and a good round sum in cash. Was she more lovely, wittier
than her peers? Not she; she came from the lowest stratum of the
people, but luck was on her side; luck, that can pull ministers down
from their chairs of state, or keep a prostitute in favour.

A custom which has gone out, much regretted by the poorer
folk, on whom this occasional pleasure was solemnly conferred by
a judicial decree, is that of 'riding' a madam on donkey-back by
way of example and punishment for the crime of "persuading
away girls of good family," as the old statute has it. All very well;
but as a rule example was made of some unfortunate in the very
lowest rank of the trade; the real culprit, pander to princes, prel-
ates, rich foreigners, and even philosophers, went scot-free.

This was the order of the ride, as my memory recalls it. First
marched a drummer, and a sergeant after him armed with a pike;

then came a groom leading an ass by the bridle, on which was
mounted, her face towards its tail, the madam, or matchmaker,
her head crowned with plaited straw. She bore a placard on her
breast and shoulders which read in huge letters, "Procuress."

Imagine the joy of the crowd yelling on either side of this procession, tossing stinking caps in the air, and closing up behind in a
tumult of bawdy rapture. Happily it is some years since we had
anything of the kind in Paris; happily, because the only effect was
to put vile ideas into the heads of those who witnessed it; and the
placards, read aloud and commented on freely, were offensive to
decent people and young girls. Besides, what purpose could it be
supposed to serve? Women of that kind have about as much shame
for their lives as the donkey that carries them.

I have seen one such woman laughing in the face of the mockers
who surrounded her; and heard her say, looking up at the windows
that were flung open as she passed: "There, on the second floor,
are some who dare not put their heads out; I know what I know,
and they know what I know; and they won't risk catching my eye."

If such performances now are rare, it is not for lack of principals;
but because, the chieftainesses of the clan being protected by their
influential clients, it seemed farcical to let the whole burden of
punishment fall on some poor starving wretch from the gutter,
who knew no other way to earn her bread.

It is these other women who should suffer, those who trade upon
their own beauty, or use it to further schemes of avarice or ambition. A woman's worst enemies are those of her own sex.

The madams are always more valiant than any man in dealing
with the police Arguses, perhaps because, apart from any protection they may enjoy, they rely on their sex to modify the applied
rigours of the law; and some deep-seated instinct tells them that,
for all their sinning, they have offended more against themselves
and religious morality than against the State, or at any rate the
State's political integrity.

Besides, they know that the police have need of them; and that
if the supply of their wares were suddenly to fail, the police would
have to supplement it from the highways and byways; they are too
necessary to be suppressed altogether. There is a story of one parish priest complaining to the Lieutenant of Police.

"Sir," said he, "my parish is infested with these creatures."

"Sir," tranquilly replied that official, "the town as a whole is three thousand short."

This is a curious chapter, but one which cannot be omitted from a work which purports to be a picture of manners in the capital of France; such a matter of public knowledge can hardly be neglected. But I have only set down what every man with eyes in his head can see for himself, and as for the rest, you may guess at it; mine shall not be the hand to lift the veil.

This state of things is common to all great towns. It has always existed; but today it has reached a point when those responsible for the public weal should have their attention drawn to it. Men spend themselves in debauch and without profit to the State; women betray their nature and sex, taking on all kinds of ugly twists of conduct, with which abnormality the men who frequent them are in turn infected. And then the daily spectacle of so many women openly living by prostitution is a circumstance most evident and deadly.

Restif de la Bretonne,[†] that original writer, in his *Pornographer,* sketched out a plan for courtesans of all classes, by which the traffic should be made less public, and decency be spared affront. Surely it should be possible to try out this plan, at any rate in part, embodying the change in laws more suited than those now in force to the spirit of the times? It is the publicity of the scandal that is so pernicious, and ruins the whole scaffolding of the moral order.

The first thing is to have recourse to our newest science, chemistry, which alone can deal with the physical infection these women spread; the fires of Tisiphone that lie beneath the pleasure-grounds of Venus. Reform will be difficult; it needs a man of wide views, and balanced mind; but it must come, the scandal smells to heaven.

It should not be. A woman accosts a young man in the street, displays for his allurement charms that would arouse even a grandfather; in a moment of time he is infected; and eighteen years of his family's care and hopes go for nothing. That should not be. A husband, decent, faithful, going about his business, finds in his path, prostitutes with their airs and graces, different from his wife, tempting—that should not be. Banish, for God's sake, these women from the streets; their talk is more deadly than their looks; children may overhear it, and every word is an offence. Why, since

the last act of this dirty drama must be played in secret, allow the
first act free hearing, from which the last logically follows? It is not
vice that kills, but this condoning, this eternal advertising of vice.

Administrators, read, mark, and digest the *Pornographer* of Restif
de la Bretonne.

<hr/>

*Deschamps: Marie-Anne Pugès (d. 1764), wife of the actor Deschamps, was a cele-
brated courtesan who had amassed a large fortune.
†Nicolas-Edme Restif de la Bretonne (1734–1806), a close friend of Mercier's who
also wrote extensively about Paris in this period, is often credited with coining the
word "pornography."

65. This English Folly
(DXLVIII, Le fat à l'anglaise, 2:41–43)

Just now English clothing is all the rage. Rich man's son, sprig
of nobility, counter-jumper shop clerk—you see them dressed
all alike in the long coat, cut close, thick stockings, puffed stock;
with gloves, hats on their heads and a riding-switch in their hands.
Not one of the gentlemen thus attired, however, has ever crossed
the Channel or can speak one word of English.

This is well enough; the dress is neat, and implies a most exact
cleanliness of person. But at the first sentence exchanged, the familiar Parisian ignoramus peeps out from under the islander's hat.
He will talk of how Jamaica must be seized; what does he know of
Jamaica? He thinks India is part of America. And though he dresses
like a citizen of London, head high, republican air, and so on, you
need expect from him no proper appreciation of serious questions: some poor devil of an usher in a magistrate's court could
answer you as well.

No, no, my young friend. Dress French again, wear your laces,
your embroidered waistcoats, your laced coats; powder your hair
to the newest tune; keep your hat under your arm, and wear your
two watches, with concomitant fobs, both at once. Character is
something more than dress. No, keep your national frippery, and

in that silly livery talk your fill of nothing, vent your paradoxes, and show forth the graces of your profound ignorance.

Have we nothing to learn from Englishmen other than the tailors? They have their fools as we have; but fatuity that springs from pride is less hateful than that which has its root in vanity. Their vicious men are restrained by the national genius for hypocrisy. As for their criminals, even these show some shadow of justice in their thieving; they leave you your clothing at least, and shed no blood unless they must. God forbid I should find myself in their hands; yet even our highway robbery is behind the times, it has the semblance without the spirit, like our fashionables.

Shopkeepers hang out signs—"English Spoken Here." The lemonade-sellers even have succumbed to the lure of punch, and write the word on their windows. English coats, with their triple capes, envelop our young exquisites. Small boys wear their hair cut round, uncurled and without powder. Older men walk with the English gait, a trifle round-shouldered. Our women take their headgear from London. The racecourse at Vincennes is copied from that at Newmarket. Finally, we have Shakespeare on our stage, rhymed, it is true, by M. Ducis,* but impressive nevertheless.

We no longer fear our enemies as we used. All these modes and drinks and customs would have been rejected, and with disdain, by the Parisians of thirty years ago. But have we taken the best of our neighbours for our own use? Has England nothing better worth borrowing than punch, and jockeys? Better, even, than the plays of Shakespeare?

*Jean-François Ducis (1733–1816) translated several of Shakespeare's plays into formal French verse.

66. Police Orders

(DL, Sentences de police, 2:47–49)

Some little time back the keeper of an eating-house was fined for selling his customers donkey-flesh, rechristened veal; the crime was made public, and these words added to the announcement: "an habitual offender." Now as a result there are regular municipal appointees who see that horses are buried at once, thus baffling those who came to cut a steak or two, which they sold for beef in their cookshops.

Police orders make curious reading; they reveal a world of petty crimes, incredible some of them, others daring, or fantastic, or novel. For the law cannot draw its veil over an offence until it has been committed; here is an instance.

Some shifting stage property once caught an actress's skirt, and lifted it beyond the bounds of discretion or decency; at once out came an order obliging every actress or operatic dancer to wear underpants during any appearance on a public stage. And wear them she must, be she Athalie's self, or Merope;* the law applies equally to the tragedienne and the high-kicking dancer, and is enforced upon all, from the ladies of the Opera House downwards. Thus one robed like a goddess, and respectability itself, must don this safeguard against the indignities of accident in company with young persons whose public function it is to do the splits, and in whose case it is by no means a superfluous precaution.

But these are the only women in Paris who do wear underpants. They are usual in the northern countries, and our fine ladies, eternally complaining of the cold, and eternally refusing to stay at home, might well adopt such a protection against chills and damp. Their health would surely benefit.

*Athalie and Merope were the heroines of tragedies by Racine and Voltaire, respectively.

67. Working Days

(DLXII, Jours ouvrables, 2:91–93)

In Catholic countries feast-days take up a fourth part of the year. Thirteen or fourteen holidays have just been suppressed, after a half-century of complaining; they used to come one on top of the other, five at a time on occasion, and pretty often three together. Their celebrations ought, of course, all to have been relegated to the various Sundays, but superstition was too strong, and reform stopped half-way.

Guess which great interest is most involved, and which battles most strongly against any real reform of the calendar? The Farmers-General; for holiday means, after Mass, all the *cabarets* full, where you may see men obliged by law to be idle, drinking away the money their week's labour has earned.

The people call working days those on which the shops are not shut; a distinction unknown to the more fortunate, to whom all days are the same, all proper for pleasure.

But a feast-day is the best for observation, when crowds fill the Champs-Élysées or drift along the boulevards; there you may study an infinite variety of faces and fashions, strange enough, sometimes, these last. Walking thus you may see for yourself the truth of what I have written concerning the Parisian of to-day; that careworn, troubled look of his, and the eternal show of constraint that he bears about with him. Sixty years ago foreigners wrote of him as of a happy man; they speak of laughing open countenances, of careless gaiety. To-day the newcomer to Paris, if he is honest, must admit that this is no true picture: our modern Parisian walks soberly and in sadness. I speak now of small shopkeepers and such, for this is the class most generally to be observed in the streets; their demeanour shows very clearly the constant travail and anxiety of their lives. The class below seems happier working than at play.

It is these *bourgeois* whom it interests me to watch, crowding a public garden, aimlessly walking, or idling on the benches or chairs a whole afternoon through. Amusement costs money, and since these people dare not spend they know no other way of making the time pass; the poll-tax hangs over them all, each has had his demand and his threat from the dreaded collector, and fear of it shows in all their faces.

This collector is the eternal kill-joy, a publican such as the apostles knew; a financier who now bears the King's commission, to whom the unborn child in the widow's womb is no more than another head to be taxed. The amount you pay is settled by him alone, and arbitrarily; no use to protest, "Ah, monsieur, my head's not worth much"; your head is as good as another's for his purpose, and worth so much to the King. The assessment once made is final, there is no appeal, not even for reasons of sickness or some other failure; and the dead man must pay his tax like the rest, if he is so unbusinesslike as to die at the beginning of the financial year.

68. Sermons

(DLXXXII, Prédicateurs, 2:163–70)

A monk tired of his cloister need only sit down and write a couple of sermons to procure a few hours' escape into the larger world; an ambitious priest will do the same, for thus he may catch the bishop's eye, and build up some reputation with the public. There is a good deal of competition for the chance to preach at Advent and Lent; one church may put over a thousand francs into the visitor's pocket, another a beggarly three hundred.

The woman who rents out the pews has a good deal of influence in these matters; she has a contract with the parish, and insists on popular preachers; when a favourite is safely secured and announced, she puts up her prices. The day of the first sermon she mounts guard at the church door, announcing the new tariff. Up and down the precincts she trots; there is no sitting down without her leave; she rules the sacred roost. Go into any church; if the chair-woman is humble, the preacher is indifferent; if she is insolent, sit down, you will hear your money's worth.

Every priest's dream is to preach before the Court; just as every young rhymster, scribbling his first verses, dreams of the Académie française. A Lent at Court brings in at least three thousand francs, and is, besides, very often the road to a fat benefice, even an abbey; with this further advantage, that on Holy Thursday the preacher has absolute licence to say to the King's face what he thinks of the King's conduct; and there must His Majesty sit, with his guards all about him, and hold his tongue. Some of these scoldings have passed the bounds of decency; but nothing happened to the preachers. They were only sermons after all.

The list of preachers for the various seasons is printed and distributed; you may take your choice, according to their reputations. Certain of these are favourites with the common people, while another's congregation comes behind four horses to church.

An observer going from church to church during Lent can be sure of entertainment, for while the matter of sermons never changes, the manner is capable of a thousand shades of difference. On the one hand a fat monk, swollen, sweating with eloquence, gesticulating in the dirty habit of his order; on the other a parish priest in the cleanest of surplices, with a well-cut coat below, his hair curled deist-fashion, who distributes condescendingly, and in honeyed tones, bouquets of rhetoric; dazzling with his perfect eloquence the local clergy and the devout ladies of the parish, with whom, when his sermon is done, he will take dinner. Or it may be a fanatic, for whom philosophy and the philosophers are the devil and his dam; he roars, foams, writhes with godly rage against them; but his audience is composed of Jansenists* and a few writers, who mock the thunderer's frenzies and his style behind their hands.

But whatever his method, the preacher must always be offered some refreshment after his task, when he comes down from the pulpit damp with his exertions and needing a clean shirt. The beadle brings a little sugar and wine; and then that voice which launched its lightnings down the nave, announcing judgment, anathema, eternal damnation, dwindles to drawing-room smoothness with its: "A macaroon, dear lady? Marzipan? Pray accept a biscuit." The ladies prudently forbid all further speech; he must take no risks. And then they compare a preacher's life to that of a soldier, and talk of how the pulpit too has its martyrs. The orator takes it with a smile, compliments, warnings and all; it is his moment. The local clergy congratulate him; he has given modern philosophy its death blow, they tell him, and while he cannot in honesty deny this, his acquiescence is humble.

But the preacher's highest privilege is that which secures him against interruption; his monologue, whatever its content, goes its way unanswered. Another excellent perquisite is that of purloining without acknowledgment whole phrases from known authors. Many of our orators have built up reputations on the recent excellent translation of Young's *Night Thoughts,* which they quote brazenly, a page at a time; but no journal would ever dare to publish the list.

Mr Young and his translator, Le Tourneur, preach daily in Paris and the provinces; various monks and religious are their mouthpieces and no one approves their activities more than I. I will linger in any church where Messrs Young† and Le Tourneur are to be heard; rich thought and splendid language they offer, and all from under some cowl or other.

But it is really the easiest imaginable living, this sermonizing; it needs only memory, and a good enunciation; not even the labours of composition need afflict those who know the tricks of the trade. For on Mont Saint-Hilaire‡ dwells a parchment-seller (is there a single trade that cannot be found in this amazing town?) and this man keeps the most extraordinary shop in all Europe. In one immense cupboard he has stored two or three thousand manuscript sermons, sermons on every subject collected from here, there and everywhere, which keep a number of copyists busy. So that when the young ecclesiastic, having spent much toil in search of an idea, relinquishes hope of inspiration at last, it is to this discreet shop that he comes, after dark, to find it.

The cupboard stands open, the vendor comes forward. "And what can we do to-day for your reverence? A Conception, a Nativity, an Assumption? Fifteen Last Judgments going very cheap, a nice lot of Forgive us our trespasses, thirty-two Passions—take your choice." "No," says the deacon, "it's an Immaculate Conception I want." "An Immaculate Conception! Well, but that's something quite out of the ordinary." "I must have it," says the deacon, "and one on Vainglory; then I want a Mary Magdalene—as saint, not sinner." "I can do it, I can do it, your reverence, but I've only three copies left; Mary Magdalene without her sins is nearly as rare as Immaculate Conceptions; eight francs apiece is the lowest I can do them. But anything on Charity, or the Attributes of the Deity, I can let you have very reasonably; two francs fifty apiece."

Up gets the young man on a chair, with a lantern, and turns over the mass of writings till he finds what he needs; there is no bargaining, no disputing of prices. Off he goes in haste, with a good roll of manuscripts under his gown; these he spreads out when he gets home, locks the door, and pillages right and left, a phrase here, a phrase there, until he has a patchwork unrecognizable as the work of any brain but his own. Then he is safe; then he can go into his pulpit with the firm step, and the firm voice of a man who knows what he will say next. Those few francs laid out in the shop with the cupboard are multiplied thenceforth a hundredfold.

When a cleric has put together in this manner a Lent and an Advent, twenty sermons or so, and learnt them, he is as sure of a living as any actor who has got by heart the same number of parts; and may tour the provinces in much the same way, finding pulpits to thump as the other seeks boards to tread.

Well! A sermon, no matter how bad, is a good thing; for its appeal is to the heart, and in such a case style counts for nothing. The people, drowsing while incomprehensible Latin canticles float over their heads, take notice when a priest begins to talk to them in their own tongue. His address is a patchwork, stolen from all the orators that ever lived before him, bought by the yard from the owner of that admirable cupboard; no matter, the people need instruction in religion, and get it by this means. The preacher has only to speak his borrowed words so that they can be heard; they sink of themselves into the hearts of his congregation and there do their work of tenderness or warning. And thus the wares of that shopkeeper on the Mont Saint-Hilaire go journeying over the length and breadth of France. . . .

*The Jansenists were a group of rigorous Catholics, followers of the seventeenth-century theologian Cornelius Jansen (1585–1638)

†Mercier was especially fond of the English pre-Romantic poet Edward Young's sentimental and lugubrious *Night Thoughts*, which his friend Pierre Le Tourneur (1736–88) had translated into French in 1769.

‡In Mercier's day, the north slope of the Mont Sainte-Geneviève in the Latin Quarter was called Mont Saint-Hilaire.

69. The Parisian and the Londoner Compared

(DXCIV, Contraste des Parisiens avec l'habitant de Londres, 2:207–10)

The customs and character of these two peoples, eternal rivals in the paths of genius and glory, offer certain remarkable contrasts which it may be both salutary and interesting to note; for thus they may, by sharing their discoveries, enrich each other; while emulation in the domain of art can bring nothing but profit to both; not only that, but the results of this competition between the two peoples in the arts of peace must surely benefit humanity. The prejudice which so long held them asunder is beginning to yield to the progress of philosophy, which tempers the gusty winds of politics; and it may be that the time is not distant when they shall see eye to eye even on those questions which still divide them.

True, there never were two neighbouring nations more utterly dissimilar. Nature has contrived a moral separation deeper even than the physical boundary by which the two are divided, of a quality to set the observer wondering. Calais and Dover might be in two worlds; in certain matters the contrasts and contrarieties are absolute.

But the spirit of philosophy, which considers the good of the world as a whole before that of any one nation, strikes a balance between these two opposing national prides, and gives each his due, without attempting to allot the palm to either. Philosophy says, very wisely: The exchange of ideas is the best and most fruitful commerce of all; greatness springs from this, rather than from the bloody soil of battlefields.

This is well enough, but persuasion might go further. There should be some unequivocal proposal for an alliance between the two, a new and lasting treaty which should be for the good of both peoples. The vulgar minds of politicians may see in such an alliance matter only for laughter; but it would be a real gain for all that, while these old protocols to which they cling are deadly.

These people see no further than their own noses; light dawns, change is all about them, changes and dawning of which they are oblivious, but which of their nature necessitate a different kind of

union between the peoples. A philosopher who reads his history
has no difficulty whatever in realizing that hitherto all statecraft
has been at fault.

If, by a constant exchange of ideas and a more complete understanding of each other's character Englishmen and Frenchmen
could somehow break down the old jealousy which hitherto has
blinded them to their true interests; if for a moment they would let
themselves breathe freely, forgetting prejudice and preconceived
ideas of each other, they would discover soon enough that their
mutual antipathy was wholly without foundation; that a breath of
goodwill could blow it away; and that, on the contrary, their mission is to pool their resources of energy and intelligence, and together, by reason of their natural superiority over other nations,
take their rightful place as leaders of Europe.

This consummation, so plausible to the philosopher, so devoutly
wished by all far-seeing statesmen, would extend the realm of
knowledge, bring plenty to the peoples, and set the world a new
and innocent and admirable example of behaviour.

England may seem to have more to offer in the way of peaceful-
ness and the decent conduct of domestic life; but then, what prevents the Frenchmen from enjoying these blessings? They might
be his if he would choose comfort and commodity rather than his
present silly luxury, which kills true happiness and wastes energy
and money.

There are many customs of our sensible neighbours that we
might adopt with profit to ourselves; their immense resourceful-
ness is not revealed at first glance, nor will prejudice admit that we
have anything to learn from their inventiveness, which so agree-
ably surprises visiting foreigners; only true concern for the public
good could make us sharers of these benefits.

We are an industrious people enough; and yet for handicraft,
and scientific daring, and dexterity in manufacture and design we
must confess the English have the best of it. They are happy, too,
in their government, which respects the rights of man while en-
forcing obedience to the law. They have done, now, with civil disorder; they have emerged triumphant from a crisis in which the
strength of the national character was most astoundingly displayed; may we learn to borrow of them that which we as a nation

need, enlightenment, and the wealth of their art; and double our own treasure, by sharing with our neighbour! That would be a golden age, when the nations should stand forward upon merits rather than upon strength, mentally deriving and bestowing such advantages as their natural situation and laws, and the trend of national thought, will allow.

Already our women have adopted a headdress symbolizing the union of England and France; and there is, to my mind, more sound common sense shown in the invention of such a hat than in all the diplomatic scribblings of all the chanceries.

70. At Table

(DXCVIII, Table, 2:222–23)

Three o'clock is the only dinner-hour now, and all meals are shorter. An invitation to supper means half-past nine, and you dare not appear a moment earlier at any private house. Kill time somehow; stay and yawn at home by the fire; anything is better than to appear in public before the canonical hour.

It looks well, and more sought-after, to arrive just before the butler makes his entry. Nowadays there is no announcement, no "Dinner is served!" The man merely appears, and bows in the doorway.

Why then give suppers? To show off one's cook, one's china and plate. And why serve different wines? There is not a moment to taste them; you are no sooner settled in your chair than you must push it back and rise; the host has shown you his riches, that should be enough for you. All this bears hardly upon that traditional starveling, the poet, who nowadays goes hungrier than ever. Farmer-general or duke, the great houses are all the same, all frugal; even the financier trims his stomach to the mode.

What a theme for a satirist! And why has not one risen to sing these latter-day meals, all too succinct? For the good old days of eating are over. Courses come and go, changing swiftly as scenes at the opera. Only at the table's foot one stalwart remains, helping himself, deaf to his neighbours, repelling with deliberate scowl all conversation that might interrupt him at his task—an Academician, no less, making the most of his time, regretting the days of Charlemagne, when four hours at table was considered the thing. Strong-minded, these immortals! Watch him at his food; what goes into his mouth is better worth your attention than what comes out of it.

At table, and by candlelight, our women look their best, and love to shine. Their heads at present are all the same colour; for some time there was a difference of opinion, whether the fashion should be dark hair or blond, until at last they settled it by choosing red. They get this ardent effect by the skilful use of some cosmetic, that gives not only the colour of the hair, but the complexion to go with it.

71. Bicêtre

Simpson's translation combines sections from two of
Mercier's chapters, "Bicêtre—(DCIV, 2:243–54) and
"De la guérison des maladies vénériennes à Bicêtre"
(DCV, 2:255–59). Paragraphs have been marked
(B) or (D) to indicate their source.

H ere are received persons of both sexes infected with venereal disease, on their producing a permit signed by the Lieutenant of Police, which is only granted after their illness has been certified by a surgeon from the Hôtel-Dieu.* There is no fixed number of patients; the hospital accepts as many as it has room for at one time. (D)

Here again, greed of gain makes light of the founder's wishes. A chief attendant, who has assumed the title of Governor, exacts from every sick person who presents himself for treatment the sum of forty-eight sous, two francs forty; and if they cannot pay, out they go, despite the Lieutenant and his permit. The results of this inhumanity may easily be imagined. Only fifty men and as many women are admitted at a time, unless for some special reason, the

extreme gravity of a case, they are obliged to exceed these numbers; but a hundred is nothing compared to the numbers of gan-
grenous people perpetually clamouring for admission. These poor
wretches are doomed; they must die, or rather fall to pieces still
living; the virus gnaws like an invisible creature at their entrails,
their symptoms change, their appearance becomes monstrous, too
horrible to contemplate; and as the disease gains ground they lose
their chance of ultimate cure. (D)

There is some talk of this scourge becoming innocuous; you
hear people saying that it is nothing like so virulent in its effects as
it used to be, and that modern science has conquered it. I wish
such talkers could visit this prison, and see for themselves the ravages brought about by ignorance, or passion, or lust. . . . (D)

You must wait your turn for treatment in this deathly place, and
have your name down as long as eight months before admission;
even so, your turn may be still longer delayed, and the virus waits
for no man. This gap between infection and the beginning of cure
is so well known, and the numbers of aspirants to treatment is so
great, that often prostitutes and the men who frequent them come
up for examination and as it were book a bed before any symptoms
have shown themselves. Moralist, what of this? Consider it; and
then on with your preaching. (D)

I have known fathers who, instead of relying on threats of hell
fire and confessors' remonstrances, have brought their sons to this
place and shown them just what the unclean liver may expect, letting them ponder the spectacle of men and women herded together, a prey to the most shameful and hideous of all maladies;
sometimes this extreme measure has succeeded where milder
courses failed. (D)

So much for the hospital; as to the prison, the name of Bicêtre
is a byword. Debtors are incarcerated here, beggars, and madmen,
together with all the viler criminals, huddled pell-mell. There are
others, too; epileptics, imbeciles, old men, paupers and cripples,
who, not being criminals, are known by the generic title of 'good
poor'; to my mind they should find refuge elsewhere, apart from
the rogues their neighbours. (B)

I had a word with one of these good poor men.

"What would you like, my friend?"

"Oh, monsieur, if I had only a sou a day I should do very well. Then I could pay off the others, and only sleep three in a bed."

"And if you had two sous?"

"I could have a glass of wine twice a week."

"Three sous?"

"That would buy me a bit of meat every third day."

The Englishman who was with me gave him, at these words, enough to sleep alone and pay his meat and wine for eighteen months at least. I should like to give this Englishman's name; the movement of pity was admirably prompt. (B)

Bicêtre is situated on a hill, between Ville-Juif and Gentilly,† about a league out of Paris; nothing could be better than the air of this part, and the site is far less unhealthy than that of the other Parisian hospitals. In fact, if the waters of the Seine could be diverted and brought there by some sort of conduit, no better place for a large hospital could be imagined. As it is, they rely on wells, and there are canals which bring water from Arceuil for the prisoners and sick; but the staff use Seine water, which a cart fetches daily for their use. (B)

One of these wells is interesting, and indeed one of the sights of the place, by reason of its great depth and the simplicity of the mechanism by which water is brought to the surface; there are two buckets; one goes up full, as the other is emptied and sinks. Some time ago a dozen horses used to be set to this task; but by an act of wise economy, and which has benefited everyone concerned, the hauling is now done by certain of the more robust kind of prisoners; it delivers them from complete and dangerous idleness, keeps them in health, and by these means they can earn a pittance, and so supplement their food. M. Le Noir‡ was responsible for this reform, which might even be extended in its scope; for occasionally the supply of water fails, and the sick have to go without their baths, which is a misfortune all round, while the water that is brought through lead pipes is, as everyone knows, unsafe to drink. (B)

The population of Bicêtre varies in number; it is more considerable in winter, since a good many very poor men find work in summer, but are destitute in the later season. The winter reckoning must be about four thousand five hundred persons. . . . (B)

Madame Necker,[§] when her husband held office under the
Crown, came in person to investigate the wards, and was profoundly moved at the sight. The ward called after St Francis was so
putrid, the air was so foul, that the most intrepid visitor could not
tolerate it for long, but fainted after a breath or two of the stench.
(B)

In this place six people to one bed was the rule; and these, lying
entirely untended amid the excreted filth from their own bodies,
soon died of one another's diseases. Madame Necker had great
influence and used it to such purpose that other beds were provided which held only two patients at a time, and were arranged in
cubicles so that the pestilent smells were kept to some extent at
bay by a partition of wood. (B)

There was one dreadful ward where five hundred men were confined together, with their misery and the deadly legacy of past vices
in common. Food was brought to them at the point of the bayonet;
it was the most abominable abyss of corruption which perhaps has
ever defiled the face of the earth. It exists no longer; and I am glad
to think that I, by the descriptions in my book *The Year 2440,* had
some hand in rousing public opinion to its horrors. There are dor-
mitories now; and the appalling risk of contagion is lessened, that
was like the torments of Mezentius, a live man bound to a
corpse.... (B)

Coming in the air smells stale; but in this matter all hospitals are
the same, there is no help for it.... (B)

We pass to the solitary-confinement cells; the prisoners in these
dungeons are allowed only a small iron instrument, with which
they work patterns in straw. These cells are in stages, one on top
of the other, and the man at the bottom of the pile is considered
best off; he does the selling, and makes the others work for him; it
is a most enviable position. (B)

A new prisoner arriving has no notion how to set about this sort
of work, until a companion in misfortune, invisible but equipped
with a little mirror, by signs puts him in the way of it. They are
infinitely clever at managing these mirrors, see each other's faces,
speak, and correspond by signs; the man at the top can communicate in this way with his fellow furthest away from him. (B)

They elect one of their number to keep watch, and he, mirror
in hand, flashes news to his companions of anything notable to be

seen through the narrow wicket at the entrance. "A woman!" goes up the excited cry, "dressed in such-and-such, short or tall"; at once all the prisoners are at their barred gratings to inspect the visitor by refraction; thus, by means of one mirror tilted this way and another at an angle, every man can look at her, while she herself has no idea that she is an object of interest, or that the men are eyeing her and beckoning. (B)

The only recreation permitted to these men is the reading of the *Gazette de France.*** Twice a week a great silence falls, and then the one with the loudest voice bawls out the news through his grating. As each name is mentioned, the others break in. "Ah, I knew him," or "I saw him once," and their commentaries are by no means devoid of humour. (B)

The designer of these cells had in mind two main considerations; to provide some sort of drainage on the one hand, and an easy approach to the chapel on the other. The chapel, then, is the heart of the hive; the men go to Mass on Sundays. (B)

Police spies who fail in their duty are sent here, not as warders but for detention; they are not, however, put with the other prisoners, for the very good reason that these latter, if they could get hold of them, would tear them limb from limb. Theirs is a vile trade, and one for which there is no pity; and yet, strangely enough, so many of these are the merest boys—think of it! A spy, an informer, and not yet turned sixteen! I think that of all the sights the place provides, this is the most horrible, for it calls up the ugliest speculations; what can their lives have been, to drive them to such extremity? And what of those who accept and train their services, and corrupt them, so young? (B)

There are subterranean dungeons, cut off from the light of day and the sounds of the outer world, save for a couple of tiny outlets in the roof. There, for forty-three years, dwelt the accomplice and chief witness against Cartouche; to this was his sentence of death converted; this was his free pardon. He counterfeited death three separate times, only in order to be carried up the stairs, and breathe clear air; and at last, when he did shuffle off his mortal coil, the doctor would not believe it, and stood out against removing his iron collar. Having lived forty-three years in this death, there seemed no reason why he should not go on for ever. (B)

From time to time there are mutinies at Bicêtre. One 1st of February, in the year 1756, the prisoners confined in that wing known as Little Ditch chose the hour of vespers as the most favourable to their project; and after knocking down the sentry, actually got as far as the guard-room, where they found weapons; but the sentry had had time to blow his whistle, at which all the guards came running. Two of them were killed in the ensuing fight, and fourteen of the mutineers. Of these latter some few escaped, but were caught and brought back; it was their uniform of coarse grey cloth, the prison dress, that betrayed them. (B)

Asked why they had risen, they answered that they had been for some time, and for no reason, kept on short rations, a very little bread, with a scrap of meat once a week; and said that they had no ill-will against any but the governor and the superintendent, who had saved on their charges' poor bellies what they afterwards spent on their own. They were tired of life, they said, and despair had driven them to what they did. (B)

Tired of life; the authorities took them at their word, and hanged a good many; others were whipped, and afterwards kept more closely confined. . . . (B)

There are guilty men enough in this hateful prison; but there are poor men too, and the condition of these sets the mind thinking. . . . (B)

The beasts of the field have places to lay their heads; not so the poor. By the laws as they stand every inch of earth, every log of wood is the property of someone or other; the poor man sleeps in an open barn on sufferance; property pursues him from the town's centre to the fields; every particle of food or handful of soil is owned, is not and never can be his. Man, in modern societies, derives his body from Nature, but has no place to live and breathe. They grant him space to die in, but never room to live. So many have, literally, only their physical strength with which to serve those who make their laws; and the have-not is always, and necessarily, the enemy of those that have. He has no resources, the have-not; he must be sick before anyone thinks to help him; he gets free burial, true, because his decomposing body would be a danger to society. They give him space to die in; would it not be better to help keep him in health, instead of neglecting him till the last extremity of sickness is on him? (B)

Every day the number of these people grows; every day the

wheels of that immense and dangerous machine called government policy go whirling round, and grind exceedingly small the
defenceless and the weak. Where lies the remedy? The evil is old,
and deep-rooted. Men of goodwill do what they can to discover a
solution for our troubles; which can only come, I think, through
the operation of time, and the growth of wisdom, grace, and pity
for their country in the hearts of our rulers. What harm is there in
trying out, or in voicing at any rate these ideas of reform? A hundred plans may be useless, the hundred and first worth while; in
which case no one will grudge money spent in buying the book
that propounds it. (B)

*The Hôtel Dieu was the main municipal hospital, located on the Ile de la Cité.
†Ville-Juif and Gentilly were villages south of Paris.
‡Jean-Charles Le Noir (1732–1807) was Lieutenant of Police from 1744 to 1785.
§Mme Necker (1739–94), born Suzanne Curchod, was the wife of Jacques Necker,
royal finance minister from 1777 to 1781 and again from 1788 to 1790.
**The official newspaper, the *Gazette de France,* founded in 1631, had a monopoly
on news about foreign affairs and the Court.

72. Carrabas; and Pots-de-Chambre
(DCXXIII, Carrabas, pots de chambre, 2:324–28)

The majestic carrabas, to the initiate, is an eight-horse affair
which takes six and a half long hours to travel twelve brief
miles. It is the Versailles omnibus; in its elongated cage of wicker-
work twenty persons shift and struggle for an hour before they can
fit themselves, and when the machine at last jerks forward all the
heads go bump together, so that you fall into a Capuchin's beard
or a wetnurse's bosom. Its wide iron steps betray every mounting
ankle, young or old, to the enquiring eye. Twice a day, slowly but
by no means sweetly, this vehicle conveys the lackeys of the lackeys
of the Crown—for what else is Versailles, as Duclos* says, but a
great servants' hall, with no topic of conversation but the master?
Also new-born babies, off to nurse with a Norman foster-mother,
set off in the carrabas twenty-four hours after birth, though the
jolting, God knows, is trial enough to adult bones.

Smart carriages, flashing past this toiling monster on the King's highway, look back in pity, and well they may; it is difficult to see how its denizens can belong, even in the humblest capacity, to the brilliant Court. If the day is sunny, you arrive grilled to a turn like a steak; if wet, moist and steaming, like a soup. And thus, at the gilded gates of the amazing palace of the richest sovereign in Europe, are set down such Parisians as desire to gaze upon the majesty of the throne.

When the clumsy and unsightly vehicle meets, as sometimes it does on its journey, the King's own equipage, the contrast is more absurd than words can convey; it is as though the aged original of all wheeled things had been mummified, and brought out beside the newest invention to point the moral of progress. Yet Henry IV, that good king, had nothing better than this; you may find him writing to Sully:† "I cannot be with you to-day, my wife has the coach." Two hundred years have indeed brought changes!

If you disdain the carrabas, the only resource left is one of those vehicles known from their general appearance as *chamber-pots,* which are certainly more comfortable but also more exposed to the weather. Engaging one of these, you find yourself equipped, to your astonishment, with pages; for the driver, who gets no wage, and must earn his money how he can, will have offered to carry four other persons at twelve sous, sixpence a head, two on the box and two on the step behind; the former are known as monkeys, the latter as rabbits.

Arrived at the golden gates, all four descend, dust their shoes, settle the swords upon their hips, and in they go to survey their rulers, guessing at princely character from princely features, acting the genuine courtiers off the stage. They slip between a couple of dukes, and in the wake of some magnifico in too much of a hurry to note his following, monkey and rabbit enter the state apartments, where at their ease, like lordlings born, they watch the royalties eat.

Both the detestable vehicles aforesaid, though they weary and bruise their occupants, hold the right of way, there is no other choice of conveyance; neither in lazy cart, light gig, nor roomy *fiacre* may you ride to the palace. Reader, need I state that this is yet another of our interesting monopolies?

Yet the tormentors are eloquent; they foreshadow those sorrows that lie in wait among the splendours, their unwelcoming contours warn you to turn back, at least those of the carrabas do; the moral of the *chamber-pot* is quite other, and no one heeds it; years, prayers, lives are spent in the attempt to drive this moral home.

Here it is; your petty ambitious, your intriguer, your lickspittle, your visionary with plans for the fortunes of France in his shabby pocket—tumble them about in these inhuman receptacles, they go to Versailles for what they can get, they deserve no better treatment. But we others who travel hopefully, enquiring innocents out for a day's sightseeing of statues, royalties, seeing the lions fed; what use to us are fine roads if we may not travel them how we please, if our enthusiasm is chilled by the sheer discomfort of the journey; and what need of officials have we, when we choose to drive out and see for ourselves in his own palace our own king?

The carrabas visitor to Versailles, safe home again in his province, makes a great tale of it, a fairy-tale, exaggerated beyond believing, of how he was received there. He did see the King, the princesses, the royalties at dinner, so much is true; but he embroiders this plain theme of fact with many and circumstantial lies, which ignorance and credulity take for Gospel. Exaggeration is legitimized, the wildest invention finds credit; our traveller can stuff his geese of compatriots with any nonsense he pleases. He will talk of the Queen's charm, how she asked for news of the province; which purely imaginary recital gains him great esteem there; and repeating this, his fancy takes fire, until at long last he comes to believe it himself.

The most impossible stories of Versailles find currency in remote Gascony, or in Swiss taverns, rumours so incredible on the face of them as to make it more a wonder that ears can be found to heed than tongues to tell them. It is a chain of senseless ribald lying—for the Swiss in his cups outdoes even the Gascon in that kind of thing. Fairy-tales, old wives' tales, Arabian Nights tales—these enormities surpass them all, but are heard in respectful silence, and grow more ludicrous with every repetition and every drunken comment.

They played once at Court some farcical dialogue, an encounter between one of these intrepid liars and some credulous provincial; never was truer comedy. But this constant talk has created already in certain quarters belief in an extravagance so legendary that how the details can have entered any sane person's cranium is hard to imagine; however, there the legends are, widespread, and credited without reservation by persons otherwise rational; it will be an uneasy task to uproot them.

*Charles Pinot Duclos (1704–72) was named royal historiographer by Louis XV in 1750.
†Maximilien de Béthune, duc de Sully (1560–1641) was Henri VI's principal minister. He restored government finances after the religious wars of the sixteenth century.

73. Pedestrian
(DCXLV, Aller à pied, 2:406–9)

An ignoble creature; that is the definition we are coming to. Nevertheless, men of genius in all walks of life still stick to shoe-leather. Wits may be carriage-folk, but genius goes afoot.

When a man, rich in intelligence but poor in pocket, leaves a drawing-room where those with carriages still chatter, and crosses the courtyard, its clean flagstones flecked with foam from the bits of idle champing horses, he must slip, blushing, between the motionless wheels to where his old creaking *fiacre* or hackney coach waits out in the street, and there in its ramshackle carcase hide his shame. If the lamps of emerging gilded chariots light up his unhappy vehicle, no bows are exchanged; he would not dare from his ignominious depth to salute those passing ladies, with whom six minutes back he talked so freely. His coachman's moustaches are enough to damn even a *fiacre* hired by the hour; and damn its passenger too, were he Plato or Homer.

For a carriage is the goal of every man that sets out upon the unclean road to riches. His first stroke of luck buys him a cabriolet, which he drives himself; the next, a *coupé;* the third step forward is marked by a carriage; and the final triumph is a separate conveyance for the wife. As his purse rounds, comes a cabriolet for the son, then one for his man of business; the steward drives in one to market; soon it will be the cook's turn to handle the ribbons; and all these diabolical vehicles, given over each morning to the impu-

dents below-stairs, dash and clatter their way through our footpath-
less streets as though fiends were at their tails.

A doctor's first move is to set up his carriage. It is nothing to
look at, he houses it outside his front door in the portico, which it
completely fills; the horses are almost in his very waiting-room, his
coachman is turned seventy; no matter, all the quarter knows he
keeps his carriage. Out of his door he comes, with his powdered
wig and his black coat and his septuagenarian on the box, and
indeed until he has driven off there is no getting in or out of his
house; again, what matter, he is a carriage-doctor, he will never
lack patients. . . .

Nowadays the young man of fashion, instead of investing his capital in a country cottage, or a library, or a mistress, sinks it in a
carriage. For a while half his income goes in upkeep; then all at
once the carriage becomes cook, cottage and mistress to him; every
night he drives out, sees ladies home, escorts them to their boxes,
and next day to a race meeting. Twice a week he offers gallantly
the loan of his horses, while husbands, that uncivil race, eternally
and senselessly busy, monopolize without complaint the conjugal
vehicle. A man with a carriage is a made man. He is *liaison* officer
for all the picnics; his horses and his person—never simultaneously, however, and for good cause—contribute to the ladies' pleasure. And so wives, since the fashion of husbandly neglect set in,
have refused to receive or consider any young man suspected of
going on foot; which decision seems reasonable.

For how can a woman exist without horses? In the brief space of
twelve little hours she must be seen at the opera, a review of troops,
any fair that may be open; must dance, and must gamble, to say
nothing of ministerial receptions, which no woman dare miss, any
more than she can afford to be ignorant of the latest fashion in
dancers. Our women of to-day, eternally restless, eternally on show,
have lent to existence something of the mobility of their own features.

Thus a provincial's first duty, on ten thousand francs a year, is
to set up his carriage. It will cost him three hundred francs a
month to begin with, and he will have no use of it whatever; his
friends will see to that. He pays, and continues to walk. Lucky man;
for this single display of tactics will so advance him, that taking it
all round, he will find his carriage an economy—that is, if he is

liberal with it. If, obstinately, he refuses to launch out, to horse himself, that is the end of him.

Certain young men only drive in the winter season; in summer they walk, loudly extolling the weather. The fact is, their budgets will allow no more than a bare eighteen hundred francs for transport. Forced to choose between the seasons, you may see them up aloft in a caped coat on the 1st of December, from which eminence they meekly descend somewhere about the end of May, when everyone goes out of town. But it is really none too easy, this problem of which season to choose when one has only eighteen hundred to spend; there are excellent arguments for both, between which there is no deciding. And so the young man combines in his person both Pollux and Castor, now Olympus receives him, and now the gutter with whose mud he alternately spatters and is spattered.

But merit, talent, genius, probity, all the virtues imaginable are nothing if they go on foot. Suppose the contrary, stupidity and all the vices served up in an elegant equipage, and then see the doors fly open, welcomes everywhere and the rank taken for granted. Poor humanity! But this is the way of it.

74. Kisses, Greeting
(DCLI, Baisers, Embrassades, 2:437–39)

We Parisians kiss easily and often; it is the commonest form of greeting. Certain of these embraces, descending unexpectedly, can be provoking, as when a man you barely know, or dislike, or have entirely forgotten, suddenly clasps you in his arms at the street-corner. The greeting kiss has its varieties; it may be tentative, or timid, or fully and completely done, according to the person and place; for you are never quite sure if the privilege is allowed, and there are no rules save inclination and caprice. One man opens his arms, which another evades; the movement may be one of surprise, or of distaste; there is no way of knowing.

We kiss, however, outdoors and in. Our *bourgeois* women expect to be, and are kissed. A mother takes the salute, her daughter drops a curtsey only. Next time you buss the mother heartily, and so acquire the right to lay your cheek against the daughter's.

There are certain pitiless embracers who kiss long and close, a frightening process to young girls, and one which the man of delicacy must deplore. He but brushes his lips against their cheek; he dreads that very closeness, and the spark it may set leaping. Others are less nice; you see their great jowls thrust against young gentle faces like stones upon a posy; your man of feeling loathes it, the whole business of kissing in public is distasteful to him. Better not take her hand, better not touch her at all, than kiss with the world looking on.

Women kiss their best, and with intent, when they greet each other in the presence of men; they do it for the victim's benefit, to show how well and admirably they can grant favours when they choose. But these kisses have a touch of insincerity, eye and lip do not match for ardour, and though the affair goes off with a smack there is nothing in it of the two necessary spices, secrecy or abandonment.

It should be forbidden to kiss children. Pimples, snuff-blackened noses, prickly chins, all make assault upon their delicate skins, careless how they may hurt or tarnish the cool sweetness of a child's cheek. These people would not finger a man's new tables and chairs, yet they see nothing odd in laying hands on his five-year-old daughter. I hate the trick of swooping down upon a child; it lacks decency, to my mind; it is as revolting as to see innocence brought in contact with vice.

In England there is none of this. Men do not kiss, they shake hands, with no doffing of hats and antics as in our streets, where two men encountering behave like actors in a farce. But when an Englishman is presented to a woman he must kiss her, and not on the cheek, either, but square on the lips, a proper kiss. Englishwomen, used to this way of saluting, no doubt find our foreign greeting, mere cheek against cheek, chilly, even insulting.

New Year's Day is always the signal for an outburst of kissing, both family and formal. Astounding, the amount of public caressing got through on that day! But if you watch the performers, you will notice that the wider the arms are stretched the less they grasp. All this cold ceremony, these imperfect shadows of—when the

with it—a most precious favour, should be done away
Parisian, to look at him, has a heart for all the world;
y~~ ~~rely the man he clasps so closely is, or ever could be, his
friend!

75. Bureaucracy

(DCXCVI, Bureaucratie, 2:572–73)

Translated by Jeremy D. Popkin

A word recently coined to indicate, in a clear and concise manner, the overgrown power possessed by simple clerks who, in
the various offices of the administration, make up and push forward all sorts of projects, which they find most often in dusty draw-
ers in the offices, and which they favor for reasons of their own,
good or bad.

They are all the more powerful with their pens because their
actions are never visible, whether they act out of prejudice or out
of passion, and because they earn neither glory for the good they
do nor shame for the evil they cause, which means that they are
bound to consider their own narrow personal situation.

As a result, these assistants without dignity rarely have an ele-
vated soul. Their pride is tied up and concentrated in petty matters, and becomes insulting. If they are inept, their mistakes, like
those of doctors, are covered by shrouds; if they are intelligent, the
arrangement of an administration divided into too many small
units only allows them to accomplish a little, because they are too
far from the center of things, which is out of their control, but
which is the only place from which regenerative measures could
be taken.

Nevertheless, one would have to have little understanding of the
human heart and its hidden weaknesses not to realize that the taste
for arbitrary authority must necessarily develop in anything called
an office. Furthermore, there is a kind of conspiracy by which the

employees charitably aid each other in building up their ir_p~. tance.

We don't want to make fun of these office workers, whose only compensation for the good they may do is their own good conscience, since credit for their work always goes to someone else and they never acquire a public reputation. We believe that they all have a certain sense of order in their minds, a quality that is always precious and that tends to bring excessive pretensions back to the norm. All we wanted to do was point out the generally recognized fact that these ministerial offices have such great power, and power that is so generally felt, that the people has created a new word to describe it.

76. Mixture of Individuals
(DCCXVII, Mélange des individus, 2:622–28)

Translated by Jeremy D. Popkin

Paris is made up of a multitude of provincials and foreigners, among whom the real Parisian, whose ancient race was good, credulous, but not foolish, is disappearing. To be born in Paris is to be doubly French; those born there have a dusting of urbanity that doesn't exist elsewhere.

These provincials, come from their villages or small towns, are even more avid for odd sights than the real Parisian, and form crowds everywhere. When someone tried to put something over on the Parisians, by telling them that a man would walk on the surface of the river, or tunnel under ground like a mole, etc., the only ones fooled were shopboys and a few employees who are always attracted by anything that distracts them for a moment from their long and boring tasks. The slightest pretext is enough for them to interrupt their tiring occupations. A few idlers start a crowd, and curiosity swells the group; but wouldn't indifference be even more condemnable, when it is a matter of an accident, an injury, or a murderous quarrel?

The inhabitants of Paris are thus never indifferent to what is going on around them. The slightest unfamiliar object stops them in their tracks. Let someone lift his gaze to the sky and look at something, and you will soon see several others stop and look in the same direction, thinking they see the same thing. Little by little the crowd will grow, all of them asking one another what they are looking at. Let a canary escape and perch on a windowsill, and the entire street is blocked by the crowd, and the moment it flits from one lantern to another, cries and acclamation go up all around; people fill every window; the momentary freedom of the little bird becomes a spectacle of general interest.

Let someone throw a dog in the river, and the banks and the bridges are immediately covered with people. Some take an interest in its fate; others say something must be done to save it, eyes follow it wherever the current takes it. This spirit of curiosity is colored by sensitive feelings. Often the crowd separates two fellows who are fighting, and the women lecture them so forcefully about the advantages of peace and concord that they become reconciled again on the field of battle.

Clowns and performers need only to do a couple of turns to attract an audience, but it disappears as quickly as it forms: most of the passers-by watch for a minute and head off shrugging their shoulders. Nothing is easier than attracting the Parisian populace, but the slightest thing sends them off again, and the wandering phalanxes of the streets are not really the petty bourgeoisie of Paris, but a mixture of fellows who, coming from small towns or the suburbs and being unfamiliar with things, pause to steal the time that belongs to their employers and their jobs. Study this group standing around: out of a hundred, there will be forty domestic servants and thirty apprentices.

Those who do heavy labor are almost all foreigners. The Savoyards brush mud off pedestrians, polish floors, and saw wood; almost all of the Auvergnats are water-carriers; the Limousins are masons; the Lyonnais are porters and sedan-chair carriers; the Normans, stone-cutters, pavers, and peddlers, they repair broken china and sell rabbit-skins; Gascons are wigmakers or surgeons' assistants; those from Lorraine are itinerant cobblers, known as *carreleurs* or *recarreleurs*.

The Savoyards live in the suburbs; they are organized in communal groups, each of which is under the leadership of a chief or old Savoyard, who looks after and teaches these young children until they are old enough to look out for themselves.

Wise rules have been laid down for these young Savoyards and other children who work for the public, whose education and religious training used to be completely neglected. Catechism classes, charity schools, and shelters have been set up, where they also get more practical assistance. No matter what some hard and short-sighted people may say, the greatest gift one can give to people is that of religious belief, because it is a consolation and makes up for everything else in the case of beings whose days are taken up with work and the imperious requirements of necessity.

Savoyards, common laborers, water-carriers, those who will work for anything, porters, clothes-brushers gather in groups on the street-corners; there, while waiting for jobs, they play jokes and elbow each other. When rulers go to war, the effects are felt all the way down to peaceful cottages. When porters fight, they bump into the respectable passer-by, who has nothing to do with their rough games, and who swears at their manner of amusing themselves. Thus the peaceful or distracted person is sometimes hurt by these undesirable good-for-nothings, with their big feet covered by iron-toed shoes, who move like towers when they are set in motion.

Those dangerous fools who go around holding under their arm a large cane that turns with them and is always ready to put out your eye also belong in this category: you are lucky to get off with a scratched face. Others have iron-tipped sticks that land on the feet of those they happen to encounter. One has to have seraphic patience not to riposte with the cane in one's hand, carried nowadays in place of a sword, that useless item that has been wisely abandoned to soldiers, to the vile agents of the tax collectors, and to those doormen known as Swisses. Instead of dueling swords, we have walking sticks, but why can't they be managed in a civil fashion, without putting our neighbors at risk?

Next one sees the apprentice wigmakers, popularly known as *whitings*, because they are covered with flour from head to toe; if you are wearing a black suit, you want to avoid them, lest you be bleached and greased; woe to those who only have a black suit! These whitings are barbers and hairdressers in the morning, and perform surgery in the afternoon. They have had to be forbidden

La mort aux rats mes Dames.

27:   5.ᵉC:

Rat-Catcher. The rat-catcher, shown in this early
eighteenth-century engraving by Louis Poisson, plied his
trade in the streets, like the Savoyards and others Mercier
described in this article. Poisson was one of many
engravers who made such series of illustrations, known
as *les cris de Paris* (Paris street cries). Unlike Mercier's
Tableau, these engravings usually showed individuals
isolated from their urban context. (Courtesy The Lilly
Library, Indiana University, Bloomington, Indiana)

to come to the surgery schools except in street clothes; otherwise, the royal operating theatre would have looked like a dirty wigmaker's shop. They used to show up at the Saint-Côme surgery schools this way; from the moment the whitings arrived, they took over the rue des Cordeliers, and it was impossible for any man who cared even slightly about his clothes to go through this street, or even those nearby.

When these apprentice surgeons are in the amphitheater, they have an object worthy of emulation in front of their eyes; then they look up, they see the bust of M. La Martinière, who rose from the rank of wigmaker's apprentice, or *frater*, to the rank of first surgeon to the king. The whitings take pride in such a founder, who has not forgotten them in spite of his success.

The millers, the bakers, the porters of La Halle who sling sacks of flour around are also sprinkled with white, but they are not as impudent as the whitings. The charcoal-burners, their opposite numbers, turn aside a little, even if they are carrying heavy loads, to avoid getting black on you. I like these fellows; their eyes stand out and are expressive. The famous adage, "A charcoal-burner is still master in his own house," comes from them. One day, I was accompanying Jean-Jacques Rousseau along the riverbank. He saw a Negro carrying a sack of coal; he started to laugh and said to me, "This man has found the right job, he won't need to wash up, he has found his place; if only everyone was as lucky as he is!" I can still see him laughing, and following the Negro coalman with his eye.

These carriers of coal have a copper medallion, which is no cleaner than their hands and their faces.

With this mix of individuals, the city needs a perpetual movement of industry, continual and sustained activity, temptation for the rich, luxury trades, and some of the vices that follow from them (for the first law is that one must live). The price of food and the necessities of life have gone up, but wages haven't risen in proportion. Thus the abundance of gold and silver has only reinforced the selfishness of the rich, who have been able to afford many pleasures for a cheaper price.

What does one not see in the classified advertisements? A crowd of men without jobs, who have been to school and have even worked for lawyers and notaries; individuals who know Latin,

French, German, English, history, geography, mathematics, and
who have nothing to eat. But anyone who knows how to serve at
table, polish, care for a horse, drive a carriage, travel long dis-
tances, will always find a suitable place.

77. Plumage
(DCCXXXI, Plumasserie, 2:670–71)

At one time the feather-merchant consecrated his art to the
decoration of churches; his wares adorned the persons of
kings, princes, and their ambassadors, or the actors who represented these potentates on the stage; nodding plumes awed the
populace from the dais during processions. Then—transfor-
mation; women seized upon these adornments of divinity, of royalty, and set upon their own heads the emblem before which poor
citizens had been used to kneel. Feather-shops flourished. Husbands found themselves confronted with a new expense; and since
real plumes last no time, there was nothing to show for the money,
a delightful consideration to women, and one which chiefly en-
sured the success of the fashion.

They take the air, these ladies, whole groups of them in tall open
carriages, drawn by half a dozen horses, and from a distance the
effect of the wavering colours on their heads is brilliant; but the
least shower brings all this bright plumage down in ruin about
their ears, and lends erstwhile exquisites the lamentable air of wet
hens. Dry, they draw all eyes; damp, they are lucky if they escape
public mocking; they know it, and hide their heads, so recently
diminished, shame-faced as though they had affronted the public
eye with shaven skulls. This one excursion may have cost something like sixty thousand francs; husbands, what of it? You must
pay. And until you can control the clouds and command the sun,
you must continue to pay, so put a good face on it. What, grumbling, when the cost of feathers runs to a mere five louis apiece?

Poets, of course, have celebrated the fashion, each in his manner, complimentary or satirical; but the women are proof against
epigram. They have their own way, while the poets talk.

78. Whiskies

(DCCXL, Wiski, 2:694–96)

Tall vehicles imitated from the English. These, in our narrow paved ways, are comfortless, dangerous, and unsafe, even to the extent of vomiting forth their own drivers now and again; they are altogether too high-built to be reliable.

Drunkenness, and the crimes due to it, should never be condoned; the old law of Pytacus, from which our own might take example, punished the drunken criminal twice over, once for his condition and once for his crime. Then what of these misdemeanours committed soberly, daily, boastfully, and all for the sake of a minute saved between one pleasure and another? What use is it to talk of law, when the most necessary of all laws, and the easiest to announce, lags behind the circumstances which imperiously demand it? These vehicles, whiskies, cabriolets, any name you please, kill a couple of hundred innocents, and our officials are too busy devising new taxation to deal with the few young fools who are responsible. Personal safety is as precious to a man as his political freedom. What use is our imposing judiciary if it must stand by, a mere ornament of State, while the gutters of the capital run with citizens' blood, and sheer unthinking butchery dishonours the Kingdom's proudest city?

Public protection for the individual, is not this the first of all laws? Yet a poor devil of a footpad does less harm with his knife than such young fools, driving their whiskies, committing their daily daylight murders with entire impunity. . . . I will not go so far as to say that the pedestrian should take matters into his own hands where these juggernauts are concerned; all private vengeance is illicit; but it might be no bad thing if one of these days the people were to pull some silly fool off his box and impress upon him the dangers of furious driving by smashing his whisky to atoms before his eyes.

On Easter Day 1788 I saw a woman and a priest run over, and killed instantaneously; I repeat, Paris is dishonoured by this criminal indifference to the lives of her citizens. But our streets are safe, the authorities remind us; a man may go about his business without fear of a knife in his back. What good is such protection? Where lies the difference in terror between knife and wheel? Of the two, the knife is more merciful, for a wheel may cripple without killing, and leave you to suffer a dozen deaths. Ordinary caution suffices where footpads are concerned, but against these moneyed murderers in their tall tumbrils no vigilance avails. . . .

79. A Closed Cemetery*
(DCCLIII, Cimetière fermé, 2:732-35)

Translated by Jeremy D. Popkin

As we have said, more than 3,000 bodies a year were buried in the Cemetery of the Innocents, in the most crowded part of the city. The dead had been buried there since the time of Philip the Fair. Ten million bodies at least had decomposed in this little space. What a melting pot! A market where fodder and vegetables are sold has been built on top of these human remains. I never cross it without becoming lost in thought. If the dead could speak, what stories they would tell! What does our century have to say that can compare with all these forgotten deeds and the different personalities vanished into the night of ages? We know nothing of our ancestors.

Infection attacked the life and health of the inhabitants of this narrow enclosure. Recent advances in knowledge have made us aware of the danger of the mephitic influences that afflicted the houses, and which could become worse over time.

General complaints, decrees of the Parlement of Paris, the wishes of the magistrates were unable to bring about the suppression of these cemeteries, because this abuse, intimately connected with religious ceremonies, had put down roots that even the law could not suddenly get rid of.

But the Innocents cemetery, which gave off fumes that several scientists had warned against, finally became a subject of concern for the government, and, after many efforts that were necessary to satisfy conflicting interests, it was closed, though not without difficulty. It is so hard to accomplish any kind of change for the better!

The danger had reached a critical point. In houses next to the cemetery, soups and milk went bad in a few hours. Wine became sour if it was left in open casks, and the miasmas from the corpses threatened to poison the air.

It was high time to set up a barrier against the mephitic emissions that this cavern of death gave off. The gas from corpses is a powerful poison that affects the whole organism, and infects every form of life it comes in contact with. Its effect on organic substances is frightening. The liquid that oozes out of dead bodies is more dangerous than that from poisonous plants, if you touch it; it kills on contact. Just resting one's hand carelessly on a wall damp with this moisture meant exposing oneself to the venom, even though it only came in contact with the surface of the skin.

In order to purify the air in a neighborhood where freshly prepared food immediately spoiled, a ditch filled with 1,600 bodies had to be disinfected.

There are few scenes more difficult to describe than the work that was done in this bonepit. It had to be covered with a layer of several inches of quicklime, and the holes also had to be filled in; they also had to be kept separated from each other, so that the gas could not become concentrated.

Picture flaming torches, this huge grave opened for the first time, the different layers of bodies stirred up, the remains of bones, scattered fires feeding on the boards from the coffins, the moving shadows cast by the tombstones, this fearsome enclosure suddenly lit up in the silence of night! It woke up the inhabitants of the area, and roused them from their beds. Some stood half-dressed at their windows; others came down to look; people from all over the neighborhood arrived. In this disorderly crowd of the astonished and the curious, youth and beauty appeared. What a contrast to these tombs, these lugubrious flames, these remains of the dead! Young girls stood at the edge of these opened graves; the rosy cheeks of youth could be seen next to the most deathly objects. This ghastly cavern of death saw in its midst beauty just roused from sleep, whose half-naked foot trod on bones.

*The Cemetery of the Innocents, founded in the Middle Ages, was located on the Right Bank, west of the Rue St. Denis. It was closed in 1780.

80. Mariage à la Mode

(DCCLXXIV, Comment se fait un mariage, 2:795–800)

To his daughter, sitting at her dressing-table, who that very moment has learned from her maid that her marriage has been arranged, enter Papa.

"Well, miss; so you didn't sleep a wink last night?"

"No, Papa."

"I thought as much, I could tell by your eyes. Now, this won't do. A girl ought to look her best the day of the contract. No sleep—that's the way to make yourself look a fright."

"I wish I did look a fright—" sighing.

"Do you indeed? Is that why you're putting on this sulky expression? Now, don't let's have more schoolgirl foolery. Proper modesty's all very well the day of the contract; but there's a difference between modesty and sulks, and at this moment you look most damnably sulky."

"I look as I feel."

"Then the sooner your feelings change, and your looks with them, the better. Smile, I order you."

"How can I?"

"How can you? Why not? What's so formidable about marrying a decent, well-bred man, with a nice fortune into the bargain?"

"Well, I suppose he is, if you say so; but it's dreadful to be handed over like this to a perfect stranger."

"That's good! A stranger, eh? And aren't you just as much of a stranger to him? No, no, my dear child, believe me, the only marriages which turn out badly are the love-matches; chance is not so blind as love. Why, you might know a man ten years, and yet not know him; men are deceivers ever—and women, too. A man's a very different fellow after he's been to bed with you from what he is before; you never can tell how he'll behave. It stands to reason; he doesn't know himself. Chance, pure chance. Take your mother and myself: we saw a good deal of each other before—well, and what do you think she said—afterwards? She said I'd deceived her; and I told her she'd given me a surprise, if it came to that. But now we get on pretty well; we had to get over it, and we did."

"Papa, what strange advice!"

"It's the sort of talk you'll hear in the world; and the world, let me tell you, is no fool. Poor people need all the love they can get, if they're to jog on together; but a couple that's better off only need to be civil to each other to live comfortably; their money does the rest. Come, now; make up your mind to it, and show a little spirit, and a smile or two; you'll see, it won't be so bad!"

Having spoken, exit Papa. The daughter, who cherishes a hidden passion for some young man or other, writes to him that she is to be married against her will, and bids him look forward to the time when, after the knot is tied, their love will find a way. She signs the contract, preparations for the marriage run their usual course, six weeks later she has the satisfaction of receiving her lover in her own drawing-room, and the last person to know of it is the husband. But if by ill-luck he were to make some protest, she would have ready a most convincing little scene to prove that he ought never to trust his own eyesight.

Jewellers, silversmiths, drapers, *modistes,* all take an interest in any marriage; but nowadays there is another artist to be reckoned with, a man whose price is above rubies, and who contributes more to the happiness of the home than any moral writer. When a young lady about to be married remembers any tender but disturbing incident of her past, and prefers that her husband-to-be should have no inkling of it, she does not trust wholly to the wisdom of Solomon, that wise man. For virginity has signs whereby it may be known; on this point she is as knowledgeable as Buffon* himself. And she wants to start well with her husband. She has heard it said that there was a resurrection. What we don't know won't trouble us. An oath of fidelity doesn't have to be retroactive; one makes promises for the future, which one keeps if one can.

So off she goes, like every other young person troubled with such doubts and hopes, to the shop of a certain Maille, at nightfall. He sells a vinegar whose effects restore confidence to her and inspire it in her husband, and which has done a good deal, in its way, to promote domestic harmony. For appearances are everything in this world; they are the only reality.

M. Maille has no need of a calendar to keep him informed of those months in which marriages may be celebrated.† Towards the end of Lent, and later, of Advent, the frail and charming creatures come to him; and if now and then a husband is deceived, it is all for the best, that no shadow of the past may come to trouble future happiness. A pretty hand steals out, seizes the bottle of restorative, pays; and then, with no other sign, the customer goes. The artist is too much a man of the world to stare; besides, the suppliants are disguised, veils hide their blushes—if they blush. A pamphlet, instructive but highly moral in tone, is wrapped up with each bottle of astringent, so that no words need be exchanged; and thus the traces of assault, or of surrender, are effaced, and it is a virgin who, crowned with orange blossom, walks to Hymen's altar eight days later.

At least, so far as the husband is concerned. Chemists can bring about marvels of regeneration, conjugal felicity is based upon certain of their discoveries; and in Paris, at any rate, brides owe to them their happiness, their triumph, and their peace of mind. Provincial ladies, alas, are not yet so favoured; such artists as they have are not to be compared with the inestimable Maille; and I for one deplore it, thinking sadly of the specious lies, the unconvincing explanations, all of which one of his flasks might save them; a bottle so small that it can hide in the palm of the hand!

And so, you ladies, who tremble for a husband's happiness, and for yourselves lest knowledge should lead to disillusion, consider, when you see upon his pots of mustard M. Maille's name linking the crowns of three European potentates, that in just such a manner does he link many a happy household, refuting suspicion, quelling doubt; by his art mistrust finds no place in the abandon of conjugal caresses. For her who knows not Maille, there must be some little dissimulation, which her happier sister may disdain. With this latter the husband knows himself victor, as indeed he is, though not the first.

Forty years ago the courtiers had a saying—"Honour is like hair, it grows again." At Versailles nowadays, as in Paris, honour and tresses are not the only ornaments that renew themselves. The other day a woman, unmarried, and not young, proposed to a certain man that she should have a child by him, out of wedlock. A child was born in due course; the father put in a claim to marry the mother, and brought his case into court. She, however, would have none of him, and scornfully asked how much compensation he required for the trouble he had been put to in seconding her efforts at maternity. He lost his case, each party paying its own costs.

*Buffon: see note to Chapter 24.
†" . . . those months in which marriage may be celebrated."—The Catholic Church forbade marriage ceremonies during Lent and Advent.

81. Crébillon* and His Son
(DCCLXXV, Les deux Crébillons, 2:800–808)

I was nineteen, and at that time the renown of the elder Crébillon was at its height. His tragedies were compared with those of
Voltaire, for in the public mind every genius must have his rival;
this balancing of one against another somehow distributes the
weight of criticism better.

There was a time when, so backward was this nation in all literary
matters, only four names were admitted to literary discussion—
Racine, Corneille, Crébillon, and Voltaire. It seems incredible now,
the thought of all those dusty disputes on these men's respective
merits, yet so it was; and I, being young and unwilling to take my
opinions ready-made, found myself unable to admire their tragedies quite so unreservedly. There seemed to me something too
formal, too constrained and uniform about them all, the fault of
the convention in which they were written, and which, enamoured
as I was then of vast and undisciplined conceptions, I could not
find to my taste. I used to read the Abbé Prévost's[†] novels, which
gave me more pleasure than all the tragedies of the past hundred
years put together.

Still, Crébillon had a great name, and I was eager to see him. He
lived at that time in the Marais, Rue des Douze-portes, where, one
day, I sounded his knocker; there followed an outburst of barking
from fifteen or twenty dogs inside, who surrounded me as I entered, and escorted me in none too friendly fashion to the poet's
own room. The staircase was foul with the excrement of these
brutes; they announced, and ushered me in to their master.

His room was bare. A pallet bed, two stools, seven or eight tattered armchairs—this was all the furniture. I saw for an instant as
I came through the door a woman's figure, four feet high and
three wide, disappearing into the next room. The chairs were all
occupied by dogs, all growling. The old man, with bare legs and
chest and head uncovered, was smoking a pipe. His eyes were very
large, very bright blue, his white hair scanty above a most expressive face. He quieted the dogs with some difficulty, and, whip in
hand, obliged one of them to quit his armchair and make room
for me. He took his pipe from his mouth a moment, civilly, to greet
me; then replaced it, and without a word continued to smoke with
a satisfaction which his mobile features most vividly expressed.

He remained in silent meditation some time, his blue eyes fixed on the floor; then spoke a word or two. The dogs growled, and bared their teeth at me. At last he put down his pipe, and I asked him: "Monsieur, when shall we see your *Cromwell?*" "It is not yet begun," said he. I asked if I might be privileged to hear a verse or two. "After one more pipe," said he. At this the woman I had seen before came in, a bandy-legged dwarfish creature, with the longest nose, and the brightest most wicked eyes I ever saw in my life—the poet's mistress. The dogs evidently respected her; she was conceded a chair, and sat down facing me. When the second pipe was finished, Crébillon recited a few incomprehensible verses from some romantic tragedy or other not yet written; I could not make out a word of the plot, nor yet its development, but the lines were in the nature of fierce reproaches to the gods, and denunciation of kings, for whom he had no love. He seemed a good old fellow, wrapped up in his thoughts, and no talker; his mistress's expression bore out the malicious promise of her eyes. His lines spoken, the poet filled another pipe, while I talked with the woman. My eye kept wandering, intrigued by the extreme shortness of her legs; his shins on the contrary were bare as an athlete's, resting after his turn in the arena. I rose at last to go, and the dogs rose too in a body, barking, and escorted me to the street door as before. The old poet scolded them gently; love showed through the harshness of the words. No other man could have borne to live in an atmosphere so polluted with dogs' filth.

I remembered enough of my classics to remind him that Euripides too was a dog-lover, and that he was in a fair way to outlive that other ancient playwright, Sophocles; he was at this time eighty-six years old. I had the luck to please him, and he gave me a tiny piece of pasteboard on which, in very fine characters, was inscribed his name; this card was a kind of passport to one of his plays; but since Voltaire saw to it that these were not often performed, I had nine months to wait before I could put it to any use. The old man had warned me that it might be so, and told me the reason, as he conceived it; he spoke of his rival as "a very wicked fellow," in tones of entire benevolence.

Two or three years later I made the acquaintance of his son. He was the very shape of a poplar, tall, slender, very different from the robust solid build of the tragic poet. Nature can never have grafted two such dissimilar men upon the same stock. The son was amenity's self, kindly, civil, and forthcoming; he had a tang of satire

now and then in his talk, but only pedants and other public offend-
ers were touched by it. We agreed together very well. He had seen
something of life, and more of women than any other man before
or since; he adored but disdained them. He talked well, and spicily,
often regretting the Regency, that period of good manners; we
had nothing comparable, he said, today. Our literary tastes, too,
were the same. He told me once in confidence that he had never
been able to get through all his father's tragedies, but hoped to
finish them one day. French tragedy, he declared, was the most
astounding farce the human mind had ever conceived, and he
used to laugh till the tears came at certain more ponderous performances, and at a public which persistently regarded every stage
monarch as a reflection of its own King at Versailles. That stock
character, the captain of the bodyguard, alternately trustworthy or
treacherous according to the author's convenience, filled him with
irreverent joy, and he always liked to know the name of the actor
cast for this part, who, *ipso facto,* became his favourite. Janissary to-
day, revolutionary to-morrow, the pivot upon which the whole plot
invariably swung, this personage by the end of the season had overturned more thrones than he had followers at his back; three times
a week with admirable precision he accomplished the downfall of
some Tarquin or other. Crébillon loved this character, his look, his
walk, his attitudes either of loyal respect or impassioned defiance;
and admired the philosophic indifference with which, according
to the exigencies of the situation, he turned his ever-ready sword
this way or that.

The younger Crébillon was Censor Royal, and also censor on
behalf of the Lieutenant of Police; it was part of his duty to read
all the street-sellers' ballads, and all the broadsheets. There were
unbelievable quantities of these published at that date; heroic cou-
plets fell like rain upon the public, and Crébillon approved them
all unmoved, and with unfailing charm of manner. He never kept
an author waiting, not even a singer from the Pont-Neuf, and was
invariably helpful, accessible, and courteous. He it was who advised
me to leave verse alone.

His door was open daily to a crowd of would-be licensees, rhyme-
sters and beginners. He said to me one day: "Wait here with me
till a quarter to one, that is the poet's hour; stay, it may amuse
you."

I sat myself down. A bell rang, Crébillon opened his door to an author, a lively young man with good manners, who introduced himself gracefully, took a chair, and a manuscript from his pocket. They began to talk, and the youngster acquitted himself well.

"And what part of France do you come from?" asked Crébillon, who, be it remembered, read and approved some forty to fifty thousand verses a year.

"From near Toulouse."

"Good. Leave your manuscript with me; then you can either call again tomorrow, or else send for it; the licence will be ready."

When the young man had gone Crébillon took up the paper he had left, and said, not looking at it:

"I have not read a word of this. You saw the author, he speaks well and easily. What will you bet that his work is quite worthless?"

"You judge rather hastily, surely?"

"See for yourself; read it."

Sure enough, the manuscript was quite nonsensical.

The bell rang a second time, the door was opened to a second author. This time the visitor halted in the doorway, unsure of himself, bowed poker-fashion, then shambled forward awkwardly, blundering against the little table on which the censor's luncheon was laid, and nearly knocking the whole thing over. It was a feat of stage-management to get him into a chair, he backed away from every civil offer; at last we had him seated. He began, then, to stammer and trip over his own tongue, answered at cross-purposes, and finally, after six minutes of this, abruptly pulled out of his bulging pocket the manuscript he had been eyeing all the time, dislodging by the sudden movement his hat and cane. He then looked about for his parasol, suspicious as though one of us might have made off with it; knocked my leg with a clumsy movement of his sword; and at last with the utmost difficulty managed to bring out a few words about haste, and great obligation, and what someone or other had told him about Crébillon's kindness.

This latter accepted the paper with his invariable courtesy, did what he could to put the poet at his ease, and at length came out with the same question as before:

"And which is your part of the world?"

"Near Rouen, monsieur."

"Good. Leave your work with me, you shall have your licence in a day or two."

Crébillon escorted him to the door, found his parasol for him, and guided him gently to and through the doorway. His unfailing clumsiness even here did not desert the visitor, who turned left instead of right, tripped on the stairs and fell down a step or two; all the while, with true Norman politeness, pushing his host away with his hand. At last he was gone.

"And that animal," said I, "has the impudence to write!"

"Wait," answered Crébillon, "you have seen and heard him, but you know nothing of him. Now I am willing to bet that his work is not without merit."

"You know him then, do you?"

"I've never set eyes on him before. Well, let us see."

We read what he had brought; and in fact that graceless Norman had written something worth while; something with style, and ideas. I was astounded at my friend's perspicacity, which he explained to me thus:

"I have had many years' experience; enough to teach me that nineteen out of twenty southerners write trash, while of those who come from the north, half are worth reading to start with, and likely as not improve as they go on. The worst verse is written between Bordeaux and Nîmes; in this latitude all poets are vile, there is not an idea among the whole tribe of them. But the northerners have sense, and a talent for self-expression which only needs bringing out."

I have often had occasion to apply this test, and the results have generally justified Crébillon's opinion. The south (with exceptions, of course) does not breed writers.

One more memory of him I must recall, an incident which goes to prove his courage, and the regard he had for the craft of letters and for me. In January 1771 I published a play called *Olinde and Sophronie;* certain lines were construed as a criticism of the behaviour of Chancellor Maupeou,‡ who at that time was at war with the magistrates. On the 20th of January the Parliament of Paris was dissolved; two days later my play appeared in print. The public put its own construction on some of my lines, and applauded them by way of vengeance on the unpopular Chancellor. The ministry, at that date none too lenient, proposed to bring me into court. Crébillon, who had licensed the play, instead of yielding to this pressure from above, stood out against it, defended me, and took the whole responsibility on his own shoulders. His generosity and firmness saved me a good deal of unpleasantness. But he had a genuine love for all men of letters. I have often heard him say that for all their vanity they are in general the most reliable kind of men.

In his works he very delicately and surely dissects the human heart and its sentiments, more especially those by which the other sex is guided; for it is characteristic of a woman that while she can read any man like a book, her own heart is to her *terra incognita*. Crébillon the younger was a skilled painter of women; he studied his models with care; and his touch for all its delicacy probes none the less surely, and sometimes goes deep.

*Prosper Jolyot, sieur de Crébillon, known as Crébillon *père* (1674–1762), was a well-known dramatist. His son Claude-Prosper Jolyot (Crébillon *fils*) (1707–77) wrote licentious novels and also served as a royal censor. Mercier became friends with both early in his career.

†Antoine-François Prévost (1697–1763) was one of the most popular French writers of the first half of the eighteenth century. His sentimental novels influenced the entire generation of pre-Romantics to which Mercier belonged.

‡René-Nicolas Maupeou, chancellor of France under Louis XV, led an effort to strengthen royal authority by undermining the powers of the *parlement*, the kingdom's principal law court, in January 1771.

82. Hôtel des Menus

(DCCLXXVIII, Hôtel des menus plaisirs, 2:813–16)

T his is the slang name for it; the Hôtel des Menus-Plaisirs, the King's diversions; really it is a warehouse where all the scenery and decorations are kept that are used on great occasions. Inside, chaos is come again, catafalques* for special funerals and ballroom furniture lie cheek by jowl. They are neighbours, and you may read the initials which signify—"For His Majesty's Pleasure," on the scaffolding of a bier. The mere putting together of all these odds and ends costs more than to buy new whatever is wanted. All the opera-girls, at least all those with influential protectors, are allowed to take their pick of the satins and other stuffs for dresses; they can never have too many *toilettes*. When the master has dined and his servants feast on the leavings the amount of waste is made clear; in just the same way any frugal-minded citizen must deplore the waste of time and good money upon ceremonies and shows.

The Hôtel houses a school of declamation; would-be actors learn their trade there under the tutelage of older actors, who take the title of professor.

A short while ago this place took fire, but there was no great public excitement; there never is, when it is State property that is in question. The people call this sort of accident, a receipt written in charcoal. There will always be money to make good the loss, they say.

But those who did take this particular fire most seriously were the Capuchin fathers, who were very helpful in saving the splendours of the three theatres. One, with a helmet on his head for ease of carrying, rescued a scimitar, and Medea's wand; another bowed beneath the weight of a pile of satin petticoats and Mercury's caduceus, making the oddest contrast with his cowl and beard. A third, with a druid's costume over his habit, rescued the rays of the Sun-king's chariot under the impression that they were set with diamonds. All these consecrated fingers handling such profane objects, for the first time no doubt, were proof enough of the old adage; Necessity knows no law; but even though the flames were raging it was too ludicrous to see these monks laden with indecent costumes, bearing off busts of indelicate deities in their arms, and generally lending what aid they could to the naked gods and goddesses of a pagan world.

Not less remarkable is the fact that a good many of these reverend fathers have, at various times, met their death in theatre fires. What a fate! To die by burning in the very building against which you lately launched your pulpit thunders. It would seem only decent to dispense them from attempts at rescue, where the building concerned is one wherein all the principles they try to inculcate are set at naught.

The Grey Friars are fire-fighters too, and as zealous as the Capuchins; but they, finding themselves passed over, draw attention to their feats of charity by means of an announcement in the *Journal de Paris*.[†]

Ever since the fire at the Opéra, all the theatres are obliged to keep a staff to deal with any possible outbreak. There are firemen, and a water-tank, and a bell to warn them when their services are required. Some practical joker once rang this bell in the middle of a tragedy; the whole place was flooded in a moment, and there was a good deal of grumbling from soaked actors and damp audience; but nobody could complain that response to the warning was not prompt.

Fire seems the fate of theatres, all the world over. Every year somewhere in Europe two or three go up, and yet nothing, not even the possibility of an appalling death, will keep people away from the play; this love of the theatre runs through all classes and conditions of men, and is carried in some cases to extremes.

But the playhouse which of all others would be most deadly in a fire is the variety theatre in the Palais-Royal, which backs on to a double line of wooden shop stalls; it is quite appalling to think of what would happen if a stray spark were to take effect here. True, the theatre has its firemen, who are alive to the danger, and keep most careful watch; but a spark is small, and the theatre itself is no more than matchwood, painted and gilt.

However, there are places which fire might very well consume without much loss; I mean the smaller theatres of which I have already spoken. I heard once, in one of their pieces, two men plotting to kill a third; says the first murderer: "The river tells no tales," meaning that they might very well drop their victim over the parapet of one of the bridges. Surely it would be better to have two licensed theatres, two rival theatres if you like, than let the people listen, for want of better stuff, to such curious maxims as this?

*A "catafalque" was a temporary scaffolding used to support the coffin during elaborate funerals.
†The *Journal de Paris,* founded in 1777, was France's first daily newspaper.

83. Turkeys
(DCCXCI, Dindons, 2:851)

D o you know how our turkeys come into Paris?"
    "Not I."
    "I'll tell you, if you'd care to hear."
    "Gladly."
    "It is really quite interesting; I always like to know a little of how our administration works."
    "Oh, turkeys come into that, do they?"
    "Certainly, it's all organization. Well, these birds, thousands of them, are sent off in charge of one man, with a long stick. They keep together; he never loses one. Of course, they don't get along very fast, six miles or so a day is the most; and that means starting at sunrise. Cluck, cluck, off they go, and somehow or other they get along."
    "That's the main thing."
    "They may cluck as much as they like, but they have to keep together, and so at last they come to the end of their journey."
    "And so to dinner."
    "What! Don't you think it's rather remarkable, all these turkeys, travelling hundreds of miles, and only covering half a dozen miles each day?"
    "Remarkable? No, why should I? I know some that do twelve miles an hour. It's true mine travel by express coach."

84. Prodigies
(DCCXCIV, Fortes têtes, 2:858–62)

I know only two persons worthy of the name, and one is the servant at an inn in the Rue des Boucheries, where they serve dinners at one franc thirty. To each customer, she serves soup, boiled meat, *entrée,* roast meat, sweet, and fruit, never once mistaking the order of the dishes, and with a vigilant eye on the man who tries to get more than his due. She must keep all the extras in her head; one customer likes his pint of wine laced with spirit; another prefers instead of the sweet a second helping of roast, for which he has to pay a sou or two more.

Well; and this astonishing woman remembers every mouthful, every order; there is no plate that is not ineffaceably engraved upon her memory; she knows who has had a half-bottle, and who half a litre. Blandishments are wasted on her, flattery is vain; and your bill when it reaches you could not be more exact if it had been drawn up by the Chancellor of the Exchequer.

She serves, daily, one hundred and ten persons; that is to say she gives out six hundred plates, five hundred dishes, bread in like quantity, spoons, forks, bottles and napkins; and never a mistake in all the lot. Does not this show a power of calculation positively Newtonian?

She is everywhere at once; not only serving, but calling the orders through to the kitchen, and infallibly distributing the dishes as they come. She never looks at you; she recognizes your voice; and on that one fact, that peg, she hangs the whole character so far as it is known to her; so-and-so eats fast, so-and-so takes his time. She is phenomenal, not only for her memory, but for her quickness in moving, clearheadedness, and dexterity; for example, there is not time to set down a dish, she lets it fall in front of you from above, but so adroitly that nothing is spilt. Knives and forks emerge magically from her pockets; a bottle of wine sails over your head onto the only place on the table where there is room for it—for there is not much elbow-space; and though the bottle seems to come down with a crack, it never breaks, so skilled is her handling.

She remembers the customer who came once, six months ago, and where he sat and what he was wearing; and she knows the exact moment when each finishes his meal. She can tell a cheat by the look in his eye; and, by his demeanour, knows, who will try to pocket the dessert apple instead of eating it there and then or leaving it on the plate.

Having served you, she takes the money for the bill, and there is in her element. You had this or that extra, she tells you, and you have exactly nothing to say; she would be on to any kind of trickery at once. Then she puts in her own claim to the tip of two sous, one penny; if you withhold it, your miserly face will never be forgotten.

Back she goes to the dining-room at an unbelievable pace; for five hours on end she is never still one moment. She is plump, but

CHAP LXX

Restaurant Scene. Food and eating were among Mercier's
favorite subjects. This illustration depicts a crowded
restaurant, like the one described in this chapter.
(Courtesy Library of Congress)

light on her feet. No man who attempted to take advantage of
both her hands being full would wait long for his punishment;
vengeance, in the form of boiling sauce, would be on his head in
a moment. Now, gentlemen, mathematicians and geometers, I defy
you here and now to perform, for six hours by the clock, what this
woman does unthinking all the year round! . . .

85. December 1st, 1783
(DCCCII, Le premier décembre 1783, 2:886–89)

A memorable date. On this day, before the eyes of an enormous
gathering, Charles* and Robert rose in the air; so great was
the crowd that the Tuileries Gardens were full as they could hold;
the gates were forced. This swarm of people was in itself an incom-
parable sight, so varied was it, so vast and so changing. Two hundred thousand men, lifting their hands in wonder, admiring, glad,
astonished; some in tears for fear the intrepid physicists should
come to harm, some on their knees overcome with emotion, but
all following the aeronauts in spirit, while these latter, unmoved,
saluted, dipping their flags above our heads; what with the novelty,
the dignity of the experiment; the unclouded sun, welcoming as it
were the travellers to his own element; the attitude of the two men
themselves sailing into the blue, while below their fellow-citizens
prayed and feared for their safety; and lastly the balloon itself, superb in the sunlight, whirling aloft like a planet, or the chariot of
some weather-god—it was a moment which can never be repeated,
the most astounding achievement the science of physics has yet
given to the world.

To an observer, the most moving part of it was this common
emotion of pity and fear, by which admiration and joy became half
pain; I heard men there reproaching themselves for their own
vivid pleasure in witnessing so fine, yet so dangerous an experiment; and who, if by some mischance an accident had happened,
would have blamed themselves as murderers. I believe there was

no single heart in that great assemblage that was not touched by the courage of the two aeronauts, men like themselves; no heart that did not send up a prayer for their safety. Pity; interest with no touch of self; tender-heartedness; such were the virtues I saw around me, while in the skies courage, and invention, and daring drove above the clouds. I thank God who gave me to live through that moment of emotion so strangely blended; the deepest, and most living, and most entirely satisfying moment of my life.

What of Montgolfier?[†] Is he only the successor of previous experimentalists, or has he by chance hit upon some simple yet forgotten or undiscovered fact of physical science? Whatever the answer, to my mind Blanchard[‡] should have the glory; for when the physicists abandoned their experiments he would not be deterred, but went on, in faith and constancy, and with a high degree of technical skill, towards the goal; the parachute is his invention; to him we owe the pioneering of the air, the conquest of space; thirty-four ascents he has made, travelling head erect and without blanching through the perils of the eagle's highway. We owe him perhaps our proudest view of man.

And yet—one short year, and the enthusiasm was over. A third ascent drew hardly a single watcher; and I believe I was the only one to regret—without, however, much surprise—this sudden change. A Parisian will not respond to the same stimulus twice. Only the man who sends his imagination up in the wake of the experimenter, to wonder at the new world of knowledge that he in his flying ship may discover—the flying ship, so long the scorn of fools; only such a man keeps his enthusiasm and his admiration unchanged. For aviation is the most marvellous of all the gifts of science, and its discoverers must rank with the greatest of the sons of science, since they challenge Nature in a field as yet untrodden, and risk their lives to wrest her secrets from her. This same courage has found recognition in every other direction; the navigator, the botanist, the man who explores the bowels of the earth or the deeps of the sea—all these have their reward. Then why not this newest discovery? We have posterity to think of.

Courage is the guiding power of all enterprise; it has changed the face of the universe, and revealed to man not only his own limitations, but his own potentialities; it has brought, many a time, the wheel full circle. Courage! That it is our highest quality, none but a fool will deny; and it is as much to be reverenced in Blanchard as in a king.

*J.-A.-C. Charles (1746–1823) was a pioneering balloonist. He employed two brothers named Robert as assistants; it is not known which one accompanied him on this flight.
†The Montgolfier brothers, Joseph Michel (1740–1810) and Etienne (1745–99), were also among the first to make balloon flights.
‡Jean-Pierre Blanchard (1753–1809) made the first balloon crossing of the English Channel in 1785.

86. Diversities

(DCCCIX, Diversités, 2:908–12)

The three-cornered hat, turned up Swiss fashion, leads the mode, while the round hat sinks out of public favour; it is because the former is more becoming, and lends its wearer an air of frankness, self-confidence, and pride. . . .

The King's zebra, in his collection of curiosities, has become the model for dress; materials are all striped; coats and waistcoats imitate the handsome creature's markings as closely as they can. Men of all ages have gone into stripes from head to foot, even to their stockings. . . .

The present fashion of women wearing their hair long is a nuisance, the backs of armchairs and carriage cushions suffer by it; all the same it is pretty to see their hair curling on their shoulders and to the waist; it has become the criterion of beauty.

Pleasure is the chief public preoccupation; national events do pass through our talk, but only as topics of the moment, not of moment. Three or four days is enough to discuss the fall of a ministry, after which actors and plays resume their sway as the only matters worth discussing.

"And how," asked Louis XIV of a courtier, "do you make love?"

"Sir, I don't make it; I buy it ready-made." This is the most usual method, and according to present experience, the most economical too.

Stock-exchange gambling is the order of the day. There is no pretence about it, and no shame; impudence is the first requisite for success, and success justifies itself. But the fun begins when some gambler, having acquired some four hundred thousand francs by sheer luck, tries to set up as Aristides the just man.

A son still retains some semblance of respect for his father. His parents brought him into the world for their own pleasure, and he now proposes to investigate it for his own; this is the prevailing sentiment, but it seldom as yet finds verbal expression, except when some elder ne'er-do-well makes a ribald song about paternal authority, which the youngsters repeat. "It is appalling to think," said a wise woman one day in my hearing, "that everything we do or say at this moment will one day be history."

The Hôtel de Ville (where the State-guaranteed annuities and interest on loans are paid) is to the *bourgeois* as the bakers' shops to the people. Are the doors open? Is payment prompt? No need to worry about public affairs. The poor neighborhoods start to grumble when the price of bread rises. The investors speak ill of the Court if there is any delay in payment, any least hitch in securing their money.

One day I overheard a baker and a stationer arguing about the importance of their respective professions.

Said the first:

"If it weren't for me and my oven, where all the hosts are baked for Mass, there'd be no Corpus Christi day, and nothing for the people to pray to."

Said number two, the paper-maker:

"All very well, but I can better that. A couple of spoken words make a God of your flour and water; but the stroke of a pen makes gold of my paper, good for any amount you please, and all over Europe."

Their audience at this point, scandalized but quite unable to decide which should have the palm, led off both disputants to the nearest wine-shop, saying as they went, in a noncommittal manner, "Ah, well, faith can work miracles, nobody denies that." And in fact the Parisian has complete faith in the printing press. Loans, lotteries, he puts in for them all, quite unable and unwilling to believe that speculators are out to swindle him; and he shows no impatience to know the upshot of the most important negotiations and events, even those which concern him personally. He has only his one answer for everything, now as heretofore; laughter.

Gunpowder has changed everything. No use, now, to go to Roman history, or Greek, or even our own history, for examples of conduct. Artillery means a different method of approach to the problems of government; only by gaiety, by eloquence, the sharp swords of wit and the battering-ram of patience can we attain our ends.

The Parisian knows that his well-being is a matter of concern to his masters; he has no real fear of famine. He knows that the prestige of the capital must be maintained, and has faith in the watch and the police so far as his personal safety is concerned; and so he supposes that calamity can never touch his city, important as she is to the whole State; and is confident that, come what may, the curtain at the Opera House will go up as usual at the appointed time.

In other towns, where there is no opera to distract attention, the inhabitants are apt to display a good deal too much interest in public affairs. More theatres, then; more distractions for the capital, since we are come to such a pass that the only cure for luxury is a hair of the dog that has bitten us. And let us abandon to the capital's sole use the talents and the gold which should be the lifeblood of our nation; this money, these talents can never flow back whence they came, can never again serve to quicken the soil. Then let them serve the nation's genius for splendour and the arts. In those at least we stand supreme, and draw from the other European kingdoms willing tribute.

87. Jockeys

(DCCCXII, Jockeys, 2:917–19)

A fashion which comes to us from across the Channel, and changes *en route;* for no man servant is ever allowed into a woman's bedroom in England.

Our jockeys, however, go where they please, and at any hour.

They go out to service early, and small, and never seem to grow an inch after, though sometimes their poor little bones take on a twist.

What purpose is served by these pallid boy-children of thirteen or so? What experiences ripen, while leaving them young in years? For where a child should be bashful, these are bold. They are libertines in the bud, the innocence of childhood has long since departed, and the very stunting of their growth proves them subject to passions too violent for their undeveloped bodies to withstand.

The last place you may look for a blush is on the jockey's cheek; he moves at his ease among women, eyeing them with a hardihood that ill agrees with his meagre face and limbs; dissipation leaves its traces even upon his breath, and the man in him has died before ever he came to virility.

They are unhealthy, too; you never see one of these boys that looks robust. Why? Because he has no chance to be anything but a weakling. Corruption of manners has gone far, and this fashionable vice they serve is deadly. No need to say more; but I might write all I know, yet never compass the whole truth.

How changed, from the gallantry of even sixty years back! It is incredible how different we are, how material we have become in all our thoughts and ambitions; as for sex, we are all one nowadays.

Jockeys frequent the smaller theatres, as do the younger prostitutes, whose fate has been the same as that of these boys. In these booths you may see, and marvel at the sight, adolescence and debauchery hand in hand, lust too young to impose its will upon frailty. On these boards—the price of entrance, by the way, is now reduced—the very lowest and most corrosive stuff is shown, stuff very much to the taste of the youngsters; who, when the player's dirtier jokes are left in the air, cap them aloud, or give them their appropriate indecent ending.

Granted that you always see the same audience at these places—happily; that only a very small percentage of the nation takes its pleasure there; and that the women who frequent them are ruined already. Still, it is in these places that the fashion of the change of sex in clothing first started; and women put off gentleness with their skirts to rival the heady passions of men.

Dress should be characteristic of sex; a woman's clothing should distinguish her from us, she should be all woman from head to heels; for in so far as she imitates men she loses herself. Now this notable change in fashion, be it observed, dates from the mode in jockeys, and the subsequent rage for such theatres as these and such plays.

Is there no remedy? Must we rush on unchecked towards calamity? But fashions and Governments have nothing in common. I am not so sure. Fashions have power to change the national taste, and so the national way of thinking. We have our financiers now, with whom money is the only standard; these abominations go forth gilded into the world, with the appalling power and weight of money behind them. It is only since the mania for gambling in stocks that these creatures abound, nerveless, too-knowledgeable poor little animals as they are. The jockey is the last and ugliest folly of our women.

I should need a stronger pen to give a true description of the harm that jockeys, and riding-coats, and public gambling, and vile plays have done. The man-milliner, contriving his revealing muslins, is hailed as 'divine.' I repeat; since they have learnt to gamble with exchanges and toy with these children, our women have no use for men save as the vile necessary servants of their shameless lusts.

88. Palais-Royal

(DCCCXX and DCCCXXI, Palais-Royal and Suite du
Palais-Royal, 2:930–35 and 2:935–43)

U nique; nothing in London, Amsterdam, Vienna, Madrid can compare with it. A man might be imprisoned within its precincts for a year or two and never miss his liberty. Plato suggests just such a prison, a place in which the captive would be held safe by his own wish, needing no constraint of chains or warders to detain him.

They call it the capital of Paris. Everything is to be found there; a young man with twenty years of life behind him and fifty thousand francs in his pocket need never leave it, not even wish to, like Rinaldo in the palace of Armida;* but whereas that legendary hero only lost time and fame, our present-day swain would probably lose all his money as well; besides forming such a habit of the place, that he could never be really happy elsewhere. It is like a tiny very rich town at the heart of a greater city; a temple of vice, the brilliance of whose votaries has banished shame; no public place in the world is more exquisitely depraved, or mocks the blush of innocence more cruelly.

It is a pity that the building had to adapt itself to the shape of the site; an oblong would have been better than the present square, which gives it, of all things, the look of a cloister. But the actual building of it was magically swift, too much so for the public, which began to make uncivil comment. The august proprietor, reproached with the amount the place would cost to put up, answered with some wit: "Not so much as you think, I get most of the stones thrown at me."

Anything you set your heart on having can be found there; you can improve your mind as you wander, learn physics, poetry, chemistry, anatomy, languages, natural history, and the rest of the sciences. You will find there women less learned than the bluestockings of the Hôtel Rambouillet,† to whom knowledge is a toy, like their parrots or their poodles; and everywhere are meeting-places, clubs, where you can talk or listen to music just as you please.

The word club sets me thinking, and this is as good a place for my thoughts as any other. Reader, a digression with your permission. We will come back later to the Palais-Royal.

Our fathers knew nothing of the club; it is a part of English life which has crept into ours, and is naturalized now is Paris. [*Mercier's note:* It is not in the French character to take these sorts of social pleasures lightly. The Frenchman, as an individual, may be wild as a hawk; but put him with half a dozen of his fellows and mark the instant change to gravity of demeanour.] There is good talk in these places, and much to be learned; . . . history, poetry, chemistry, any topic is welcome; they are academies, composed of persons of all grades of society, who have as interest in common their love for knowledge and for art.

In just such a circle I began to develop my literary heresies. "I have been reading these demigods of yours, and I will not bend my knee," I told them. Then there would be attempts to convert me, which ended, often as not, in the one who came to pray re-

maining to scoff with me. I can imagine no greater happiness than
to talk freely with men who can follow your mind, who understand
your meaning before it is spoken, and whose interests cover a wide
field. Often when a question seemed to have been talked out, it
was exciting and stimulating to find some undiscovered aspect of
it, and start the discussion anew. There is nothing like this sort of
talk for sharpening a man's wits, or for bringing out truth; for the
putting together of two opposing minds will often set flying sparks
of new and excellent ideas. No, this is a pleasure which kills the
taste for others more vulgar, or for company less good; company
in which, since the matter is too trivial for real discussion, one
holds one's tongue, and as soon as civility permits, makes for the
door.

I am not so absurdly prejudiced as to suppose that there is no
good talk outside the capital; or that the clear sun of the arts shines
only on Parisians, while the provinces are illumined only by occasional wandering stars; I leave such silly dogmas to the genuine
Academicians.[‡] It is none the less a fact, all the same, that the mind
of man, pressed like a grape by the teeming interests of the city all
about him, gives here a more abundant yield. Ideas come more
easily to birth, and are themselves more fruitful here; they must be
strong enough to withstand the buffetings of criticism, and remain
firm in contact with the thousand different and changing individualities which crowd the townsman's life; characters in Paris are
more sharply distinct than in the provinces, and sometimes more
eccentric. There is a kind of peaceful quality in the life of the
smaller towns, where day follows day smoothly as a river flows; but
the capital is a storm-tossed sea, eternally troubled by contrary
winds.

The Academicians of the Louvre reserve to themselves, with
laudable modesty, the right to illumine that palace with their intellectual splendour; there, with forty guardians about her, thrones
French literature. But the despots are not absolute; there are re-
bels who laugh at, or who refuse to recognize, their sovereignty.
There are innumerable small academies, which do more than the
official guardians of the arts to make art known, to which the
younger men come, and find pleasure in the exchange of ideas;
there is a reading first as a rule, followed by talk. These readings
are becoming more and more popular.

I confess I detest such academic bodies where members are named by royal letters patent, and feel drawn far more towards these other more spontaneous societies, to which entrance is free, not hampered by childish and preposterous ceremony, the ritual of an urn with votes; and which pass no sentence of exile, for the sole crime of thinking and writing like the abbé de Saint-Pierre[§]. Let us have more of these societies; let us talk, and never, never join an Academy, for if that should happen, it would be the end of us. Our frank use of words would turn to jargon; our friendly emulation to jealousy; and soon we would dwindle down to a mere rivalry of pride in littleness. I have laughed, just lately, to see one or two friends that I thought were strong-minded taken in by the popular illusion that talent must have its label and sit at a green-clothed table before you can be sure that it is genius.

[*Mercier's note:* As I write comes the news that all clubs are suppressed by order of the King, except such as hold their meetings in private houses. These, having no body, so to speak, of premises, are presumed not to exist.]

(DCCCXXI, Suite du Palais-Royal)

Everything is to be heard, seen, known there; a young man can get a very fair education just by requesting it. But there are dangers too. Vice holds sway there; and what the young fellows learn in public they take with them into their private lives, so that society now is rotten and shameless to a degree never before known. The indecent parade is never done. Vice holds court at all hours, and for all purses.

In Athens, the Phrynés** had their own temple; so have those of our day; and, despite a recent attempt to oust them, they still practice their trade within these walls. They are back again, triumphant, and more indecent in their solicitations than ever before.

Like the prostitutes, the stock-exchange dealers meet here three times a day; money is their one topic, and the prostitution of the State. . . . They gamble among themselves, in the *cafés,* and you may see their expressions changing under the stress of gain or loss. A pretty Pandora's box is the Palais-Royal, and of the best workmanship, as that was; but we all know what Vulcan's treasure-chest let loose when it was opened.

Sauces hold their place here by the side of science. Clothes for the pretty ladies in one window, and in the next certain surgical instruments, particular to pretty ladies, these too. Toys whose fashion is dead in a day, instruments to reveal the eternal truths of astronomy—the same shop sells them both. One man, dazzled, staring at the display, says to himself with a groan: "If only I could buy!" Another looks, and laughs, and says with a smile, "What a devil of a lot of things a man can do without!"

All the would-be voluptuaries and *gourmets* lodge here, in rooms that Roman consuls and Assyrian monarchs might envy. No sound of anvils here, or tinkers' hammers; the only scents are those from the kitchens or the coffee-roasters; this place would kill the genius of ten Cromwells,†† twenty Guises, thirty Masaniellos.

The *cafés* are full of men whose sole occupation, which keeps them employed all day long, is the hearing and subsequent retailing of news; which comes in one colour, and goes out another after they have done with it.

It is a most expensive place; prices here are triple, quadruple the prices anywhere else; and yet people come, and pay, especially the foreigners, who love having everything the heart of man can desire assembled in one place, under one roof, for their pleasure. The Palais-Royal can provide in a moment, and without time wasted in searching, every necessary for any station in life; this gives it an immense advantage over shops in other quarters of the town, which already seem to have taken on a kind of savour of the provinces, so dull their streets are, and so unpeopled.

But the rents, which by reason of the intense competition are far too high, are ruinous to the shopkeepers; there are constant bankruptcies among them, dozens of failures. The barefaced swindles engineered by these men are scandalous and happily unique in France; they sell you copper-gilt for gold, crystal for diamonds; even their woven stuff cannot compare with the really valuable and solid materials sold elsewhere; it is as though the absurd height of their rents excused them from common honesty; and you never discover that you have been cheated until it is too late.

The young men go about in groups, pallid, impudent, bold of eye, no very cheerful sight to a philosopher; you can hear them coming from one end of the place to the other, by the tinkle of chains for the two watches they wear; they go from one window to another in this labyrinth of ribbons, silks, pompons, flowers, dresses, masks, rouge-pots, and hairpins in packets six inches long or more, eternally moving, eternally idle, a prey to all the vices; seeking in vain to hide, under an affected arrogance of demeanour, their entire unimportance to the world.

The Tartars' Camp is the name given to the two unfinished galleries which still await their marble columns; these should look superb; they will put the finishing touch to the building. In these galleries the women walk two by two to catch men's eyes dressed in the latest spoils of the milliner, mad modes too, some of them, which last a day or two, and then are forgotten even by their own inventors. The names of these fashions would fill a dictionary of several volumes folio; however, we have no such useful guide as yet. . . .

It is the plain women as a rule who are the best dressed, and this is as it should be. This is no place for the *bourgeois* mother between her two daughters, or indeed for any decent woman; the prostitutes with their bold eyes, and dress, and their talk as they pass, are enough to drive any other class of women from the place.

This building, which would be the easiest imaginable prey to fire, is the resort of frail youth; but middle age is the highest bidder. The crowd is mainly young; the little theatres draw their audiences from the Palais-Royal, the great houses not so much, since the Opéra and the Français maintain some outward respect for decency. These youngsters have an unmistakable look of their own; a tired look, a look in which are revealed passion without energy, and an untouched heart. The traffic of the senses, the decline of the race, the irreverent disregard of children for their parents, who in their eyes had best die soon and share out their money—this confusedly, not wished in so many words, but wished in effect; these are the horrors that stalk naked through the galleries; a father is no more than the silly begetter of his son, a mother no more than a duenna to be tricked. You may hear adolescents talk thus, poor creatures of the new morality, corrupt already beyond redeeming, and less wise in their generation even than their parents.

Here they declaim vile verses from that vilest of plays, *La Pucelle*,[††] and not only the poet's verses, but his principles; yet the rest of Europe had nothing to say to Voltaire, who wrote for gain, and seduced a reputation rather than deserved it; who influenced morals, which he corrupted, more profoundly than minds, which he professed to enlighten; in short, the man of all this world of men most unlike and most violently opposed to Jean-Jacques Rousseau, whom he slandered and persecuted, and who wept at his death. There should be a statue of Voltaire in the very centre of the gardens of the Palais-Royal. . . .

There is a passage in Horace[§§] which gives the picture of this resort to the life; but even he says nothing of the rooms above the galleries, let out to lovers not by the hour even, but for so many minutes at a time. I think this specialty of ours would have surprised even him, and moved him to step aside, to let Juvenal take the pen.

It is so easy to buy pleasure here; what wonder that men do so buy it, and forget all other ties, the marriage-knot among them; that association unique among death's contracts, which gives free rein to passion, yet whose basis is the concord of good friends!

Still, this ugly traffic is not indulged at all hours of the day; there are times when a semblance of propriety reigns, and some respect for public decency and order. Towards five o'clock in spring and summer, and in the morning before eleven, women of the other classes may walk in the gardens without fear of being accosted. A lovely woman is the loveliest thing in nature; and at these times she may move at ease, giving pleasure and receiving it, but honestly and unafraid, in the walks of this fairy-tale palace.

The circus is the most graceful, and the most original piece of architecture in all Paris. It is not, perhaps, to be compared with the circus of ancient Rome, except in joke; but then it is not intended to be used for any of the same purposes as that antique model. It is a temple in miniature, so much may safely be granted; an underground palace where people may gather for their pleasure, which might have come into being at the wave of some enchanter's wand.

The Prince—this is the general opinion—ought to add some hundred and forty columns to this building; it would be the loveliest, then, of the capital's palaces; and the capital itself, if it goes on at this rate, will in a century or so be the marvel of Europe.

But the police are kept busier here than anywhere else in Paris;

the Palais-Royal, with its gardens and dependencies, manages to give them more trouble than the rest of the town put together.

*Armida, a sorceress, cast a spell on the knight Rinaldo in the Italian Renaissance poet Torquato Tasso's epic, *Jerusalem Liberated.*

†The Hôtel Rambouillet was the palace of a seventeenth-century noblewoman who made it a center of literary and intellectual conversation.

‡The "Academicians" referred to here were the forty writers appointed to the royally sponsored *Académie française.* Mercier, who was not a member, considered them a stodgy group, unworthy of their special privileges.

§The abbé de Saint-Pierre (1658–1743), best known for advocating a system to guarantee international peace, had been expelled from the *Académie française* for criticizing Louis XIV.

**Phyrnés: an elegant term for prostitutes.

††Oliver Cromwell seized control of the English government during the Puritan Revolution of the 1640s. The Duc de Guise had plotted to make himself king of France during the religious wars of the sixteenth century. Masaniello was the leader of a revolt against the king of Naples in the seventeenth century.

††*La Pucelle:* a mock-heroic poem about Joan of Arc, by Voltaire, notorious for its bawdiness.

§§Horace and Juvenal: Roman poets. Horace's satire was relatively restrained; Juvenal was more outspoken.

89. Rent-Day

(DCCCXLIX, Payer son terme, 2:1021–27)

How many of you turn pale, my poor, but dearly beloved Parisians, when you read this chapter title! The words have a lugubrious sound. The landlord is the one creditor that must be paid, no matter who goes without. You arrange with your dressmaker to pay her half, which even so means a profit for her of a hundred per cent; your hairdresser knows very well, and admits freely, that he is always the last to get his money. The waiter from the corner *café* who comes to bring you his employer's bill is soon done with; you need only give him thirty sous and tell him to treat himself to a variety show. [*Mercier's note:* All Paris is, properly speaking, a superlative variety show; but I mean now a tiny theatre called the Variétés Amusantes, which is a thorn in the side of the players at the Comédie française. They loathe this little theatre more than all the rest put together.] You can arrange matters with your grocer, your butcher, your tailor—even, with your moneylender; but never, never, with your landlord.

It is due the eighth day of every third month; and if you have not the money ready, next day at seven in the morning he is on your doorstep with:

"To-day is the ninth, and here is my bill." If you hesitate, he goes on: "It's every man's first duty to pay his rent." Then he looks about him. "Of course, if you can't find the money just now I see you have a nice pair of mirrors, I might raise something on those; or there's that commode, my brother-in-law would make you a fair price for that."

This man, himself a tenant, is the most pitiless creditor of all, and the most regular visitor on quarter-day; but he too is squeezed by the actual proprietor, who owes money to the builder, who owes money to the tax-collector, who refuses to wait, and winds up the matter by issuing a writ in the King's name; for he can get a triple payment if penalties are imposed.

The quarter-days are in January, April, July, and October, and somehow or other the landlord's demands have to be met. Households are upside down on these days; and if you fail with your money, the next thing is a bailiff at your door with his warrant stamped and all complete. It is the busy time for these men, what with writs to serve here, and seizures of property to carry out there. The principal tenants are privileged; but in the poorer quarters where money is hard to come by, there is much threatening, and talk of bailiffs, and locking of entrances; besides some nocturnal vigilance on the part of the principal tenant, who has to find the rent himself if subtenants disappear without paying. It is a major crime, this non-payment of rent; the only unforgivable sin.

A woman who earns her living in questionable ways, but pays her rent, gets the name of a decent honest girl; while she who keeps her landlord waiting for his money may be a model of all the virtues, but will get no credit for it. Morality is a matter of paying on time and your landlord keeps his hat on with those who owe him a day over the quarter.

Every three months sees some three or four thousand families on the move; these are the people who cannot find the money for their rent. They shift their few pieces of furniture from garret to garret; each time they move without paying they have to leave a piece behind, so that at the end of two or three years they have not a stick left. The poll-tax* collector, who is forbidden by the regulations to have compassion, takes the last of their possessions.

But when the rent is paid there is jubilation in a thousand poor homes; credit is good with the baker and the greengrocer when the critical day is safely past; the poor creatures have three months' respite, which to them, living from hand to mouth as they do, seems an eternity of surcease from anxiety, a happiness the rich can never know; but as the next quarter comes round, the whole business begins again. The first of the month leaves you a bare seven days' grace; only those with a rent of three hundred or so are allowed a fortnight to pay.

Sometimes it so happens that one of these poor housewives, knowing some days before the rent is due that she can never raise the money in time, sends her daughter to the hairdressers, where she lets out her locks for the apprentices to practise on; the poor child, like a modern Iphigenia,† submits her innocent head to the torturers, who twist her hair and singe it, paper it and prink it; burning her ears with the inexpert tongs, tearing her scalp with their mishandled combs, they inflict upon her a twelve hours' martyrdom at twenty sous the day.

There she sits in the chair with a tormentor on either side, and experience which brings more tears to her eyes than pence to her pocket, while the tyros perfect their education. Above her poor smock towers the *coiffure* of a duchess. She goes barefoot, with her head bowed beneath the weight of three pounds of flour and two of pomade; and the whole effect of this edifice will not even be becoming; no man masters his profession in one flick of the comb. Thus poor mortals suffer, enduring indignity and pain, that the goddesses may be superbly crowned.

Poor Iphigenia! For she must go through the streets with her cross upon her head, and hear the mockery of the people as she passes; everyone knows this expedient, everyone recognizes whence the contrast comes, of towering head and bare heels. She

must endure a whole fortnight the torment of the tongs, the pulling down and re-erecting of the tall structure ten times a day; but
at least she will have earned the full sum for the terrible rent-day.

No, my ladies, no! This dressing of hair is an art, which only the
experience of years can teach; and the artist has practiced long,
and at the expense of many other heads, before your tresses came
to be so knowledgeably piled. Tears have been shed in his white-
powdered studio, and other women have sat with clenched teeth,
that he might learn to lend your locks that natural curl, and bring
them gracefully on to your shoulders. Did you know this? Or knowing, do you care? Not greatly, I think. And yet, these others are
women too, who have suffered for your sakes; your beauty springs
direct from their wretchedness. That is worth remembering,
surely. Unless—my God! unless the thought of it lends savour to
your pleasure.

At present, the chief tenant is responsible for the poll-tax of all
the sub-tenants; an eternal cause of dispute. You cannot change
your lodging without showing your receipt, and the tax-collectors
can and do trace evasions back to Noah's Flood. The only escape
is into a monastery or a furnished room, where you may leave it all
to your landlord, and laugh in the faces of all the ravening collectors in the kingdom.

The cinder-man, the bottle-collector, the rubbish-sorter, the old-
iron and old-clothes men, each one of these has his fixed address,
and pays his tax. At midday, when the streets are crowded, you
wonder how all these people are to find beds for the night. The
town is like a hive, where each insect has its cell; but in these
human hives the cells are by no means equally distributed. Here
you see ten human insects in one; while another insect can house
animals to draw him, and cooks to feed him richly, and has sixty
times the amount of space to himself.

During the past thirty years ten thousand new dwellings have
been put up, and there are eight thousand rooms empty; the reason is, that nowadays convention stands in the way of a choice of
lodging; and people need more room, live more extravagantly
than they used. It is difficult to tell whether the population in the
past forty years has increased or decreased; probably, I think, the
latter. There is far more competition for small places; you will find
a hundred applicants for a couple of rooms at a hundred and fifty

francs, while the great house at twelve thousand stands empty for months; all things considered, the poor man pays more in proportion for his lodging than the rich, and so on all down the line; this fact is the most incontestable, the most deplorable, and the saddest of all those my book has to offer; any insistence on it, here and elsewhere, is an attempt to din it into the heads of those in whose hands rests the order and administration of our city; our liege-lords present and to come. The wisdom of human laws is shown in their concern for those who have no other protection; it is by their compassionate regard for these that posterity will judge the lawmakers and kings.

*"poll-tax": a head tax, assessed on all residents of Paris.
†In the story of the Trojan War, Agamemnon sacrificed his daughter Iphigenia to ensure the success of the Greek expedition against Troy.

90. The Height of Buildings
(DCCCLI, Hauteur des maisons, 2:1033–34)

There had to be some limit set, it was altogether necessary; people were piling their dwellings one on top of the other; so now the limit for height is seventy feet, not including the roof. Unhappy householders in certain quarters get neither light nor air by reason of these extravagant buildings; others waste time and breath toiling up stairs as interminable as Jacob's Ladder. Poor people, lured to the attics by small rents, which are all they can pay, find that their water and wood comes dearer because of the porterage; others must light a candle to see to eat their midday dinner.

This towering up of the houses contrasts strangely with our narrow and tortuous streets. All the main thoroughfares are too wide for the occasional traffic they carry; but these others, in which a dozen vehicles may be struggling at once, are so insufficient that there is constant confusion.

The Mont de Piété* is the only exception to this new rule, to which private houses all are subject. Neighbours of this tall structure who complained only got a fresh decree and a rap on the knuckles from the surveyors for their pains. The fact is, this place houses so much of the portable property of the public that it needs all the room it can get; its contents are estimated, by and large, at something like forty millions.

Fire in this depository would send the remaining effects of all the poorer citizens up in smoke; a happening too appalling to contemplate.

*The Mont-de-Piété was a municipal pawnshop, where the poor could get small loans in exchange for articles of household property.

91. Shoemaker
(DCCCLVII, Cordonnier, 2:1045–47)

In he comes, and drops on his knees before a lovely lady.

"You have a perfectly shaped foot, Madame la Marquise; but"—taking up the shoe she has slipped off, and which is not of his manufacture—"but who makes your shoes? you got them in town? I thought as much; there's no sense in these fellows. Look at that arch, did ever you see a finer? And all spoilt by a shoe that might have been built by the Visigoths. Is that a little dust I see? You go walking, Madame la Marquise? In that case the weight should come on the toe. Yes, I shall be proud to make you anything you wish, I have the sketch of your foot, and I shall put your order into my foreman's own hands, a very quick worker he is, and skilful. You'll find no pressure anywhere. I take my leave, Madame la Marquise."

This prince of shoemakers wears a black coat, and a well-powdered wig; his waistcoat is of silk; he looks more like something in the legal line than his own.

His less distinguished colleagues go about with grimy hands and wigs not in their first youth; their linen stinks; but then they have not his clientele, they work for the vulgar, composing in their gross way Visigothic shoes. Astonishing, the difference between a great lady's footgear and that of a schoolmistress!

In the year 1758 I used to pay just half what I do now for a pair of shoes—the same shoes. The leather nowadays is less good, but

they are better cut. *À propos;* all you young medical st\
surgeons, barristers in the bud, and authors unfledged,\
and apprentices in the arts of finance or geometry, he\
envy; in my young days we went to the play—which after all is part
of a man's education—for one franc apiece; you pay two francs
forty. This increase has not come about gradually; simply one day
the price went up to double. These variations in prices are of interest, because they affect a man's way of life, and explain the real
difficulty some have in making ends meet; a wise Government
would realize and foresee this.

There is a brotherhood of shoemaker-monks, a community living, as the apostles did, by the work of their hands; making shoes
and singing psalms, occupations by no means incompatible; indeed, our present-day religious do wrong to dissociate work from
prayer. Brother shoemaker is far more in the tradition of Christ's
disciples than any fat monk housed in a palace.

The brotherhood gives good value for money; that is as it should
be, Christians are or ought to be honest men. They complain of
the new tax on leather; it is too heavy, they say, for trade to bear;
but though they grumble it is in all humility, and with due submis-
sion to the King's decree.

Ninety out of a hundred citizens never dream of paying cash for
their shoes; the workman, no matter how poor, must give credit,
or lose customers.

92. The Eight Social Classes
(DCCCLXI, Les huit classes, 2:1060–63)

Translated by Jeremy D. Popkin

P aris has eight distinct classes of inhabitants: princes and great
lords (the least numerous), professionals,[1] financiers, mer-

---

1. Mercier uses the word "robe" for this group, which normally refers to the
judges of the *parlement* and other major law courts, but his discussion in the following paragraph shows that he is actually referring to the privileged educated professions as a whole—law, the Church, and medicine.

chants or store-owners, artists, artisans, manual laborers, servants, and the poor.

One needs to distinguish between three groups under the heading of professionals: the legal professions, the Church, and medicine. The legal professions compose a numerous cohort of individuals, who all seem to suffer from the most terrible appetite. The Church supports a crowd of lesser clergy, whose black swarms fill the theology schools. Medicine itself is divided into different groups of healers, who scurry from house to house, their lancet or their remedies in their hands, either to reassure people who are in good health, or to treat the sick, *Hippocratically, Galenically, or Paracelsusistically*[sic].

Financiers can be classified from the head of the tax-farm to those who make personal loans for a week at a time. Exchange brokers, these new crocodiles, are in the middle of this ravaging and detestable group, which will soon be treated with the contempt it deserves, because its excesses are increasing.

The spirit of commerce and trade is degraded in Paris, and doesn't have the proud and haughty tone provincial merchants affect. Since great nobles never pay cash, merchants have to go regularly and humbly entreat them or their servants. Oddly, even though they don't pay their bills, they are continually sought out as customers; it's because in the end they pay double, and since merchants themselves live on credit, they do business on this basis. If they aren't paid, merchants declare bankruptcy. The risks merchants take, in buying on credit on the one hand, in order to sell on the installment plan, makes them suspicious, fearful, and dishonest. Once they have taken on these characteristics, they never lose them; they reflect them in their actions, their behavior, and even in the way they show off their wealth. In vain they try to give themselves airs; their affected and clumsy ways invariably give them away.

The artists are above them, even though they are less wealthy; they have an independent spirit that gives them easy and gracious manners. Because they use their creative faculties more, they have better taste in what they do. Painters, architects, and sculptors are never anything more than artists, while musical composers are on a higher plane.

Out of ignorance, the *bourgeoisie* confuses artists and men of letters; there is a great difference between them. The man of letters is far more than an artist: if Corneille and Molière had had their arms cut off, they would still have been Corneille and Molière. Men of letters form a group apart, the nobility of letters.

The artisans seem to be the most fortunate of all these groups. Making their living from their industry and their skill, they are content with their place, which is as sensible as it is rare. Without ambition and without false pride, they work only to support themselves and to be able to enjoy themselves; they are straightforward and civil to everyone, since they have to be able to do business with people of all conditions. Artists' lives are dissipated and sometimes immoral; that of artisans is sober; perhaps because they are dedicated to occupations that are more useful than the arts that cater to luxury, they are compensated by a clear conscience and a tranquil life. A woodworker strikes one as more trustworthy than a painter of enamels.

When one considers with a philosophic eye the idlers and the useless people who belong to these different classes, such as the male and female nobles who claim descent going back to *Adam,* the lesser nobles who go around with certificates testifying to the heroic deeds of one of their ancestors, the court clerks, ushers, bailiffs, paper-shufflers, and thousands of other personnel who live off taxes, and when one adds to them all those people whose sorry occupation is at least a double burden to the country, those men with belts across their shoulders, whose noble occupation is to guard hares and rabbits, those *rentiers* who live off their investments and whose only employment is to vegetate, and then coachmen, postillions, grooms, and then if you also add the numerous colonies of monks, canons, chaplains, all people who like to eat, you will be in consternation when you realize how few are occupied with bringing forth from the earth things that are really valuable, the only genuine wealth. It is nevertheless these working men who constitute the wealth of a state, and, without them, everything languishes, everything declines, everything dies.

In London, one speaks of the majesty of the English people; in Paris, one does not know what label to give them.

CHAP.CCCCXLVII.

Water seller. Mercier made many references to the
suffering of those who depended on casual trades, like
water-selling, but in fact he remained an outsider to their
world. In "The Eight Social Classes," he makes only
passing reference to any groups beneath the prosperous
artisan milieu into which he had been born. (Courtesy
Library of Congress)

93. Gutters

(DCCCLXIII, Les gouttières, 2:1068–70)

I f I were as long-winded as a certain writer in the *Mercure de France*,* my chapters would never get finished; happily for my readers, I am less prolix. Gutters are my theme; brief let me be.

Rain falls pretty equally on all surfaces; it is the function of the gutter to bring these scattered waters together, and disperse them in torrents from on high upon the busy streets, sousing the coachman on his box, ruining silk parasols, soaking pedestrians and loosening paving-stones.

If these rainspouts were only turned inward, towards the inner courts of buildings, well and good; but no, they unleash their waters upon the heads of passers-by. One gutter flows into another, the torrent becomes a cataract; an ounce of water weighs ten by the time it has fallen thirty or forty feet, and carries with it fragments of plaster and tiles to crack open the unwary head below.

Paris in the rain becomes one great water spectacle, with twenty thousand streams falling from an average height of fifty feet, bearing unclean memories of their native roofs upon them. Sometimes, during a storm, the weight of water is too much for a leaden gutter, which comes down bodily with its burden; wooden pipes spread out the water fan-shaped. Shelter? There is none against this concentration of rain; and even in a carriage the drumming on the roof makes you look up apprehensively and wonder if the coachwork is solid.

Why not bring pipes down the walls of houses? The water then could escape without all this fuss. Certain gutters, as they now build them, throw a perfect Niagara of water across the street, through which horses and pedestrians must pass. The people, snug under their projecting eaves, laugh to see the great man's lackeys bob down their heads, and get a second ducking from blown spray when they think the first is safely over. The fellows on the box laugh themselves, and take this mockery in good part, but they are soaked to the skin all the same; this is not one of the moments when insolence becomes them.

After the storm, half the cement that holds the street together has been washed away, the stones are shiny and smooth as a knife-grinder's wheel; then road-menders have to come and make the damage good.

These gutters are as dangerous dry as when flushed with water, for the people who live in attics use them to save their own legs, and throw every kind of ordure down them. The gutter is more treacherous on a fine day than in a storm, for the latter at least gives you warning; but you may be walking quietly with the sun on your shoulders when some stinking liquid or other comes soundlessly out of the blue and soaks you; and the Commissary of Police can do nothing, if the disgusting stuff has come from the gutter; there is a fine for throwing anything out of the window, but the gutter is privileged. If you take the law into your own hands, you will find yourself defendant in an action for assault.

And there are other risks. Cats, valiant lovers, turbulent fighters, choose these projecting eminences for their lists of love or combat; space for either activity lacking, down somersaults one of the protagonists, claws out, on to your head; and if you wear a cape, that is lucky for you.

They have done away with signs; now surely someone might turn municipal attention to these damnable gutters which flood and disrupt the streets, and endanger passers-by in half a dozen ways. In the Rue Saint-Jacques, which runs half-way across Paris, and the Rue de la Harpe, which is also very busy, you can always reckon on a ducking in wet weather.

As a matter of fact, these lead gutters are forbidden on all new buildings, which run off their surplus water down the walls in pipes to the street; but in most districts this by-law is ignored, or else the old buildings never fall down. At any rate the city surveyor turns a blind eye to this, as to certain other abuses.

*The *Mercure de France,* founded in 1672, was France's most important literary magazine up to the time of the Revolution in 1789.

94. Brothels

(CMVII, Lieux publics, 2:1180–81)

Are places where thieves and pickpockets come to lose their illicit earning in drink and other pleasures; for this they steal, to pay their women, and drink and take a hand at cards among their peers.

As a peasant drags carrion through his fields to lure wolves and destroy them, so the police license certain places of ill-fame, in order to keep an eye on the rogues who will surely frequent them, and thus save themselves the trouble of looking further.

These women are the recruiting sergeant's right hand. He waits his prey in a *café*, hands over his mistress to any likely young fellow that eyes her, and pays for the likely young fellow's wine, till the latter, after a day or two's debauch, wakes up to find himself a soldier of the King; obliged to shoulder arms and march under pain of the lash, until the hospital claims him and he expiates the pleasures of enlistment.

The recruiting sergeant is free with his money. He gets together a few young men in a *cabaret* and says to them as he orders a meal: "Well, friends, this is how we fare every day in the regiment; soup, *entrée* and roast, that's our usual. I won't deceive you, there's no *pâté*, and the wine's nothing like so good as this; we don't get *pâté* every day, or such good wine, but for the rest, well, it's as I say— soup, and two meat courses; ah, and a salad, I forgot that."

This sterling honesty of deceit always fetches the youngsters. "I won't deceive you, no *pâté*, the wine's not much"—that rings true; it is good to think we still have orators who know their job.

95. Grocer-druggists

(CMXC, Épiciers-droguistes, 2:1406–10)

They sell cinnamon, and poisons like *aqua fortis,* together with oil, cheese, emetics, brandy and paint, sugar and arsenic, senna and jam; statutes exist to confirm them in their rivalry with the apothecaries. When drugs and salts of somewhat similar appearance are mistaken for each other, so much the worse for medical science, and so much more the worse for the unwary purchaser of the packet. The perpetual danger of such a transfer ruffles no single sheet of foolscap in the bureaux of our rulers.

Drugs and spices, both are retailed by the same individual; his assistant doles out now a handful of raisins, now a lump of Glauber's salt; soap or emetics, prunes or extract of viper's flesh, the same scales serve for all, to weigh out food and nostrums alike. If the assistant fails to interpret the chemical characters on a box, if he cannot read at all, if he is entirely unfamiliar even with the look of the different drugs and so by mistake hands out something deadly, nobody cares, nobody protests, and the victim of error is quietly buried next day. But the statutes of his mystery are peremptory; the druggist has a right to purge his quarter, and sell groceries into the bargain.

These grocers sell ground pepper, done up in a twist of paper; and the dishonest ones make it go further by mixing in a little dog-dung, which being blackened and powdered blends perfectly with the pepper; so that the innocent Parisian savours his food, not with the spices of Malacca, but a product very different from what he supposes, and what he pays for. . . . The only precaution against this kind of trickery—they pound up horse-beans from Auvergne, too—is to have the pepper ground under your own eyes; otherwise the grocer will continue to put this revolting indignity upon your palate.

Watching these shops, they seem perpetually busy, always someone in and out. The Parisian poor have no store of provisions, they buy in fractions, two ounces of this, one ounce of that, at a time; they never have a good piece of cheese in the house, nor a whole pound of sugar, nor a pint of oil. They never have in hand more money than will see them through the day, and so they go on buying in tiny portions for their dinner in the morning, for their supper at night. They buy their wood, too, very dear, faggots and drift-wood about double what it costs the *bourgeois;* they are for ever obliged to be carrying it, and having the logs split, and the kindling chopped small.

For a purgative, in the same way, they go to their grocer, who is cheaper than the apothecary, and think they have made a good bargain; the grocer may be dangerous, but he costs far less.

Hence this eternal procession of servants and boys, carrying their tiny packets of groceries or drugs, wrapped in paper, of which these tradesmen are great users, always buying up spoiled sheets from the printers, so that the despair of authors and booksellers is their delight. Without the grocer and the butter-woman we should be crowded out of our houses by the ever-congesting mass of paper.

The Chevalier Blondeau,* going about among these shops, and examining with care all such papers, bought by them by the pound, has rescued a perfect treasure of charters and deeds that otherwise must have perished as envelopes, and wrappers. Among these lost deeds he recovered the actual marriage contract of Louis XIV. Time, mice and the worms attack and destroy these proud parchments on which human genealogies depend. Such and such a famous house goes down in ruin because an old paper has been twisted up to cork an apothecary's flask; or some poem at which Europe might have wondered, humbly holds an ounce of snuff for the nose of an undertaker's mute. A nation's genius, a family's origin are alike unprovable when the documents are gone; when through ignorance, or fire, or some extraordinary chance precious papers have been destroyed or sold for what their weight will fetch.

In four hundred years, time will have dealt so with all our books, except such as have the luck to be reprinted. Book of mine! Will this be your fate? Or will you set up a bold front, brazen, diamond-hard, to resist the destroyer, together with the viable labours of our Forty Immortals?

*Claude-François Blondeau de Charnage (1710–76) published a collection of historical documents.

96. Mealtimes

(MVIII, Heures des repas, 2:1466–67)

Road-menders, plasterers, stone-cutters and the like, take their chief meal at nine in the morning. Louis XIV dined at midday, as colleges still do, and the provinces. Thirty years ago one o'clock was the hour; now you dare not sit down before three-thirty. In those days one plate served two persons, and one glass two lovers; now, though each has a plate to himself, civility obliges the hosts and hostesses to issue their invitations judiciously, so that a woman still may find herself next her lover at table. Supper comes half an hour before midnight, and visits an hour or so before that; you are sure at that time to find people at home, for our women go late to bed, and avoid daylight as much as they can. . . .

Dessert is served on our tables with the decorations proper to the season, winter or summer as the case may be; in January frost is *de rigueur*—artificial, naturally; it melts in the heat of a room, however, like the mere product of nature. I have seen on a table twelve feet long, a frozen river flow, trees bud, flowers bloom, and spring don her green robe.

As for the decoration they call *sablé*, which goes with dessert, how unimaginably childish it is! They make it of powdered white marble, which is dyed any colour you please. *Sablé* comes within the social province of the proper butler; a butler ignorant of the only correct decoration for tables will never get on.

Paris society cannot be properly regulated until the hour for the chief meal is fixed for six in the evening, and the opening of the theatres for nine. With these hours a man might have a clear day for work, time to do it well and take pleasure in it.

97. Seats in the Pit

(MIX, Parterres assis, 2:1468–71)

N owadays you may sit in all the pits, except that of the opera. As generals dispute whether open order or close ranks are best for an assault, so this question has been argued, whether the pit shall sit or stand at a play. Authors, real theatre-lovers, and all sane people are for seats; but if the benches are to be narrow and close-packed, if the allowance of room makes for cramp in all patrons over middle height, it is better to stand, providing the managements allow freedom of movement.

When the two great theatres suddenly hoisted their prices from twenty sous to forty-eight (which the public suffered in silence) a little thought might well have been given to the spacing of these benches; but in Paris the public has no spokesman. Years of grumbling do nothing to shake an abuse, no matter how trifling; and so our pits continue in vile discomfort, as if it were not enough to pay forty-eight sous, and have the fixed bayonets of a guard behind you. Satisfy the Minister and the actors by all means, but give the playgoer his modest licence to sit as he likes, with room enough to keep the cramp out of his legs.

Another thing; these pits, holding five or six hundred persons, are literally places of detention; no entrance, no leaving, without a turn of the key; you must knock to get out, no matter for what purpose. This is one more of those incredible slaveries to which our public submits, and which may well make the foreigner hold up his hands; for in case of fire it would take some minutes to break down the doors. The doorkeepers are slow in answering the signal; and there are certain ill-regulated souls who find it difficult to enjoy a comedy under lock and key, hedged in by muskets. Six hundred men held in durance by three women! Englishmen, Germans, Russians, Poles, what think you of this dragooning of people who have paid for the privilege? Some truths are not credible.

It would save money to have all the theatres in the same quarter. The actors would gain, for there would be a constant go and come of playgoers, who care very little what they see, so long as it fills a few hours of their leisure. As matters stand, you arrive at your chosen theatre to find it full; its rival is at the other end of the town, and if the journey does not put you off altogether, it cheats you both of time and pleasure. Pack all the playhouses together, and you confine the din and confusion to one quarter; the others are left in peace. There is no menace to pedestrians of five carriages abreast, and the would-be spectator is not disappointed. The competition thus provoked would be stimulating too; but to perfect the noble art of entertaining the privileges of the various companies must go. Art must be free—save, naturally, for the censure of morals, to which every Government has a right. If this were done we might see actors on our stages, and not gentlemen-in-ordinary-in-waiting, singular creatures who at present, God knows why, find themselves the interpreters of Molière and Corneille. . . .

Since seats were allowed the pit has become noisier than ever, exercising a good-humoured tyranny over the actors, who put up with it, but whom it tries pretty high. This struggle between actors and patrons is something curious and new, and at times is more diverting than the play itself. The din persists for hours, and the pit at any rate enjoys itself; the soldiers, since a recent order, never intervene.

It is the pit which pays the nation's debts of gratitude, welcomes great men, and does what it can to reward them; greatness in any sphere here finds recognition. The King of Sweden arrived one night at the opera after the curtain had gone up; the pit in no time had the curtain down, and the overture given again for his benefit.

No other nation has this gift of spontaneous gratitude for greatness. The feeling, the enthusiasm, is fired in a moment, and out breaks the applause, unpremeditated. No other people expresses itself so charmingly, with such vivacity and grace. The most delicate allusion is seized, the wit of the crowd follows the subtlest turn of phrase, and like a volcano erupting, out floods the applause, single-voiced.

Perhaps the Athenians only might compare in this with the French. A just man appearing on the stage, all eyes would turn to Aristides. When Themistocles* showed himself after the battle of Salamis at the Amphictyons, every man rose; and Alexander, lord of the world, at his zenith of glory, longed for the accolade of Athenian hands.

---

*Aristides and Themistocles were Athenian political leaders. The assembly of the Amphictyons regulated issues concerning worship in major Greek temples.

98. Drunkards

(MXXI, Ivrognes, 2:1514–16)

A peasant or an artisan who takes a drop too much in his village is sure to get home safely enough; his wife arrives, gives him the rough edge of her tongue, and out of the pothouse he goes. But Paris is nightly re-entered by squadrons of drunkards staggering in from the suburbs, rebounding from walls. At the hour when the theatres are disgorging, the most dangerous time of all, back they come. In vain the semi-blind leads the blind, each step is perilous; and the heart of every decent citizen is in his mouth watching their progress through the traffic.

It would be a good thing, and humane, if every owner of a coach or carriage were to refrain from using his horses on Sundays and feasts, or else were to give his coachman strict orders to drive with every care, for no doubt about it, these days are the most fertile of all in accidents.

Drunkenness as the result of too much good wine is pardonable up to a point; the drinker pays for his fun with a headache, and keeps his bed; what passes understanding is how our Parisians will insist on new wine, sharp, raw, detestable, and pay through the nose for it.

Beer, such as the Dutch and English drink, is good for the workers; here the stuff they swallow is pernicious beyond belief. It is the thing I marvel at most in the capital, this consumption in quantities of wine so raw that the more educated palate cannot swallow a spoonful of it. In other countries excessive drinking is an inconvenience, true, but a passing one; here it is a hideous thing, horrifying, and why? Because the stuff, being a mixture of grapes and other things from here there and everywhere, affects the digestion, and therefore the reason, sooner than any other liquor can do; and I can honestly say that of all the abuses of our time the one which I most profoundly deplore, which I would repress and punish with real severity, and first of all, is this adulterating of the people's wine.

Drinking is the source of endless disorder. A workman has spent thirty or forty sous in no time, and those thirty or forty sous mean the loss to his family of four or five four-pound loaves, that might have kept his children for a week.

I should like to see small beer, as they call it and drink it in

England, brought into common use in France; it is refreshing, and
as good as food; our people would do better than with these green
wines they are for ever soaking.

Wine-drinking darkens the skin and the outlook of a nation; we
grow petulant on it, quick to unreasoned action, and so have none
of that steadiness and *sang-froid,* that considered calm of more
northern peoples.

However, in Paris wine still holds sway, and an observer may wonder, is it worth while to sacrifice everything, woods, corn-bearing
fields, to the vineyards? Call it how you will, slave labour tends and
harvests the grape. Beer, however, is another thing, and would do
us Parisians good if we could take to it; its strength can be calcu-
lated, it is a food, and healthier than the green wine which makes
people behave so violently that they end up in the magistrate's
court.

But what's the use? If the people were to change and welcome
beer at their poor tables, down would come the tax-collector, and
up would go the price until it came as dear as Burgundy. In the
brasseries the cost of a glass is nearly at wine level already.

99. Clocks
(MXXII, Pendules, 2:1517–18)

E very chimney-piece has its clock; a pity, I think; a dismal fashion. Nothing is more dreary to contemplate than a clock; you
watch your life ebbing, the pendulum ticks off each second that
is yours only as it passes, and then is yours no more. Clocks are
everywhere, in every room you see them, and apparently nobody
finds them disturbing, though they mark most mercilessly the
flight of the hours; clocks like little temples, or with domes of
gilded bronze, or perhaps globes of white marble, with the figures
running round like an equator.

Observing one of these clocks, I found that its capricious owner
had more than once changed the gilded figure on its top; the
movement was not affected, the hands performed their office

none the worse, and I could not but reflect that in other spheres of activity the size and shape of the gilt figure is of no such vast importance; so long as the inner mechanism of the bureaucracy functions all goes well, and the figure in the head office becomes mere ornament.

Luxury has run the whole gamut of imagination in devising these superfluous splendours, it can go no further; and since they are quite useless, and not even pleasing to the eye, the waste of money in such futile expenditure is heartbreaking.

100. Period
(MXXVI, Époqué, 2:1523)

This expression comes to us from the nobility. "Is it period?" they ask each other. And there is another expression, *sourcin,* or origin-man, by which they imply that a title is recent, not lost in antiquity. Yet the present-day fashion of financial scandals we owe to the minds of certain of these period pieces.

Period is all very well, but pedantry is unforgivable. It is absurd to hear courtiers talking like schoolmasters, or worse, like sergeant-majors, for they use the same voice to the everyday civil comer that they employ with their troops. Their insolence is almost royal, and quite insufferable. It is worse than any other. I had almost rather kow-tow to a lawyer.

[In the angry and disjointed chapter called "Commentary" (CCCXXIV, Légères observations, 1:852–60) we get one or two brief glimpses of courtiers' manners.

Your great man stares you up and down; he calls this *toiser.* If it offends you, you have your remedy; do the same to them. (1:423)

Meeting a prince of the blood, the correct thing is to meet his eye, and then yield place to him, there should be no other saluta-tion; he is first among his peers, that is all. He is not displeased to be stared at; recognition is a sort of compliment.

With a porter to deny you, you may laugh at duns; however, to be ruined, and loudly proclaim the fact in company, is now very much the thing.

A trick whereby you may know a courtier is his having one shoulder higher than the other, like a man of letters. Jewelled watches are quite gone out; instead, it is now the fashion at Court to wear one very large brilliant set in a pin at the neck.]

Index

Sermons, 152–55
   sellers of, 154–55
   See also Preachers
Servants, 70
Shakespeare, William, 149
Shoeblacks, 108
Shoemakers, 214–15
Shopkeepers, 71–72
Signs, tradesmen's, 44
Simpson, Helen De Guerry (translator),
   17–19
Société Typographique de Neuchâtel,
   15
Spies, 36–37, 39–40, 163. *See also* Police
Stock Exchange, 93, 199
Street criers, 133. *See also* Hawkers
Street numbers, 43
Street singers, 113–14
Sully, Duke of, 53
Surgeons, 177
Surgery, Academy of, 30
Swiss doormen, 66

Tableau de Paris (by Mercier), 1
   critical edition of, 3n, 17
   illustrations of, 19
   influence of, 17
   Mercier's characterization of, 23,
      26–27
   reception of, 15
   style of, 14
   translations of, 17–19
Tapestries, 120
Tax collectors, 48, 151–52, 212
Taxes, 48
   poll tax, 212
   street taxes, 41
Terror, Reign of, 16
Theatre, 77, 83, 225–26
   actors and actresses, 77–78, 109, 150
   advertisements for, 89
   box rents, 78
   boxes, private, 77–78
   military guards at, 129–31, 225
   pit, seats in, 131, 225
   prices, 215

   spectators at, 201
   See also Comédie française, Comé-
      diens-Italiens
Theatre Français. *See* Comédie français
Theatrical entertainments
   Variétés amusantes, 210
   Vaudeville, 83
Turkeys, 193

Vaucanson, J. de (automaton builder),
   60
Vauxhall Gardens, 82
Vehicles
   cabriolets, 168
   carrabas, 165–67
   carriages, 47, 89–90, 168
   carts, 41
   "chamber-pots," 166
   chariots, 99
   fiacres, 47, 168
   sedan chairs, 116
   wagons, 100
   whiskies, 179
   See also Cabs and cabmen
Venereal disease, 79–80, 147, 160
Versailles, Court of, 60–61, 165–68
Vestris, G. A. B. (ballet dancer), 124
Villermé, Louis-René (sociologist), 1
Voltaire (author), 16, 185, 186, 207–8.
   See also *Pucelle, La*

Westminster Abbey, 135
Wigmakers, 175–77
Wigs, 125–27
Window-boxes, 127–28
Women, 46, 55–6, 69–71, 84, 169–70,
   171, 178, 201–2
   girls, 91–92
   and marriage, 84–85
   at Palais-Royal, 207
   as shoppers, 72
   at theatres, 77–78
   See also Prostitutes

Year 2440, The (by Mercier), 4–5

Zola, Emile, 1